Understanding
Persuasion
foundations
and practice

2nd edition

Understanding

Persuasion

foundations
and practice

RAYMOND S. ROSS

Wayne State University

PRENTICE-HALL, INC., ENGLEWOOD CLIFFS, NEW JERSEY 07632

Library of Congress Cataloging in Publication Data

Ross, Raymond Samuel, (date)
  Understanding persuasion.

  Bibliography: p.
  Includes indexes.
  1. Persuasion (Rhetoric)   2. Persuasion (Psychology)
I. Title.
PN207.R67   1985   001.51   84–17993
ISBN 0–13–937053–6

Editorial/production supervision:
  Virginia McCarthy
Cover design: Wanda Lubelska Design/Filip Pagowski
Manufacturing buyer: Barbara Kelly Kittle
Business agent, Ross Enterprises: Ricky Ross

Printed in the United States of America

10   9   8   7   6   5   4   3

ISBN 0-13-937053-6   01

Prentice-Hall International, Inc., *London*
Prentice-Hall of Australia Pty. Limited, *Sydney*
Editora Prentice-Hall do Brasil, Ltda., *Rio de Janeiro*
Prentice-Hall Canada Inc., *Toronto*
Prentice-Hall of India Private Limited, *New Delhi*
Prentice-Hall of Japan, Inc., *Tokyo*
Prentice-Hall of Southeast Asia Pte. Ltd., *Singapore*
Whitehall Books Limited, *Wellington, New Zealand*

Contents

Preface   ix

PART I
FOUNDATIONS

1 **The Study of Persuasion**   1

Influence, Motivation, and Persuasion *2*
Democracy and Persuasion *5*
Attitudes and Beliefs *8*
Ethical Persuasion *17*
Summing up *26*
Study Projects and Tasks *27*

2 **Human Motives and Needs**   31

Our Biological Foundations *32*
Our Psychological Foundations *37*
A Theory of Human Needs *43*
Summing Up *48*
Study Projects and Tasks *50*

3 **Sources of Influence**   53

Credibility *54*
The Self: Concept and Presentation *63*
Summing Up *68*
Study Projects and Tasks *68*

4 Theories of Persuasion   71

Classical Rhetoric *73*
Consistency Theories *82*
Theories of Behavioral Perception *90*
Summing Up *97*
Study Projects and Tasks *99*

PART II
PRACTICE

5 Audience Analysis   101

Audience Psychology *102*
Mob Mentality *113*
Audience Adaptation *117*
Summing Up *123*
Study Projects and Tasks *125*

6 Organizing the Message   127

General Postulates and Principles *128*
Strategies of Arrangement *133*
Summing Up *157*
Study Projects and Tasks *158*

7 Reasoned Supports of Persuasion   161

Emotive and Rational Supports *162*
Forms of Logical Support *163*
Forms of Reasoning *165*
Elements of Argument *169*
Fallacies *172*
Sender-Receiver Considerations *177*
Summing Up *178*
Study Projects and Tasks *178*

8 Campaign Persuasion   181

Social Movements *182*
Campaigns *185*
Mass-Communication Aspects of Campaigns *192*
Codes and Regulations of Conduct *194*
Summing Up *198*
Study Projects and Tasks *199*

APPENDICES

A Model Speech Outlines   203

B **Model Campaign Analyses** **217**

Index
Author *227*
Subject *231*

Preface

Teachers and scholars of persuasion still suffer from the political and social manipulations of the 1960s and early 1970s. The behaviorally oriented communicologists were often viewed then as evil causal-logical positivists teaching and researching absolute *laws* that would only further such Machiavellian manipulation of others. Although the behaviorally and empirically oriented social psychologists have mostly shrugged, an energetic and vocal group of communicologists have not. From among them a newer, interaction-oriented, receiver-oriented, projectionist view has emerged. Predominant in this view are assumptions about how we derive or negotiate *rules* that help or allow us to make choices about what action we will take. Critics of this projectionist view note a confusion, rather than an oversight, about what to do with messages and what to do with ethics.

There is also the old problem of the one and the many: rules theory fits interpersonal influence better than it does large-audience or media communication. Our best communication scholars, and even the eclectics among us, are divided on this theoretical (or pretheoretical) difference of opinion. "If this were my book [*Persuasion Theory and Context*, Reardon], I would not so readily embrace the rule-following model as the keenest scalpel for dissecting the persuasion process."[1]

This little book, which is more interested in one-to-many persuasion, finds it perhaps easier to adopt a pragmatic, pluralistic, multidisciplinary framework than would those who are interested solely in interpersonal influence.

---

[1]Gerald R. Miller, quoted in Kathleen Kelley Reardon, *Persuasion Theory and Context* (Beverly Hills, Calif.: Sage Publications, Inc., 1981), p. 11.

This book does find generalizations or lawlike universals valuable, but does not consider them to be worth very much without analysis of and adaptation to the audience. Logical empiricists who deal with statistical confidence limits of .05 are conceding that they have a specific chance of being wrong, and so their generalizations or laws can hardly be considered absolute. The danger that these generalizations may be *taught* that way is real, but that danger may largely be offset if one thinks of (and teaches) them as axioms or theorems conditioned by context. An *axiom* or *postulate* is simply a probable proposition or principle that is assumed to be true. *Theorems* build systematically on axiomatic assumptions and, like theories, are more amenable to empirical testing. The axiomatic notion allows for a more comfortable borrowing of behaviorally generated principles and laws, as well as constructs or rules, however determined. It allows one to utilize both the explanatory power of a rules orientation and the predictive power of widely accepted or demonstrated theoretical statements. Most important, it allows us to look at messages as intrinsically valuable stimuli and at ethics as necessary rules for the practice of persuasion.

For some scholars, ethics poses a dilemma between social pragmatics and one's pretheoretical orientations: "we are suggesting that a preoccupation with ethics may indicate an underlying assumption that persuasion is a unidirectional, causal form of influence designed to victimize choiceless people."[2] The *process* notion of communication has been with us for a long time now, and we have applied probability theory to causality for an even longer time. Our communication texts all stress *choice,* and so does our national association, which is concerned that we may *not* be occupied *enough* with matters ethical.

For all our concerns with epistemology and metaphysics, one should not shy away from the other major traditional divisions of philosophy: ethics, logic, and aesthetics. The text addresses ethics and logic as important parts of persuasion. A famous teacher of antiquity, while suspect as a logical positivist (and male chauvinist!) made his view on ethics crystal clear:

> Persuasion is achieved by the speaker's personal character when the speech is so spoken as to make us think him credible. We believe good men more fully and more readily than others: this is true generally whatever the question is, and absolutely true where exact certainty is impossible and opinions are divided . . . [the speaker's] character may almost be called the most effective means of persuasion he possesses. (Aristotle, *Rhetoric,* I, chap. 2.)

Eclectics are neither *evil* "logical positivists" nor cavalier "rational epistemologists," not solely "laws theorists" and not just "rules theorists." In this multidisciplinary, pluralistic framework one values empirical generalizations whether stated as rules or laws. One respects an individual's role in

---

[2]Mary John Smith, *Persuasion and Human Action* (Belmont, Calif.: Wadsworth, 1982), p. 315.

negotiating and processing rules and constructs, and one views ethical message strategy as an important part of persuasive speaking.

This short preface and the book that follows reflect some accommodation to the recent and substantial upheaval in communication and persuasion orientations. Since persuasion, and especially attitude theory, is also rooted in social psychology, the text has tried to deal with upheavals there as well.

None of the new directions and debates suggest that all traditional "discovered" knowledge is false and unimportant. Nor should one infer that all knowledge, "interpreted" or "experienced," in the newer, projectionist view is *all* that is important. Because some knowledge has different epistemological roots or is not currently receiving a lot of attention is not good reason for leaving it out. The classic works on attitudes, consistency theory, human needs, message organization, audience analysis, and ethics are still enormously valuable. They remain part of what persuasive speakers and educated listeners need to know.

This book does, then, reflect the changes and issues of current interest in the field of persuasion. The chapter on campaign persuasion reflects the findings of contemporary scholars of rhetoric. Attitudes are defined in modern, more technical language, but the classic Allportian ideas are not ignored. The discussion of theory reveals involvement with attribution and social-perception processes, as well as the influence of newer pretheoretical orientations of communication scholars.

This text is not meant to be an encyclopedia of current research on persuasion. It includes, however, many references to recent work and also the classic references. Nor is it simply a description of where the field is and what the arguments are. This is an introductory book. It is meant to provide an eclectic perspective that hopefully reflects the new through contextual redefinitions and philosophical reevaluations of the old. As John Dewey might have stated, the philosophic goal of this book is to mediate between the stubborn past and the insistent future. It is pragmatic in that it approaches persuasion by asking not primarily "How do we know it?" or "What does it all mean?" but rather "What is it supposed to do?" and "How do we do it?" It approaches theory for help in explaining and predicting. Gerald Miller puts it well:

> If the goals of explanation, prediction and control are to be achieved, empirical generalizations about human communication, whether they be cast as rules or laws, must be sufficiently parsimonious to permit their comprehension and application by scholar and practitioner alike . . . to say that human beings, as a whole, are marvelously complex does not imply that *none* of their important communicative behaviors can be explained by recourse to relatively simple antecedent mechanisms.[3]

---

[3]Gerald R. Miller, "Taking Stock of a Discipline," *Journal of Communication,* 33, no. 3 (Summer 1983), 34.

This book is intended as a practical introduction for students and speakers concerned with rhetorical communication. Difficult simplification has been attempted to make it readable and interesting, and above all practical. The real hope is that students using it learn the crucial importance of rhetorical communication as an agent of social control in a complicated, pluralistic society.

Contemporary rhetorical criticism dimensions found in Chapter 8 are improved, thanks to the efforts of Professor Bernard Brock of the Wayne State University staff.

Other books by Raymond S. Ross:

Persuasion: Communication and Interpersonal Relations, 1974.

Speech Communication: Fundamentals and Practice, 6th ed., 1983.

Essentials of Speech Communication, 2nd ed., 1984.

and with Mark G. Ross:

Relating and Interacting: An Introduction to Interpersonal Communication, 1982.

Understanding Persuasion
foundations
and practice

1
The Study of Persuasion

Influence, Motivation, and Persuasion
        Influence
        Motivation
        Persuasion
Democracy and Persuasion
        Campaigns
        Social Compliance
        Leadership
        Interpersonal Relations
Attitudes and Beliefs
        Definitions
        Attitude Clusters
        Range of Attitudes
        Functions Attudes Serve
Ethical Persuasion
        Clues
        Choice
        Status
        Distorting or Falsifying Evidence
Summing Up
Study Projects And Tasks

INFLUENCE, MOTIVATION, AND PERSUASION

Influence

To understand *persuasion,* we must first understand *influence* and *motivation. Influence,* the most general term of the three, refers to a power that affects a person or a course of events, usually indirectly or intangibly. Influence is something that causes: it might cause a change in the character, thought, mood, or action of someone. Influence sometimes implies a degree of control over the thinking and actions as well as the emotions of another. We tend to think of influence as being mostly in the affective domain. It can be positive or negative, human or nonhuman, intentional or unintentional, ethical or unethical. Lighting, music, pictures, and other mood-setting devices are capable of influencing us, as are other people, of course.

Social influence, as used by psychologists and communicologists, normally refers to a change in one person's beliefs, attitudes, behaviors, and emotions due to the behavior or presence of another person.

Motivation

Motivation is a more complex term, and is the heart of many philosophical and psychological theories about why *organisms* behave and think as they do. Motivation pertains to any stimulation or inducement that leads to an act. Here we are most interested in *human* motivation, but many studies have also been done on why animals do what they do. There are at least three basic answers to these questions, and they subsume the dozen or so primarily social-psychological theoretical approaches. Freudian psychoanalytic theory and other drive theories suggest that *tension reduction* or *need reduction* is the basis of motivation. *Goal achievement* is the answer suggested by social-learning and achievement-motivation theories. Humanistic psychologists like Maslow and Rogers, as well as attribution theorists like Heider and H. H. Kelley, assume that human motivation is based on *growth, mastery* of the environment, and a need for *self-understanding.*

Some of these views of human motivation are quite mechanical and materialistic. Others, such as those of the humanists, are mostly cognitive (*thought*-oriented). The interests of their proponents vary from defense mechanisms (the Freudians) to self-actualization (the humanists). All of these lawlike theories have something to offer students of persuasion. Some, as we shall see, seem better suited to broader communication interests. None is inherently wrong, and all help us, often in quite different ways, to better understand what motivates us.

These various theories suggest that we are motivated both by need and by plenty. Success and satisfaction foster motivation; so do failure, dissatisfaction—even threats. Thus we have avoidance needs as well as growth needs.

Human motives have been defined by David Krech and Richard Crutchfield as survival, security, satisfaction, and stimulation.[1] They group these motives into deficiency motives (survival and security) and abundancy motives (satisfaction and stimulation). *Deficiency motivation* is characterized by the need to avoid danger, threat, disruption, and discomfort. *Abundancy motivation* is characterized by the desire to grow, discover, create, enjoy, and achieve. (Motives and needs will be covered more extensively in Chapter 2.)

Although those doing the theorizing about motivation are interested in the results of intended and applied motivation, they are not restricted by intention. Those who study motivation are interested in any stimulation or inducement that leads to an act, whether by accident or design. Further, they are essentially amoral—that is, not particularly concerned with notions of right or wrong, pleasant or unpleasant. "Your money or your life!" would certainly be motivational and influential for most of us, but as we shall see shortly, it is not persuasion in the sense that communication scholars view it.

Persuasion

Persuasion is certainly concerned with *social influence* and *human motivation,* but it is a much more restrictive term and a more arbitrary one. In the multidisciplinary framework of communication theory, *persuasion* is a change process resulting mostly from shared, symbolic, thinking activity. The interaction and coordination between source message and receiver is critical. While this text is concerned mostly with messages, the effects of persuasion are in the volitions, thoughts, and behaviors of the receivers. This suggests that humans have some choice in these matters, a theme that we will pursue later in the chapter when we discuss ethics. This transactional view is captured by Mary John Smith, a rules theorist: "Persuasion . . . is a symbolic activity whose purpose is to effect the internalization or voluntary acceptance of new cognitive states or patterns of overt behavior through the exchange of messages . . . a process of persuasion has occurred when people internalize the meanings they assign to messages in an atmosphere of perceived choice."[2]

In our view, persuasive messages attempt to influence *how* receivers choose or decide which information to process. This implies the utility of strategy and theory and the criticality of audience analysis. Audience analysis is the theme of Chapter 5.

That persuasion, like all influence, can be unintentional seems obvious. However, it seems far more practical to talk about and assess strategies and goals that were or are *intended.* This is not to say, as we shall see shortly in our discussion of ethics, that persuaders and persuadees don't have responsibility beyond *intent.* The doctor who motivates a patient through incorrect diagnosis

[1]David Krech and Richard S. Crutchfield, *Elements of Psychology* (New York: Knopf, 1958), p. 279.

[2]Mary John Smith, *Persuasion and Human Action* (Belmont, Calif.: Wadsworth, 1982), p. 7.

and treatment and is found guilty of malpractice probably did not *intend* to do harm. An incompetent teacher may have had *good intentions.* It is important that senders understand their own persuasive intentions; it is important that receivers take care in *attributing* intentions to others and their messages.

Persuasion is rarely a one-shot effort. Often, each appeal is part of a larger persuasive plan or campaign. Participants must consider this when making attributions and drawing inferences.

Effective persuaders must analyze their audiences and predict their reactions. Likewise, receivers should analyze the sender to gain insight into his or her strategy. If choice is truly available, then most persuasion becomes self-persuasion. If we do persuade ourselves, we have still more reason to learn why we do the things we do. Knowing audience attitudes is where every good *sender* starts. Knowing oneself and understanding the techniques of persuasion is where every good *receiver* starts.

Part of our understanding of persuasion involves the realization that we are multi-motivated. We are motivated by need but also by abundancy; by logic but also by emotion; by the world around us and surely by the people around us. In persuasion the people around us are most important motivation. The intermediaries, the opinion leaders, the people significant to us often have more influence on us than the original message sender.

The situation we are in may greatly affect the interchange between sender and receiver. There seem to be four classic situations. Let us try to model persuasive communication so that it fits all four.

The four situations in which we are most apt to find ourselves are shown in Figures 1–1 and 1–2. These four situations may and frequently do overlap. They have been displayed in the form of two separate models for clarity. Figure 1–1 illustrates interpersonal and speaker-audience persuasive communication. The overlapping ellipses stress the importance of audience (receiver) analysis

FIGURE 1–1   Situation Model for Persuasive Communication

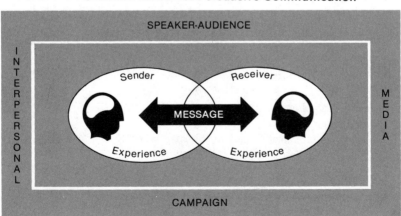

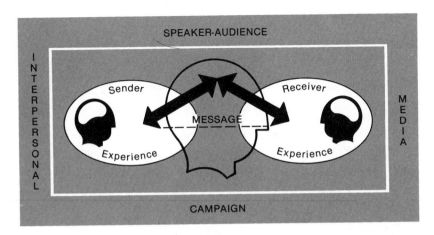

FIGURE 1–2   Intermediary Model for Persuasive Communication

and self (sender)-analysis. Persuasion does not take place in a vacuum. Some common ground between senders and receivers is essential for it to occur. This common ground is found or established through self-analysis and audience analysis. The overlap in the ellipses shows this area of common experience. Ideally, as shown in Figure 1–1, the message goes through the overlap, where the greatest understanding and persuasion are possible. The brain is where the *sender* first puts the message together. It is also where the *receiver* reconstructs the message, based on his or her experience. Experience includes attitudes, emotions, knowledge, values, and such. The double-headed arrow indicates that persuasion is a two-way undertaking, a transactional process of *mutual* influence.

In media or campaign persuasion, intermediaries are usually involved in the persuasive process. The idea that an intermediary can affect persuasion is not clearly shown in Figure 1–1. Figure 1–2 helps clarify this aspect of persuasion.

In this model, note that the sender's and receiver's experiences do not overlap. The intermediary, or opinion leader, is shown by the head that connects the experience of the sender with the experience of the receiver. This shows the importance of these intermediaries in the process of persuasion. The model could also be drawn with the ellipses overlapping. It is common, particularly in media persuasion, for the receiver to be influenced by both the sender and the intermediary.

DEMOCRACY AND PERSUASION

To make our democracy work and survive, we must rely on persuasion, whether we are settling problems, selling ideas and products, or changing people's attitudes. Ethical, religious, advertising, and political campaigns use persuasion. Persuasion is central to leadership, education, and interpersonal relations. Unless leaders and followers are rhetorically sensitive and ethical, they can pervert democracy's most effective means of social control. Our despots, demagogues, and false prophets seem to learn the superficials well, but in time they usually fail the test of ethical and responsible intent. Many start with good intentions but are somehow mesmerized by their ego and become unable to cope with change. Witness Jonestown! How do nine hundred people become so indoctrinated that they take their own lives? The carnage at Jonestown wasn't entirely voluntary, but the orderly rows of the dead pay mute testimony to the fact that these human beings had lost their will to resist the influence of another.[3] To become sensitive and knowledgeable about persuasion, whether we are senders or receivers, is a social imperative.

Campaigns

The average United States citizen has 1,000 advertising contacts per day.[4] He or she receives these appeals from people, radio, print, and mostly television. Rarely are these one-time persuasion efforts. Although each message can usually stand alone, most are part of a larger advertising plan or campaign of persuasion.

As Table 1–1 indicates, media expenditures alone are impressive. A single division of a major automobile company spends over $75 million a year on

TABLE 1–1   Media Expenditures

COMPANY	TOTAL AD DOLLARS (IN MILLIONS)	PERCENTAGE OF TOTAL DOLLARS NEWSPAPERS, MAGAZINES	TV	RADIO
American Motors Corp.	31.5	33.9	64.3	1.6
Chrysler Corp.	97.4	20.9	52.1	3.0
Ford Motor Co.	157.3	32.9	59.8	5.4
General Motors Corp.	235.3	38.9	49.9	8.0
Honda Motor Co.	20.6	39.1	56.4	4.5
Nissan Motor Corp.	49.4	28.3	59.5	11.7
Toyota Motor Sales U.S.A.	41.7	29.3	61.0	6.0
Volkswagen of America	45.5	37.4	61.2	1.1

Reprinted with permission from the August 1978 issue of *Advertising Age.* Copyright 1978 by Crain Communications, Inc.

[3]*Newsweek,* December 4, 1978, p. 38.
[4]*Training,* May 1979, p. 22.

advertising. All of the commercials, the car shows, the news releases—even the "punt, pass, and kick" contests—are scheduled and coordinated according to a carefully planned master strategy or campaign of persuasion. Persuasion is the business of advertising and marketing. Both consumer groups and the advertising and marketing industry work hard at policing the persuasion that emerges. The professionals know that honest advertising is pragmatically the best long-term policy. In a sophisticated society ethical persuasion is extremely practical. The student of persuasion can appreciate the intricacies of a well-planned campaign and protect himself or herself against deceptive practices. In a democracy, persuasive political campaigns sell candidates, programs, and promises. Candidates' speeches are carefully prepared to meet the main issues at the right time. Even the time a candidacy is announced is part of the campaign strategy. Demagogues sometimes emerge. A rhetorically sensitive student of persuasion can check such threats to a democratic society. Our knowledge and understanding protect us as citizens—a truly important reason for studying persuasion.

Social Compliance

Persuasion certainly helps ensure social compliance. Our legal rules, the "law of the land," are established through the persuasive efforts of our lawmakers, citizens, and lobbyists, among others. Social pressure is often capable of persuading us to comply even with programs that are unpopular, whether a dress code in school or busing students for racial balance. That some social pressure all too often causes us to break the law is painfully clear. Some compliance is gained more positively. Rewards that offset less critical personal objections may *motivate* (rather than persuade) us to comply and even adjust our attitudes: employers gain compliance with promotions, teachers with grades, parents with allowances.

Leadership

Even in a democracy, leaders and organizations who use deceit or unreasonable force sometimes emerge. Recently we have seen the emergence of cult leaders who use an unethical, emotional dependency to achieve their ends.

The ethical, democratic leader has the clout of fair rules, contracts, and law. The clout of the demagogue is not and should not be available. To fire a person a week without reason in order to keep everybody honest is a practice of the past. Unions, labor laws, social pressure, and government programs motivate democratic leaders to use persuasion. The threat of an unreasonable job loss is further nullified by supplementary unemployment-insurance and welfare programs. Employee benefits, training, affirmative action, communication programs, working conditions, and grievance procedures are the tools of the modern persuasive leader. It's the contractual threat of the strike rather than the strike itself that usually motivates changes in attitude. Most union-management problems are successfully resolved through communication and persuasion. We hear and read about the minority that are not.

A survey of 1,000 executives from thirteen major corporations found that 90 percent felt they could advance their careers by being perceptive and persuasive in dealing with their coworkers.[5] It is socially imperative that our future organizational and political leaders understand modern persuasion.

The quality of leadership we exert in the social groups to which we belong is also critical. Persuasion is a practical necessity in all group interaction. When we speak out, whether as leader or participant, we can profit greatly from the foundations and practices discussed in this text.

Interpersonal Relations

How we treat others near us determines in large part how we influence, motivate, and persuade them. Interpersonal persuasion is an important part of campaigns, social-compliance efforts, and leadership. How we perceive others—and they us—affects our personal persuasion. For all the efforts of the mass media, we still spend most of our communication time directly talking and listening to others. Improving the interpersonal messages we send and receive is in itself strong reason for studying persuasion.

Campaigns, compliance, leadership, interpersonal relations—all provide socially imperative reasons for studying persuasion.

ATTITUDES AND BELIEFS

Definitions

Attitude refers to the thoughts, feelings, and behavioral intentions that govern our predispositions toward people, situations, and things. Attitude has also been defined as a tendency to respond in a given way. This response may be *cognitive* (how one thinks), *affective* (how one feels), or *behavioral* (how one behaves, or intends to behave). According to Gordon Allport, this tendency to respond is a mental state that is organized through experience and exerts a dynamic influence on behavior.[6]

The altering of attitudes is for some the altering of a receiver's *cognitive schematic structures* as well as behaviors as a result of message processing.[7] It is

---

[5]"The Cox Report on the American Corporation," *Mainliner Magazine,* October 1983, p. 11.

[6]Gordon W. Allport, "Attitudes," in *The Handbook of Social Psychology,* ed. C. Murchison (Worcester, Mass.: Clark University Press, 1935), pp. 795–889. See also William J. McGuire, "The Nature of Attitudes and Attitude Change," in *The Handbook of Social Psychology,* vol. 3, ed. Gardner Lindzey and Elliott Aronson (Reading, Mass.: Addison-Wesley, 1969), p. 142.

[7]Smith, *Persuasion and Human Action,* p. 213.

also the current catchword in business, and an important factor of success, according to a survey of thirteen major American corporations.[8]

Other theorists view attitudes as being underlaid by cognitive schematic structures called *belief systems.* Beliefs are sets of *inferences* we make, or constructs we hold, about the world.[9] Beliefs are thought to be nonevaluative. They are also probability statements or propositions we hold about the world. Consider the following *belief* statement: Smoking and heart disease are related. This statement is a belief in that it makes a probability inference between smoking and heart disease. Now consider the following *attitude* statement that might grow out of this belief: Smoking is bad. The statement is an attitude because it makes an evaluation of one of the objects (smoking) in the belief statement. The significant point is that our attitudes are evaluative and grow out of our belief systems.

Bem argues that our belief systems have a vertical structure.[10] That is, we can engage them at different levels. An attitude that grows out of a belief we hold to be primary in our belief system is different from an attitude that grows out of a more lightly held belief. Figure 1–3 may help clarify the difference.

Figure 1–3 illustrates the notion that belief systems underlie attitudes and that attitudes are somehow related to behaviors. Note the inconsistency between the attitude *smoking is bad* and the behavior *heavy smoking.* This inconsistency may be explained if we consider the level at which the belief system is engaged.

Bem argues that in addition to having a vertical structure, belief systems have a horizontal structure.[11] In other words, various belief systems can act on attitudes and behaviors at the same time. Figure 1–4 suggests the horizontal structure of belief systems and clarifies the inconsistency between attitude and behavior illustrated in Figure 1–3.

We now have two belief systems operating on the heavy-smoking behavior. The attitude statement that grows out of belief system 2 is "Calmness is good." If our smoker holds calmness important to his or her life, health, and happiness, then calmness is probably a primary belief. If on further exploration of our smoker's belief system 2 we find a positive relationship between smoking and calmness ("Smoking makes me calm"), we can infer that belief system 2 is more deeply engaged than belief system 1.

The diagonal lines represent the relative amounts of belief-system engagement that underlie each of the attitude statements. Attitude 2 (*Calmness is good*) is more motivating than attitude 1 because it grows out of a more deeply engaged belief system. Our smoker is more ego-involved with attitude 2 than

[8]"The Cox Report," p. 11.

[9]Milton Rokeach, *Beliefs, Attitudes, and Values: A Theory of Organization and Change* (San Francisco: Jossey-Bass, 1969).

[10]Daryl Bem, *Beliefs, Attitudes and Human Affairs* (Belmont, Calif.: Brooks/Cole, 1970), p. 10.
[11]Ibid., p. 11.

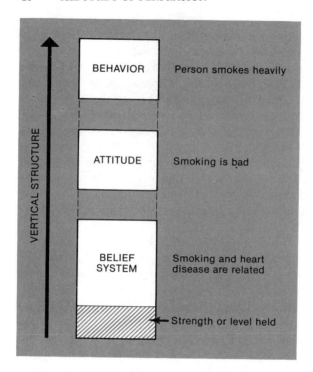

FIGURE 1-3
Vertical Attitude
Structure

with attitude 1. Attitude 2 therefore has a stronger effect on behavior (*heavy smoking*).

The smoker can smoke and at the same time have a very negative attitude about smoking. This occurs because the belief system underlying attitude 1 (*Smoking is bad*) is not as deeply engaged as the belief system underlying attitude 2. Hence, attitude 1 is less predictive of the behavior than attitude 2.

Martin Fishbein and Icek Ajzen define *attitudes* in a similar fashion, as "the sum of a person's salient beliefs about an object's attributes ... multiplied by his evaluations ... of these attributes."[12] Attitudes are thus made up of beliefs and evaluations of the beliefs. How one views the personal consequences of smoking can then affect attitude. Part of the evaluation involves social norms—what others will think about such behavior or intended behavior. The more deeply engaged the belief system, the more motivating the attitude becomes. In other words, the more primal the beliefs and the more applicable they are judged, or evaluated, to be, the more ego-involved or motivating the resulting attitude.

In our view, *opinions* are essentially the same as attitudes; for some, an opinion connotes a more superficial or less enduring form of attitude.

Values may be viewed as important goals or ends. They help hold our

[12]Martin Fishbein and Icek Ajzen, *Belief, Attitude, Intention, and Behavior: An Introduction to Theory and Research* (Reading, Mass.: Addison-Wesley, 1975), p. 399.

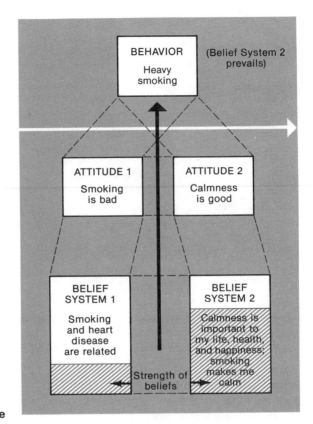

FIGURE 1–4
Horizontal
Attitude Structure

belief and attitude systems together. More will be said about values in Chapter 2.

Attitude Clusters

Our attitudes are seldom simple and seldom unrelated to other beliefs and attitudes. Larger attitudes may be thought of as a cluster of related notions, some more important than others. Some clusters contain more notions than others do. For example, consider an attitude about the use of marijuana. It could be viewed as a leaf or quasiflower having negative and positive petals sized according to importance, as shown in Figure 1–5.

If we sum the individual's positive notions and negative notions associated with the attitude, we can see that the prevailing attitude is negative (−22 versus +15), and we have a measure of strength.[13] However, we do not

13Ibid. For differing views, see pp. 229–44.

FIGURE 1–5   Attitude Cluster About Marijuana Use

have an index of the individual's personal commitment, ego involvement, or amount of belief-system engagement that underlies the attitude. Attitudes are complex. Measuring them is difficult because we cannot see them. We must infer them from what people tell us.

Range of Attitudes

Consider the statement of attitude shown graphically in Figure 1–6. The attitude represented by our flower would probably fall in category 3 on this scale. However, we're not really sure. Although illegality greatly affected this person's attitude (−9) toward *use,* he or she might lean toward legalization. Suppose a person, Sue, did check position 3 in Figure 1–6. It might seem that she would be difficult to persuade, and she might very well be if that were really the only position she favored. Suppose, however, there was a range of numbers that fit her attitude. Perhaps she could also live with positions 2 and 4. These we can label *acceptable* positions. Perhaps she found positions 5, 6, 7, and 1 unacceptable, or *objectionable* (Figure 1–7). We have more attitude information now.

Although position 3 is the *most* acceptable, her range includes the neutral position. Persuasion looks more promising now. We are beginning to get an idea of just how strong the belief system that underlies her attitude is.

Suppose Sue had a large range, or latitude, of *noncommitment,* as shown in Figure 1–8. Assuming she has enough interest or ego involvement to receive

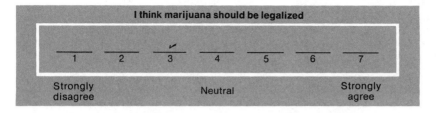

FIGURE 1-6

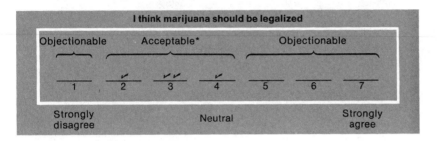

✓✓ :most acceptable position
✓ :acceptable positions

FIGURE 1-7

persuasion, we could assume she'd be easy to persuade in either direction. However, if Sue's range of acceptance were very narrow, and if her most acceptable position was still position 4, she might be very difficult to persuade. She has rejected all the other positions, as illustrated in Figure 1–9.

In general, the larger the range of rejection (objectionable position), the more ego-defensive Sue becomes and the more difficult to persuade. The larger the range of acceptance or noncommitment, the less Sue's ego is involved and the easier it is for her to change her attitude.

These three positions have been called *latitudes* of acceptance, rejection, and noncommitment.[14] This is an important concept, one that will be explained further in Chapter 4 under the heading of social judgment theory.

Functions Attitudes Serve

Attitudes appear to function differently for different persons. Moreover, they often function differently for the same individual, depending on the situation he or she is in. If we understand why people hold the attitudes they do, we are better prepared to predict how and when those attitudes might change. People may hold similar attitudes but for quite different reasons or

[14]This terminology is derived from assimilation-contrast theory. See Muzafer Sherif and Carl Hovland, *Social Judgment* (New Haven: Yale University Press, 1961), pp. 150–57.

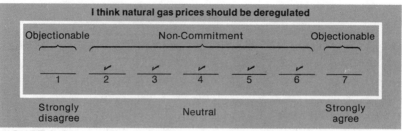

FIGURE 1-8

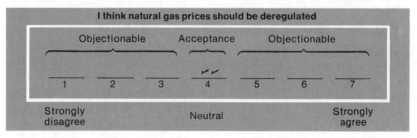

FIGURE 1-9

desired goals. One person's attitude toward liberalizing marijuana penalties might be based on the practical problems of enforcing the current law; another's on a difference in life-style.

Attitudes serve at least three general functions: referencing, self-identi-fication, and ego defense.[15]

Referencing "People need standards or frames of reference for understanding their world, and attitudes help to supply such standards."[16] We gain prepackaged norms and attitudes from our larger value systems and culture. These supply reference points that enable us to better comprehend a very complex world. When we are exposed to new knowledge that affects us, we often find our attitudes a handy frame of reference for categorizing and understanding it.

We also reference pleasure and pain, good and bad, reward and punishment. These are very practical attitudes. We adjust and modify this referencing function in very utilitarian ways. We tend to classify such things as high grades, money, and special privilege as favorable and their opposites as unfavorable. We also acquire some of our attitudes in whole or in part because of this practical referencing function.

[15]With apologies and appreciation to Daniel Katz, who identified the following four functions: adjustment, ego defense, value expression, and knowledge. See Daniel Katz, "The Functional Approach to the Study of Attitudes," *Public Opinion Quarterly*, 24 (1960), 163–204. See also M. B. Smith, J. S. Bruner, and R. W. White, *Opinions and Personality* (New York: John Wiley, 1956), pp. 41–44.

[16]Katz refers to this as the *knowledge* function.

Self-identification   Our attitudes help us define ourselves and know who we are. Some attitudes give positive expression to our value systems. We gain identity as well as satisfaction from the expression of some cherished attitudes. Our prayers in church or temple, our oaths of office or allegiance, even the clothes we wear—all help us assert and identify ourselves. When our feelings contradict our beliefs, we often have trouble with this function.

Ego defense   We often develop attitudes we think will protect our egos from conflict and frustration. These attitudes help us reduce anxieties and adjust to threats. They can help us survive temporarily trying times by taking the heat out of conflict, the pain out of frustration. When such attitudes are totally unrealistic and persistent, they can hurt us by delaying objective solutions to problems and slowing our social adjustment to the real world.

Sooner or later we all feel the pressure of differences between our personal needs and the demands of society. When we become ego-defensive and find it difficult to compromise or adjust our attitudes, we may adjust in other ways. We may distort reality to take pressure off our ego. We may lash out. We may retreat to a state of repressed hostility.

All people are subject to these physical and emotional vagaries. Evidence suggests that persons suffering from emotional disorders represent extreme variations of the same problems that occur among normal persons. The generalization that asocial, hostile, aggressive characteristics are associated with resistance to persuasion is drawn from research on such people. All of us temporarily vary our reactions and states of mind with the pressures we face (or think we face), the kind of issue involved, and our state of fatigue. People with heavy anxiety problems such as hypochondria, insomnia, or an obsession with an often unreasonable idea tend to be more difficult to persuade.[17] Our tolerance levels vary from person to person, from issue to issue, and within ourselves from day to day. We all have sensitive areas where even minor intrusions may cause disruptive reactions.

Herbert Kelman extended our insights into attitude functions and required contrary behavior when he suggested *identification* and *internalization,* along with *compliance,* as processes of social influence.[18]

Identification is a form of compliance based on a keen desire to relate satisfactorily to a special person or group. For Kelman it is a role relationship that may form a part of a person's self-image. *Internalization* is simply acceptance of an attitude because it agrees with your value system. *Compliance,*

---

[17]Irving L. Janis, "Personality Correlates of Susceptibility to Persuasion," *Journal of Personality,* 22 (1953–54), 504–18.

[18]Herbert C. Kelman, "Processes of Opinion Change," *Public Opinion Quarterly,* 25 (1961), 57–78; and Herbert C. Kelman, "Attitudes are Alive and Well and Gainfully Employed in the Sphere of Action," *American Psychologist,* 29 (1974), 310–24.

on the other hand, means accepting influence because of favorable reactions, rewards, or the avoidance of punishments, regardless of private beliefs.

Kelman categorizes the concerns one has about the social effects of one's behavior (antecedents) and also suggests classes of predictable results (consequents). The likelihood of a given social influence process being involved is a function of the *importance* attached in terms of a person's goals, the *power* of the persuader (for example, control of the means to a goal), and the *prepotency* or predominance of the induced response.

Compliance is distinguished by antecedent concern for the *social effect* of your behavior. Identification is distinguished by concern for attractive *social groups* and *anchorages* in them. The motivational base for internalization is an agreement of values, or *value congruence.* In terms of the power of the influencing source or agent, compliance is dependent upon the control the agent has over the means to a desired goal; identification is based upon the attractiveness of the agent's social role; and internalization is based on the agent's credibility. Persuasion occurs in a compliance situation through a limitation of behavioral choices toward a goal, in identification through a definition of role requirements, and in internalization through a reorganization of the individual's conception of means-ends relationships. The three processes of influence are then determined by the nature of these three antecedents.

There are three classes of consequents in Kelman's theory: (1) conditions under which the persuasion is expressed, (2) conditions under which attitude can be changed, and (3) the type of behavior system in which the persuasion is found. Behavior and attitude predispositions acquired under circumstances of compliance are discharged only under conditions of *surveillance* by the influencing agent. Responses adopted through identification circumstances are discharged only under conditions where the agent's role is of marked importance to the receiver. Behavior and attitude predispositions acquired under internalization circumstances will tend to be expressed when the relevance of issues to certain values is perceived.

Compliance responses will cease when they are no longer perceived as the best way to reach social rewards. Identification responses will be abandoned when they no longer maintain satisfying, self-defining relationships. Internalization-acquired responses will cease when they are no longer perceived as the best way to maximize one's value system.

Finally, compliance responses and opinions exist in a behavior system of specific, external demands; identification responses and opinions exist in a behavior system of expectations defining a specific role; and internalization responses and opinions exist in a behavior system of human values. If an attitude or predisposition has certain antecedents, it has predictable consequents. The distinctions among compliance, identification, and internalization are summarized in Table 1–2.

TABLE 1-2 Summary of the Distinctions Among Three Processes of Social Influence

	COMPLIANCE	IDENTIFICATION	INTERNALIZA-TION
Antecedents:			
1. Basis for the importance of the induction	Concern with social effect of behavior	Concern with social anchorage of behavior	Concern with value congruence of behavior
2. Source of power of the influencing agent	Means control	Attractiveness	Credibility
3. Manner of achieving prepotency of the induced response	Limitation of choice behavior	Delineation of role requirements	Reorganization of means-ends framework
Consequents:			
1. Conditions of performance of induced response	Surveillance by influencing agent	Salience of relationship to agent	Relevance of issues to values
2. Conditions of change and extinction of induced response	Changed perception of conditions for social rewards	Changed perception of conditions for satisfying self-defining relationships	Changed perception of conditions for value maximization
3. Type of behavior system in which induced response is embedded	External demands of a specific setting	Expectations defining a specific role	Person's value system

From Herbert C. Kelman, "Processes of Opinion Change," *Public Opinion Quarterly*, 25 (1961), 67.

ETHICAL PERSUASION

Contemporary philosophers as well as many contemporary persuasion scholars have shied away from this topic—not because they condone mendacity, but rather because of the sound of *law* rather than *rule*, the ring of *internal* rather than *interactional*, and so on. According to Sissela Bok,[19] a modern ethician, even though the lawlike admonition to tell "the whole truth and nothing but the truth" is unattainable, it is still possible to discuss virtues

---

[19]Sissela Bok, *Lying: Moral Choice in Public and Private Life* (New York: Pantheon, 1978), p. 13.

such as truthfulness and its contrary, dishonesty. Regardless of the nature of truth (relative or absolute), we can still understand that a lie is a statement intended to deceive. A liar bears a burden of proof that a lie is necessary as a last resort. We need some kind of ground rules—whether these be viewed as laws, rules, or ethical postulates—about a receiver's right to some free choice and a sender's obligation to be honest. Altruism is "in" as we write this. Perhaps we can also agree that a "healthy concern for others" also requires the ground rules stated above.

Clues

We offer the following postulates as guidance. If there is such a thing as a covering law, it would be that participants in persuasion are ethically responsible for the strategies employed, inferred, or attributed. When feedback and mutual interaction are minimal, the burden is usually on the sender. Regarding concealment and deception, Henry Ewbank and Jeffery Auer bluntly stated years ago that it is unethical for a speaker to conceal his or her real purpose, or the organization represented, pretending to speak objectively when really an advocate of one point of view."[20] This postulate or rule is obvious in some contexts but not as clear in others: a man posing as a minister to bilk a senior citizen of her money; a Marxist pretending to be a capitalist. These are unethical if the concealment or deception is *total* (there is no real clue), whether the concealed entity be purpose, organization, or point of view. But what of strategy? Perhaps rhetorically one should not be too quick to shout out one's point of view or purpose. To do so might prohibit any kind of a hearing. The emerging theorem is that you are rhetorically ethical as long as your concealment is not total or is not delayed until it has no chance of being heard.

As receivers we should be on guard and perhaps expect some over-statement when listening to a person with an obvious ax to grind—a politician, salesperson, or promoter. If that person is within the law (no false claims, slander, and so on) and does not falsely or totally conceal the purpose or the organization represented, he or she is probably meeting this ethical postulate.

Special situations   Is truth relative? Are broad, mental reservations, if not lies, allowed? Yes, say some pragmatic ethicians, in the same way that a defendant pleads not guilty, or a doctor, questioned about professional secrets, replies "I don't know." Yes, they say, because there were fair and sufficient clues within the specific context and situation. A courtroom would not allow any kind of mental reservation (a very special context). According to societal ethics, the common good is at stake here and supersedes the private good of the individual.

---

[20]Henry Lee Ewbank and J. Jeffery Auer, *Discussion and Debate: Tools of a Democracy* (New York: Appleton-Century-Crofts, 1951), p. 258.

A strict mental reservation is, in the absence of any clue, by definition a lie in any context. So too are all communications that are grossly unfair to the facts, or so subtle that they give the receiver absolutely no clue about possible alternatives.[21] The *clue* is important, as is the context. Notice in Figure 1–10 how the message is changed when the clue and the context are manipulated.

The picture at the bottom shows the true context. The other three pictures, using restricted clues, are unethical since they suggest different contexts: "man on the town," "candidate," and so on.

If moral law permits some concealing of the truth, to what situations does this pertain? What are some guidelines? First, here are some generalizations or axioms that enjoy wide ethical acceptance in a democracy:

> We have a right to do what is necessary or helpful to preserve our own personal dignity and independence.
>
> We have a right to keep our private affairs secret.
>
> We should do that which promotes mutual trust. (Doctors, lawyers, and others should not reveal secrets except in extraordinary circumstances in which the common good demands it.)

All of these generalizations deal with situations in which trust and some kind of secret puts us in a double bind.[22]

Secrets (definitions)

Secrets (definitions)   Joseph Sullivan has forthrightly delineated the ethical, lawlike principles or rules that he feels should govern the keeping or revealing of secrets. We offer them for your consideration:

> *Secret*—is a truth which the possessor may (right) or ought (duty) to conceal.
>
> *Natural Secret*—is a truth, which *from its own nature* gives the possessor said right or duty.
>
> *For example:* One's own or one's neighbor's private affairs, the revelations of which, at least in ordinary circumstances, would cause reasonable offense or injury.
>
> *Secret of Promise*—is a truth, which *because of a promise made,* possessor has a duty and therefore a right to conceal.
>
> *Secret of Trust*—is a truth, which, because of the fact that it was confided to one by another on the express or tacit agreement that having been communicated for a serious purpose it be held in trust, possessor has a duty and right to conceal.
>
> *For example:* Knowledge communicated to a lawyer or doctor, or even in some circumstances to a mere friend.
>
> *At times permits*—i.e., man sometimes has the *right* to keep a secret.
>
> *At times commands*—i.e., man sometimes has *more than a right,* he has a *duty.*
>
> *Question:* When are these times?

[21]See James Jaksa and Steven Rhodes, "A 'Content-ethic' for Interpersonal Communication," *Michigan Speech Association Journal,* 14 (1979), 80–88.

[22]For an excellent discussion of situational perspectives, see Richard Johannesen, *Ethics in Human Communication,* 2nd ed. (Prospect Heights, Ill.: Waveland Press, 1983), chap. 5.

FIGURE 1–10   Photojournalism at the Edge of the 1980s

Source: *Popular Photography,* December, 1979, pp. 79–80. Photography by Walter Oates, *Washington Star.*

Answer: a. *Man has a duty* to keep:
1. a *natural* secret—as long as
    (a) the truth is not made common property by someone else;
    (b) he cannot reasonably presume the leave of those concerned, to reveal it;
    (c) concealing the truth works no serious harm to a community;
    (d) he is not questioned about the matter by legitimate authority;
    (e) it can be kept without serious inconvenience to himself or another.
2. A secret of *promise* as long as
    a, b, c, d, as above.
    (e) it can be kept without serious inconvenience to himself or another; and even at the cost of such inconvenience, if he has—*expressly promised* to do so.
3. A secret of *trust*—as long as
    (a) *revelation is not necessary* to avert serious and impending harm from
        (1) the community,
        (2) the holder of the secret,
        (3) a third and innocent party who is endangered by the person who has confided the secret in another.
        (4) the one who confided the secret.
The reason why the obligation of keeping a secret, even of promise, ceases in the circumstances mentioned above, is because, even when assuming obligations of a strict contract, no man can reasonably be thought to intend to bind himself in such circumstances. Cf. approved authors in Moral Theology.
    (b) *Man has a right* to keep all secrets
        (1) in all the above-named cases where he has a duty;
        (2) in some of the cases mentioned where he has no duty.[23]

Choice

Honest clues protect the receiver's fundamental right of choice. Even in social-compliance situations there is usually some choice. When choice is minimal, at least there are some alternatives (the courts, when necessary). The ultimate decision of how to behave, act, interpret, or believe must in some way, however small, be left to the receiver. That choice must be a viable one. The thug with a knife in your stomach may *motivate* you to give him what he wants, but despite all the clues, he offers no viable choice. Instead, he is practicing raw force, or coercion.

Not all questions of viable choice are as clear-cut as the one above. For example, difficult ethical questions emerge from social dilemmas such as compulsory schooling versus parental rights. Some religious groups refuse to send their children to school. Voluntary busing programs clearly offer some choice. Forced busing offers much less (private schools or moving). Affirmative-action laws give employers some choices in how they may comply. We may not always perceive that we have viable alternatives. Perhaps, as the illustrations show, our choices are severely limited. Nevertheless, in a democracy choice is a very special ethical consideration for all who seek to persuade.

[23]Joseph F. Sullivan, S. J., *Special Ethics* (Worcester, Mass.: Holy Cross College Press, 1948), pp. 26–27.

Fair hearing   As receivers we have an obligation to seek out clues and choices, to question and clarify, to make an effort to give a fair hearing once we have committed ourselves to some legitimate interest in an issue.[24] We must make an effort to understand the sender's biases and intent. We should show tolerance. Fair hearing replaces force in a free society. Ewbank and Auer reminded us that "no code can be legislated or imposed to relieve the listener of the duty of analyzing the speech and deciding for himself what constitutes valid proof and a legitimate appeal to the emotions."[25]

To give fair hearing we must also analyze our range of acceptance. Are we really stuck with a "hard" attitude? Is there some latitude in our position? To give a fair hearing also means allowing the other person some chance to talk. Ethical communication doesn't outlaw aggressive arguing, but it does outlaw excessive monologuing; it does necessitate giving the sender some chance to make and explain his or her point. Fair hearing also calls for fair fighting. Sandbagging or setting people up for an obvious embarrassment borders on unethical (and often illegal) entrapment. Dragging in every superfluous issue in order to deliberately confuse is another violation of ethics.

Compliance with legitimate authority   As ethical citizen receivers we have an obligation to comply with legitimate authority and law (elected, negotiated, voted, and so forth). We needn't like it. We can try to change things. But it is only by operating within the parameters of legitimate authority and law in a democracy that we are able to make changes through nonviolent persuasive means. Strikes are by definition nonviolent. (Some, unfortunately, become violent.) Grievance procedures are clearly opportunities for persuasive changes. Laws (really rules) can and have been changed. Petition campaigns, recall campaigns, protests, demonstrations—all are part of ethical persuasion as long as they comply with the legitimate authority and rules that govern them. Specific, ethical negotiated codes and standards are discussed in Chapter 8.

Status

Culpable ignorance   The intent or attributed intent of the sender is, of course, critical to an evaluation of his or her message. Equally important is the role, or status, of the sender. A person qualified to serve and serving in a leadership role has special ethical obligations. We expect our political and religious leaders and our professional people to be responsible, regardless of their intent. An incompetent person may have good intentions. We judge such people harshly and hold them ethically responsible, even though their intent

---

[24]See Franklyn Haiman, "Democratic Ethics and the Hidden Persuaders," *Quarterly Journal of Speech,* 44, no. 4 (December 1958), 385–92. See also Johannesan, *Ethics in Human Communication,* pp. 124–26.

[25]Ewbank and Auer, *Discussion and Debate,* p. 258.

may have been good. Our laws accommodate this notion, not just for professionals but for political leaders as well. Senators, representatives, and other public figures have less protection from libel and slander than does the average citizen. (They do, of course, have their immunities.)

All of us have some ethical obligations beyond intent. Many people have been hurt by those who "meant well." All of us have some obligation to get our facts straight before sending messages that might capriciously misinform or injure the receiver. Moralists call this *culpable ignorance*—that is, ignorance, usually from carelessness, that deserves blame.[26]

We have an ethical responsibility to rhetorically analyze our situations. For one not to care how people are apt to decode a message borders on irresponsibility. A child may decode a message quite differently from a mature adult. How a particular person may interpret a particular message is an ethical consideration. Responsibility is often a frustrating question.

False pretense   A person posing as a doctor of medicine may do considerable harm through such a charade. Speaking as a qualified economist or engineer while lacking the background to do so is also dangerous and unethical. This is not to say (assuming we are not posing) that we must remain silent on taxes, wage concessions, automotive engineering, and the like. The point is that we should not mislead others about our *qualifications* to expound. The concert pianist in Figure 1–11 may be a brilliant piano player, but not an expert on foreign policy. He has as much right as anyone to speak his mind, but

FIGURE 1–11

---

[26]See Lawrence J. Flynn, S. J., "The Aristotelian Basis for the Ethics of Speaking," *Speech Teacher*, 6, no. 3 (September 1957), 179–87. See also Johannesen, *Ethics in Human Communication*, p. 30.

less so if he's *posing* as an authority or if we've paid thirty dollars to hear him *play!* There are, however, several clues for us here, and so he may be guilty of poor judgment but not unethical communication (unless he was grossly in breach of his contract). We'll have more to say about these matters in the section on credibility in Chapter 3.

Distorting or Falsifying Evidence

Lies and false facts   "He tells a lie who has one thing in his mind and says something else by words or by any signs whatsoever" (St. Augustine). To some moral philosophers, the natural end of speech is to communicate our thoughts, and a lie is evil because it frustrates the very purpose of speech. A communicator is responsible for telling the truth and for the social consequences that result if the truth is not told. This view includes not only our words but all of our nonverbal communication as well.

Sissela Bok reminds us that the consequences of lying affect not only the liar and the person lied to but also third parties, who may be affected by the deception and even the rules that are part of our social institutions.[27]

Being honest and fair to the facts are agreed-upon rules for most of us. We must play by the rules and obey the law. The use of outright lies, manufactured facts, and "dirty tricks" is thought to be unethical. Even here we encounter some problems. Prudence is a virtue.

Can the ethical person be honest without being unkind? Can he or she be both tactful and forthright? When does strategy become unfair distortion? What does *quite* mean (Figure 1–12)?

Use of emotional appeals   This is not a new ethical question. Plato and Aristotle argued it long ago. Plato counseled that emotional appeals should be avoided since they detract from the truth. Aristotle felt that it was a persuader's moral purpose, not his or her art, that made such appeals unethical. The use of emotional arguments when there is *no* evidence to support one's point is for Aristotle (and most modern rhetoricians) unethical. It is also unethical if the emotional argument clearly flies in the face of what the receivers, given time, would find in their own investigations.

In a heated interaction one is not always searching for truth. One may not intend to distort unfairly, but it happens. As receivers we should be reminded that humans are emotional as well as rational, and that free citizens have a right to sound off and frequently do. Our ethical tolerance should include a healthy discounting of legitimate emotional appeals.

---

[27]For a more detailed discussion of lying, see Bok, *Lying.*

FIGURE 1–12

Unsupported personal attacks   When a communicator attacks the character of an opponent rather than the issue at hand, that person is guilty of *ad hominem* argument (unless the character of the person *is* the issue). When *ad hominem* is used solely to change the argument from one of issues to one of personalities, as a rule it is considered unethical. Our legal system calls it *slander* if the personal charges are unsupported.

Public figures usually have less legal protection from *ad hominem* than other citizens. To argue the stage and screen abilities of Burt Reynolds by referring to him as "that self-centered, woman-chasing traitor" is a good example of *ad hominem*. Such an argument is probably irrelevant, if not unfair and unethical, if we assume that Reynolds's stage and screen abilities have no direct, logical connection to his alleged off-stage pursuits. That is not to say that every personal attack is illogical or unfair. If Reynolds were being evaluated on off-stage matters, a personal attack might have more justification. Although Reynolds might have problems getting   en with you, the same kind of unsupported personal attack on a neighbor would probably earn you a legal suit for slander (libel if you put it in writing)—clearly serious matters of ethics (and legality) for responsible communicators. To quote Ewbank and Auer: "It is unethical for a speaker to divert attention from weaknesses in his or her argument by unsupported attacks on an opponent or by appeals to hatred, intolerance, bigotry and fear."[28]

Thomas Nilsen challenges communicators to also take into account the special circumstances, the intent, and the feelings behind questions, and to combine honesty with respect for the sensitivities of the receiver. "Morally good communications are those which best preserve the integrity of the ego, contribute to personal growth, and harmonize relationships. These ends are served by communications which, in addition to providing the information needed in a given situation, permit and encourage the expression of thought and feeling, and reveal respect for the person as a person."[29]

SUMMING UP

Influence can be positive or negative, human or nonhuman, intentional or unintentional, ethical or unethical. Lighting, music, pictures, people—all are capable of influencing us. *Motivation* is any stimulation or inducement that leads to a human act whether by accident or design. It is amoral. "Your money or your life!" is motivational and influential, but not persuasion. *Persuasion* is a change process resulting mostly from shared symbolic and thinking activity. The effects of persuasion are in the volitions, thoughts, and behaviors of receivers who have some choice in these matters. Persuasive messages attempt to influence how receivers choose or decide which information to process.

Democracy depends upon persuasion to survive. It is central to our political campaigns, social compliance, leadership, and interpersonal relations. Persuasion is rarely a one-time or one-shot effort.

Attitude refers to the thinking, feeling, and behavioral intentions that govern our predispositions toward people, situations, and things. Attitudes are underlaid by beliefs. *Beliefs* are probability statements or propositions we hold

---

[28]Ewbank and Auer, *Discussion and Debate*, p. 258.
[29]Thomas R. Nilsen, *Ethics of Speech Communication* (Indianapolis: Bobbs-Merrill, 1974), pp. 88–89.

about the world. *Opinions* are essentially the same as attitudes. *Values* are goals or ends that help hold our belief and attitude systems together. Attitudes are related to various beliefs and to other attitudes. They may be thought of as a cluster of related notions. Attitudes have range or latitude of acceptance, rejection, and noncommitment. Attitudes serve several different human needs, such as referencing, self-identification, and ego-defense.

Persuaders and persuadees are ethically responsible for the strategies employed, inferred, or attributed. When there is no clue, where concealment is total, it is a lie. So too are all communications that are grossly unfair to the facts. Honest clues protect a receiver's fundamental right of choice. As receivers we have some obligation to give fair hearing and to comply with legitimate authority. We have ethical obligations beyond good intentions. We must get our facts straight. Moralists call this problem *culpable ignorance,* that is, ignorance usually from carelessness deserving blame. Using outright lies, manufactured facts, and "dirty tricks" is unethical; so too are completely unsupported emotional arguments or personal (*ad hominem*) attacks.

STUDY PROJECTS
AND TASKS

1. Interview an assigned classmate for eight to ten minutes. Then allow him or her to interview you. Prepare to introduce each other to the class. The purpose is audience analysis.
2. Analyze the following definitions of *persuasion* by speech-communication scholars and be prepared to discuss them in class.
    a. "communication in which the communicator seeks through the use of symbolic agencies, particularly language, to effect a desired voluntary change in the attitudes and/or actions of the receiver(s)." (Andersen 1978)
    b. "a complex process of communication by which one individual or group elicits (intentionally or unintentionally) by nonverbal and/or verbal means a specific response from another individual or group." (Applbaum and Anatol 1974)
    c. "a conscious attempt by one individual to change the attitudes, beliefs, or the behavior of another individual or group of individuals through the transmission of some message." (Bettinghaus 1980)
    d. "communication intended to influence choice." (Brembeck and Howell 1976)
    e. "the act of manipulating symbols so as to produce changes in the evaluative or approach-avoidance behavior of those who interpret the symbols." (Cronkhite 1969)
    f. "the co-creation of a state of identification or alignment between a source and a receiver that results from the use of symbols." (Larson 1983)
    g. "an intentional effort by symbolic means to effect change in others." (Boaz and Martin 1975)
    h. "process in which the persuader strives to establish particular relationships between his own attitudinal or behavioral states and those of the intended persuadee." (Miller and Burgoon 1973)
    i. "discourse, written or oral, in which the author controls all appropriate

communication variables in an attempt to determine the response of the receiver toward a particular choice of belief or conduct." (Minnick 1968)

j.   "human communication designed to influence others by modifying their beliefs, values, or attitudes." (Simons 1976)

k.   "communicative behavior that has as its purpose the changing, modification, or shaping of the responses (attitudes or behavior) of the receivers." (Bostrom 1983)

l.   "the activity of demonstrating and attempting to change the behavior of at least one person through symbolic interaction." (Reardon 1981)

m. "process of altering the beliefs, attitudes, intentions, or behavior of another by the conscious or unconscious use of words and nonverbal messages." (Ilardo 1981)

n.   "process in which the sender intends to exert influence and the respondent makes choices voluntarily... that takes place in a field of numerous interacting forces." (Thompson 1975) [30]

3. Define what persuasion means to you. Compare your definition with that in the text or those in project 2.

4. Develop your own verbal-pictorial model of the persuasion process. (See Figures 1–1 and 1–2.)

5. Apply the model in Figure 1–1 or the model in Figure 1–2 to a specific persuasion effort you have observed. Report what insights, lessons, or problems this exercise yielded.

6. Identify a persuasive effort you have received (through advertising, interpersonal discussion, or a speech, for example). Analyze it in terms of the definitions and concepts offered in this chapter.

7. Analyze three or four of your basic attitudes. Explain the belief systems that underlie them. Use diagrams like Figures 1–3 and 1–4.

8. Locate an attitude you have on a social issue and diagram it as shown in Figure 1–5.

[30]a.   Kenneth E. Andersen, *Persuasion,* 2nd ed. (Boston: Allyn & Bacon, 1978), p. 7.

b.   Ronald L. Applbaum and Karl W. E. Anatol, *Strategies for Persuasive Communication* (Columbus, Ohio: Chas. E. Merrill, 1974), p. 12.

c.   Erwin P. Bettinghaus, *Persuasive Communication,* 3rd ed. (New York: Holt, Rinehart & Winston, 1980), p. 4.

d.   Winston L. Brembeck and William S. Howell, *Persuasion: A Means of Social Influence,* 2nd ed. (Englewood Cliffs, N. J.: Prentice-Hall, 1976), p. 19.

e.   Gary Cronkhite, *Persuasion* (Indianapolis: Bobbs-Merrill, 1969), p. 15.

f.   Charles U. Larson, *Persuasion: Reception and Responsibility,* 3rd ed. (Belmont, Calif.: Wadsworth, 1983), p. 5.

g.   John K. Boaz and Dennis C. Martin, *Persuasive Communication* (Dubuque, Iowa: Kendall/Hunt, 1975), p. 2.

h.   Gerald R. Miller and Michael Burgoon, *New Techniques of Persuasion* (New York: Harper & Row Pub., 1973), p. 7.

i.   Wayne C. Minnick, *The Art of Persuasion,* 2nd ed. (Boston: Houghton Mifflin, 1968), p. 19.

j.   Herbert W. Simons, *Persuasion: Understanding, Practice, and Analysis* (Reading, Mass.: Addison-Wesley, 1976), p. 21.

k.   Robert N. Bostrom, *Persuasion* (Englewood Cliffs, N.J.: Prentice-Hall, 1983), p. 11.

l.   Kathleen Kelley Reardon, *Persuasion: Theory and Context* (Beverly Hills, Calif.: Sage Publications, Inc., 1981), p. 25.

m. Joseph A. Ilardo, *Speaking Persuasively* (New York: Macmillan, 1981), p. 3.

n.   Wayne N. Thompson, *The Process of Persuasion* (New York: Harper & Row, Pub., 1975), p. 8.

9. Measure the attitudes of the class on a social issue such as the Equal Rights Amendment or affirmative action, using the multiple-check system shown in Figure 1–7. Discuss analysis implications for persuasion.

10. Locate and explain one attitude you hold that is also held by others, perhaps for completely different reasons.

11. Discuss three attitudes you hold that serve the functions of referencing, self-identification, and ego defense.

12. Using the concept of ethics discussed in this chapter, describe a persuasive effort (one-shot or campaign) that you feel was unethical to some degree.

13. Analyze how you were persuaded to enter your college or university.

14. Discuss the strategy of nonviolent civil disobedience, as used by Martin Luther King, in terms of social compliance.

15. Prepare an oral report or essay in which you attempt to prove, disprove, or illustrate any one of the ethical rules listed in this chapter.

2
Human Motives
and Needs

Our Biological Foundations
       The Human Apparatus
       Systems of the Body
       Homeostasis
       Our Biological Needs
Our Psychological Foundations
       Deficiency and Abundancy
       Values as Motives
       Impelling Motives
       Affiliation Motives
       Achievement Motives
       Competence Motives
A Theory of Human Needs
       Categories of Needs
       Motive Terms and Basic Needs
Summing Up
Study Projects and Tasks

OUR BIOLOGICAL
FOUNDATIONS

For all our negotiated, rules-based rationality, we humans have need of real bread. Biologically we are tough, survival-oriented organisms, but with clear limitations. Beyond these limits, whether they be clean air, untainted food, fresh water, peaceful rest, or perhaps even a universal love, we are frail indeed.

The human biological apparatus, with its elaborate systems, has built-in requirements that must be met if the animal part of us is to survive. There are some reasonably constant laws about our internal biological environment that affect our nature. It is here that many basic springboards of human motivation are found. In this section we discuss our biological needs, along with human physiology, the critical systems of the body, and how the maintenance of a constant, internal environment (homeostasis) provides some of our most basic motivations. We are still learning from the examples of gross poverty and discrimination that we see around us that when biological needs are not being met, even our complex and serious social needs may have to stand aside for them.

The Human Apparatus

Some philosophers assume that all of us are much alike, at least in a general sense. At the physiological level this assumption presents only a few problems, for despite obvious individual differences in height, weight, color, and so forth, all people are strikingly similar. We could hardly have a science of medicine were this not true. All doctors use the same anatomy chart and all search for your appendix in about the same area.

The animal part of us appears to have a master biological plan that governs survival activity. Our brief analysis of this plan can start with the cell, which is both the functional and structural unit of the body. In spite of great variations in appearance and consistency, all parts of the body are aggregates of many of these units.[1] The body contains an estimated 21 trillion cells, which are organized into body systems, tissues, and bones. Our biological nature manifests itself in all human behavior, from abstract thinking to violent physical contact.

This human animal can run a mile in less than four minutes, adapt to weightlessness in space, manipulate delicate surgical tools, and survive at the equator or the North Pole. He or she is able to reason, build, destroy, relate, record, and communicate.

---

[1]Barry G. King and Mary J. Showers, *Human Anatomy and Physiology*, 6th ed. (Philadelphia: Saunders, 1969), p. 6. This text contains an excellent discussion of the various body systems.

For all its fantastic capacity, however, this biological nature has limitations that seriously govern behavior. We must meet our biological demands if we are to survive. Life-giving oxygen is perhaps our most critical demand; without it we have less than ten minutes to live. Air travelers are well advised to use oxygen masks when recommended. The relatively constant body temperature that allows us so much survival latitude also has strict limitations. An elevation of ten degrees for even a few hours can irreparably damage our brain cells. Body temperature is ordinarily so constant that it is one of the first indicators checked by the doctor when we sense or relate any kind of biological disequilibrium. The body is still vulnerable to infectious bacteria and other unnamed and unknown microorganisms. It cannot repair itself indefinitely and of course it ages. Survival and deprivation studies indicate that we can live without water for no more than six days and without food for no more than thirty.

Systems of the Body

The principal system of the body is the *nervous* system, which has the job of coordinating all the parts and functions of the body. It includes the brain, spinal cord, nerves, ganglia, and our sense organs. The sense organs are specialized endings of the sensory division of the peripheral nerves. The eyes, ears, and nose contain such endings. The skin contains receptors for touch, temperature, and pain. These receptors inform us about the outside world; there are others that inform us about conditions or activities within the body. The *proprioceptors* register muscle tension and sense of position. We are aware of the position of an arm or leg without looking at it. Proprioceptors in the inner ear provide us with a sense of balance. Proprioceptors also control the energy and extent of muscular activity.[2]

The autonomic nervous system controls all remaining functions of body tissues except skeletal muscles. We are not typically aware, except under emotional stress, of heartbeat, muscle contraction, digestion, and glandular secretion, all of which are under automatic control.

In short, the nervous system coordinates the activities of the body. It provides the mechanism through which our human machinery responds to the outside world in avoiding injury, obtaining fuel, and so on.

Another system circulates the fluids that transport fuel, gases, and other substances to the tissues and cells and, on the return trip, the waste products from the same cells to the appropriate sites for their excretion. This *circulatory* system includes the heart, blood vessels, and lymphatics.[3]

The heart pumps blood through an elastic system of blood vessels that is divided into three subsystems. The *arterial* system carries blood away from the heart to a network of tiny vessels called *capillaries,* whence it is collected and

[2]Ibid., p. 11.
[3]Ibid., p. 13.

returned to the heart by the *venous* system. *Plasma*—a part of the fluid portion of the blood—passes through the capillary walls to form the *tissue fluid* that supplies oxygen and nutrients to all the cells of the body and in its marvelously complex way simultaneously removes waste products and maintains a thousand different cell requirements at a constant level. The fluid is returned to the bloodstream through the *lymphatic* vascular system. Great variations in blood supply to any part of the body may be brought about by the nervous system and the interaction of other body systems. More will be said of this balancing activity under the heading of Homeostasis.

The *respiratory* system provides the body with oxygen and removes carbon dioxide. It includes the nose, pharynx, larynx, trachea, bronchi, and lungs. External respiration is breathing; internal respiration involves exchanges between the cells and the body fluids. Barry King and Mary Showers consider talking, sneezing, and coughing as accessory functions of the respiratory system.[4]

The *digestive* system prepares fuel for the metabolic functions carried out by the cells. *Metabolism* includes the complex functions involved in the release and utilization of chemical energy by the body. The digestive system includes the mouth, pharynx, esophagus, stomach, and small and large intestines. The teeth, palates, and salivary glands are considered accessory structures. In sum, the food we eat is acted upon mechanically and chemically by the digestive system so that the body may draw upon it for energy, growth, and repair of tissues.

Elaborate *urinary* and *reproductive* systems complete the systemic picture. Add muscles, bones, and glands, and we have at least mentioned the critical machinery of the body.

Physiological mechanisms within the organism may provide an explanation of physiological drives. C. T. Morgan suggests that there may be a central motive state based on hormonal factors and neural centers,[5] and studies with animals support this. Electrical stimulation of brain centers appears to reveal some cerebral control of physiological drives. A central motive state may prime or sensitize the organism to respond to external stimuli.

There is much yet to learn about our human apparatus and motivation. However, most of us would agree that everything a person *does* depends on the functioning of these biological systems. They are involved in all human behavior and have much to do with motivation.

Homeostasis

Homeostasis is the body's unceasing, automatic effort to maintain its internal environment in balance and at a constant level. A good example of this

---

[4]Ibid.

[5]C. T. Morgan, "Physiological Theory of Drive," in *Psychology: A Study of Science,* vol. 1, ed. S. Koch (New York: McGraw-Hill, 1959).

automatic corrective action is temperature regulation. When the external temperature is extremely hot, body heat is reduced by dilation of the superficial blood vessels and increased blood flow in the skin and by perspiration. During heavy exercise in hot weather, the insulating qualities of the superficial tissues of the skin may be reduced twentyfold.[6] The hotter we get, the harder our body works to cool us down. Sweating provides moisture on the skin, complete with salt to hasten evaporation. The faster the evaporation, the faster the cooling process. The body will also reduce heat by vaporizing water from the lungs, raising the temperature of inspired air, and liberating carbon dioxide from the blood as it passes through the lungs. The appropriate body parts are triggered to precise action, and at an ever-increasing tempo until a balanced state is restored.

The body's response to extreme external cold is equally automatic, selective, tenacious, and marvelous. Heat is produced by a higher metabolic rate, oxidation in the tissues, stimulatory hormonal effects, and shivering. The heat production of a person shivering is comparable to that of a person doing strenuous work. "Gooseflesh," or pilomotor activity, considerably increases the insulation value of the skin. At some temperatures this gooseflesh insulation is equal to that of a business suit.[7]

In response to a dangerously high internal body temperature caused by sickness or infection, the body will resort to shock, a kind of short-circuiting of the body systems to slow itself down and cool off. This self-regulating tendency responds swiftly to threat, never losing account of side effects.

When the body is subject to heavy exertion, the heart works at an ever-increasing rate to move the blood and its energy-giving oxygen to the muscles and to remove the acids that cause fatigue. The lungs expand manyfold and supply the rapidly burning oxygen; the respiratory system expels carbon dioxide wastes more and more quickly. While all this is going on, the adrenal glands may be called upon as a general or emergency source of energy and strength. In physical combat, when emotion is running high, even wounds heal faster. Blood clotting actually speeds up—it is truly a marvelous process.

Thus, despite deprivations, bodily threats, changing cell requirements, and unusual external conditions, the body works unceasingly to balance its internal environment. When this balance is threatened, our body systems attack the problem immediately, selectively, and with ever-increasing effort until it is restored. Amazingly, except in emergencies, all the other body states are kept in balance despite these vigorous self-regulatory actions. The water level of the blood, for example, does not get out of balance during heavy perspiration. And typically body heat is not generated at the expense of blood sugar.

Will has little to do with these homeostatic functions. Nature takes over

---

[6]King and Showers, *Human Anatomy and Physiology,* p. 381.
[7]Ibid., p. 397.

and controls them. We can, of course, assist in small ways. We can hyperventilate for oxygen or take on liquids for heating or cooling. Our role is to replenish our internal environment. When internal resources are low, homeostasis becomes biological motivation. Our cells demand attention.

Our Biological Needs

If humankind is to continue living, it must obviously satisfy certain biological requirements, like all other animals. It is essential for survival that we have oxygen, food, water, rest, elimination of wastes, and exercise. All men and women have need of these and have roughly the same limitations in terms of pain, temperature, and denial of physiological requirements. Although these needs for self-preservation and avoidance of bodily damage originate within the body, their fulfillment must come from outside once the body's reserves are in jeopardy. If the body is in a state of imbalance or disequilibrium, it will call upon us to select those things in the outside environment that specifically meet its requirements. If one is slow in meeting these internal needs, the demands intensify and the entire body mobilizes for concerted action. Our actions and behavior are triggered by our biological needs. These needs are associated with goals that offer to meet them. These goals, even at the basic level of food and water, offer us choices and behavior over which we have some control; however, whether we choose water or milk or beer, we must satisfy our basic need for fluids.

The threat of environmental pollution has given us good reasons to check on our biological needs. Also, a biological imbalance resulting from great stress, ill health, or drug abuse may cause serious problems for the human body. Biological motivations constantly affect our behavior and the intensity with which we search out related goals. Motivation—biological, social, or whatever—results in behavior designed to reach a goal thought to satisfy a need.

There is a hierarchy implicit in our various needs. As we have suggested, when the biological needs of oxygen, food, water, rest, elimination, and exercise are threatened or are not being adequately met, even our complex and serious social needs may be downgraded. Studies of deprivation suggest that people become increasingly less interested in the niceties of culture as they are systematically starved. Sex stimuli become less important when one sees nothing but visions of food. At a more subtle level, research suggests that a full stomach facilitates persuasion.[8] Salespeople have been buying clients' dinners before the big sale for years. There is much we do not know about the influence of satisfied needs and habit on the persuasion process. Gordon Allport suggests that behaviors and desires that we have persistently learned in order

---

[8]Irving L. Janis, Donald Kay, and Paul Kirschner, "Facilitating Effects of 'Eating-While-Reading' on Responsiveness to Persuasive Communications," *Journal of Personality and Social Psychology*, 1 (1965), 181–86.

to satisfy our basic needs may become "functionally autonomous"[9]—that is, motivators themselves. The striving for the necessities of life may become a need of itself once the basic needs are met. If the body's internal environment is complicated, understanding its interaction with the outside world and the human personality is doubly so.

OUR PSYCHOLOGICAL FOUNDATIONS

When there is a plethora of bread, when basic biological needs are being met, then what makes Johnny run? What are the dimensions of our social-psychological nature? We can never escape our biological limitations, yet we learn to seek social satisfactions with almost the same intensity that we seek survival itself.

To a great extent, the sources of motivation are found in an understanding of human nature and behavior. Since ancient times, we have tried to find simple explanations of what motivates people to do what they do. To Aristotle, "the proper study of man is man himself." The assumption here, as we have seen, is that all humans, broadly speaking, are much alike. At the biological level this assumption presents fewer problems; in the social realm it is more complicated. Plato argued that to study man one must investigate his environment; for Plato, man was a reflection of his society. In modern times, scholars of the projectionist view have trouble with internal causes that determine behavior; modern-day positivists can accept internal motivation if it is conditioned by probability. Most pragmatic pluralists of today tend to say that one must understand both the person and his or her environment in order to understand human behavior.

Deficiency and Abundancy

David Krech and Richard Crutchfield have postulated four principle human motives that bridge our biological as well as our social needs: survival, security, satisfaction, and stimulation.[10] As we saw in Chapter 1, these are grouped into deficiency motives (survival and security) and abundancy motives (satisfaction and stimulation). Deficiency motivation is characterized by the need to avoid danger, threat, disruption, and discomfort; its primary goal is tension reduction. Abundancy motivation is characterized by the desire

---

[9]Gordon W. Allport, "The Functional Autonomy of Motives," *American Journal of Psychology*, 50 (1937), 141–56. See also P. James Geiwitz, *Non-Freudian Personality Theories* (Belmont, Calif.: Brooks/Cole, 1969), chap. 2.

[10]David Krech and Richard S. Crutchfield, *Elements of Psychology* (New York: Knopf, 1958), p. 279.

to grow, discover, create, enjoy, and achieve; here, tension may actually be sought for stimulation. These general motivations have been inventoried in Table 2–1.

Values as Motives

According to Milton Rokeach, values act as life guides. He identifies two kinds: *terminal,* the ultimate goals that motivate us; and *instrumental,* the

TABLE 2–1   The Krech and Crutchfield Inventory of Motives

	SURVIVAL AND SECURITY (DEFICIENCY MOTIVES)	SATISFACTION AND STIMULATION (ABUNDANCY MOTIVES)
Pertaining to the body	Avoiding hunger, thirst, oxygen lack, excess heat and cold, pain, overfull bladder and colon, fatigue, overtense muscles, illness and other disagreeable bodily states, etc.	Attaining pleasurable sensory experiences of tastes, smells, sounds, etc.; sexual pleasure; bodily comfort; exercise of muscles, rhythmical body movements, etc.
Pertaining to relations with environment	Avoiding dangerous objects and horrible, ugly and disgusting objects; seeking objects necessary to future survival and security; maintaining a stable, clear, certain environment, etc.	Attaining enjoyable possessions; constructing and inventing objects; understanding the environment; solving problems; playing games; seeking environmental novelty and change, etc.
Pertaining to relations with other people	Avoiding interpersonal conflict and hostility; maintaining group membership, prestige, and status; being taken care of by others; conforming to group standards and value; gaining power and dominance over others, etc.	Attaining love and positive identifications with people and groups; enjoying other people's company; helping and understanding other people; being independent, etc.
Pertaining to self	Avoiding feelings of inferiority and failure in comparing the self with others or with the ideal self; avoiding loss of identity; avoiding feelings of shame, guilt, fear, anxiety, sadness, etc.	Attaining feelings of self-respect and self-confidence; expressing oneself; feeling sense of achievement; feeling challenged; establishing moral and other values; discovering meaningful place of self in the universe.

guidelines that motivate our everyday behavior. He has found that values vary and change somewhat according to a person's condition as well as sex, age, race, and education. Composite value rankings for American men and women (rearranged by rank) are shown in Table 2–2.

TABLE 2–2 Value Rankings (Composite) for American Men and Women

VALUES	MEN	WOMEN
Terminal Values:		
A world at peace	1	1
Family security	2	2
Freedom	3	3
A comfortable life	4	13
Happiness	5	5
Self-respect	6	6
A sense of accomplishment	7	10
Wisdom	8	7
Equality	9	8
National security	10	11
True friendship	11	9
Salvation	12	4
Inner harmony	13	12
Mature love	14	14
A world of beauty	15	15
Social recognition	16	17
Pleasure	17	16
An exciting life	18	18
Instrumental Values:		
Honest	1	1
Ambitious	2	4
Responsible	3	3
Broadminded	4	5
Courageous	5	6
Forgiving	6	2
Helpful	7	7
Capable	8	12
Clean	9	8
Self-controlled	10	11
Independent	11	14
Cheerful	12	10
Polite	13	13
Loving	14	9
Intellectual	15	16
Logical	16	17
Obedient	17	15
Imaginative	18	18

From Milton Rokeach, "Change and Stability in American Value Systems, 1968–1971," *Public Opinion Quarterly*, 38, no. 2 (Summer 1974), 229.

Impelling Motives

Our earliest textbooks on persuasive speaking compiled lists of motivational springboards similar to those above. Some of these lists are still used today. Here is one from 1908 by A. E. Phillips.

1. Self-preservation: life, health, injury, pain, disease, suffering.
2. Property: goods, lands, wealth, income.
3. Power: strength (intellectual, moral, physical), authority, influence, skill, force, energy, endurance.
4. Reputation: self-respect, pride, esteem, regard, praise, recognition.
5. Affections: desire and concern for welfare of other people or institutions, altruism.
6. Sentiments: duty, liberty, independence, honor, fairness, nobleness.
7. Tastes: aesthetic desires, beauty, pleasure, appetites.[11]

In a given culture, many people seem to react similarly to similar stimulations. However, to suggest that learning and symbolic interaction play only a minor role in such reactions or that a person has absolutely no choice is unobjective.

Affiliation Motives

Social scientists have long referred to humans as *social* animals. Social tendencies have been called *gregariousness, companionship,* and *succorance.* All have in common the seeking of *others* for help, encouragement, and sympathy. This urge to be sociable appears to be stronger in some people than in others. It does, however, appear to affect us all, particularly in times of trouble or threat. When our beliefs are seriously threatened we tend to seek out people of like mind as if to soften the hurt. It has also been theorized that some people socialize just for the sheer joy of it. Stanley Schachter said of affiliation, "Most of us have experienced occasional cravings to be with people, sometimes with good reason, frequently for no apparent reason: we seem simply to want to be in the physical presence of others."[12]

Schachter found that anxiety heightened this need for companionship. Students were told they would be guinea pigs in an experiment involving painful but not dangerous electric shock. The experiment was interrupted and the students were told that during the delay they could wait alone or wait with others. The majority preferred companionship. Misery does love company.

Schachter also pointed out that in related experiments, anxious people

---

[11]A. E. Phillips, *Effective Speaking* (Chicago: Newton, 1908), pp. 48–62. See also John A. McGee, *Persuasive Speaking* (New York: Scribner's, 1929), pp. 178–79 (for a list of twenty-two); and Alan H. Monroe, *Principles and Types of Speech* (New York: Scott, Foresman, 1935), pp. 39–53.

[12]Stanley Schachter, *The Psychology of Affiliation* (Stanford, Calif.: Stanford University Press, 1959), p. 1.

sought out other anxious people. Misery not only loves company; it loves miserable company! Affiliation apparently provides much of its own communication. Just being with other people who have similar problems seemed to reduce tension, even when no verbal communication took place.

All of us like to hear our beliefs confirmed; we like to be reassured by others who share our opinions. This is an important insight. Our desires to hear what we want to hear, or think what we want to think, sometimes take over when feelings run high or when we are desperate to reassert a shaken belief or value. Many times people themselves, apart from the issues, become important to us because they provide approval and support. Affiliating behavior may be the result of social influences that work both ways. One may affiliate because one feels strong social pressure to join, as in the case of some unions, gangs, or churches. One may not affiliate for the same reason. Or one may not join because one feels strong and secure in one's own right.

In terms of persuasion, the need for affiliation has long been used in campaigns to get us to join. Clearly, lonely-hearts clubs appeal to the need for companionship. Dishonest persuaders have often taken advantage of this need through campaigns that pretend to help suffering people. We know from experience that those who are suffering are often eager to affiliate and may be more susceptible and gullible.

Achievement Motives

Everyone usually derives satisfaction from finishing a task, completing a difficult job, or reaching a goal—in short, achieving something. All of us probably have some need for achievement. For some, little motivation is necessary; for others a great deal of effort is involved. A driving need for achievement is often found in people on their way up the professional or organizational ladder.

Our varying needs for achievement are most likely learned; they are part of our society and are related to our perceived place in it. Much has been written of the role of culture, society, and social status as a factor in the need for achievement. There is evidence, however, that people of all cultures and societies respond similarly to this need.[13] If the would-be persuader knows the origins of this need and understands how people with high needs for achievement tend to behave, he or she should be more successful, other things being equal.

An achieving society is high in achievement motivation. It emphasizes self-reliance and performance in the rearing of children and extends these values to a competitive, entrepreneurial spirit in adulthood. Societal values are

---

[13]David C. McClelland, *The Achieving Society* (New York and London: Collier-Macmillan, 1961, 1976; first Free Press paperback ed., Van Nostrand Reinhold, 1967; Irvington Press, 1979), p. 43.

more important in shaping such a society than are economics, natural resources, and the like.

High achievement needs, according to David McClelland, are typically found in the middle class rather than the lower or upper class.[14] The lower class has apparently not yet entirely aroused its achievement needs; the upper class may feel it has achieved enough. The growing American middle class's insistence on values, quality education, independence, and determination is probably a reflection of McClelland's argument. McClelland described an experiment in which students from the lower and middle social classes were observed while working on a project. When the students were told how they were doing, and also rewarded with money, the two classes were observed to perform equally well. However, when the money was withheld and the students were told only how well they were achieving the given standard, the lower-class group lost interest but the middle-class students kept on performing. The middle-class group was more interested in achievement; the lower-class group was more interested in money.

People's needs for achievement do change, not only over time but probably from issue to issue as well. Nevertheless, a persuader (or a teacher) will be more successful if his or her message is adapted to the achievement needs of the target group. For example, a person with a driving passion for achievement can be expected to be amenable to persuasion to *try harder*. This was true in all the McClelland research studies, regardless of culture or political system.

Those with high achievement needs generally prefer feedback that tells them how they are progressing toward a goal. This is useful knowledge for persuaders. People with high achievement needs are more realistic about their efforts than most, and can absorb negative feedback. This is not nearly as true of those with low achievement needs, and one should adapt one's persuasion accordingly. Those with high achievement needs also have lower affiliation needs than their opposites. When cooperation is essential, they prefer to seek expert help rather than relying on close friends, of whom they may have only a select few. Achieving a standard of excellence is more important to them than gaining monetary or other rewards.

Achievement-oriented people become more absorbed and are more persistent than others in working toward a goal. They resist rigid, authoritarian structure, but do prefer specific order and discipline. They are moderate risk takers, and are more daring in unusual, new, or unknown situations. Interestingly, both extremes of risk taking are more apt to be found among those with low achievement needs.

We should remember that human behavior has motives other than achievement needs, and is heavily conditioned by other people and the context. Most people will expend more effort toward a goal if good and

---

[14]Ibid.

sufficient reasons are put forth at precisely the right time, place, and circumstance. That some of us are sometimes more achievement-motivated also seems obvious.

Competence Motives

Most people enjoy the satisfaction of doing something well. According to Robert White, the feeling of competence or effectiveness in mastering an area of knowledge motivates us.[15] He suggests that we often overlook the significance of this feeling of competence. "Competence means capacity, fitness, or ability. The competence of a living organism means its fitness or ability to carry on those transactions with the environment which result in its maintaining itself, growing and flourishing."[16]

The negative form of this feeling, incompetence, may motivate one to helplessness, inertia, and a sense of inferiority. According to White, persistent challenge to one's personal sense of competence is a prime mover toward frustration. The threat that leads to frustration in a challenging situation is not so much the obvious defeat as the feeling of incompetence in coping or dealing with the problem. If you've prepared for an exam but somehow manage to fail it, your feeling of stupidity may very well be more frustrating than the low grade.

The sense of competence that a person brings to a practical problem helps shape one's motivation and determine one's success in solving the problem. The sender and the receiver of persuasion are well advised to consider competence as an important source of motivation.

A THEORY OF HUMAN NEEDS

Perhaps the best known *drive-motive* theory is that of Abraham Maslow.[17] It posits a hierarchy in which one must satisfy basic deprivation needs before our more humanistic needs. Although this hierarchy is often portrayed as a ladder, Maslow thought of these needs as being dynamic. That is, we are *generally* moving up or down a ladder, and while doing so we have our hands and feet on *different* rungs. We may therefore be able to fulfill our need for self-actualization while still responding to *some* of the physiological or other lower needs (Figure 2–1).

Our previous discussion of deficiency and abundancy motivation suggests that most behavior is the result of interaction among several motives.

[15]Robert W. White, *Lives in Progress* (New York: Holt, Rinehart & Winston, 1966), p. 248.

[16]Robert W. White assisted by Katherine F. Bruner, eds., *The Study of Lives* (New York: Atherton, 1966), p. 74.

[17]Abraham H. Maslow, "A Theory of Human Motivation," *Psychological Review*, 50 (1943), 370–96.

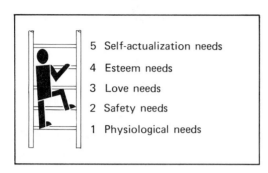

5 Self-actualization needs

4 Esteem needs

3 Love needs

2 Safety needs

1 Physiological needs

FIGURE 2–1
Priority of Needs

Categories of Needs

Maslow places needs in five general categories. In order of importance, they are *physiological, safety, love, esteem,* and *self-actualization.*

Physiological needs   These are the biological needs referred to previously. They are directly related to self-preservation. Although generally rated most important, they become less so when satisfied. A starving person may be dominated by visions of food, but physiological needs do not dominate the behavior of most of us. The primary physiological needs are oxygen, food, water, rest, exercise, avoidance of bodily damage, and excretion.

Safety needs   These reflect our desire for a sense of security and our dislike for personal violence, harm, or disease. We generally prefer a safe, predictable environment to one plagued by unforeseen events. This protective desire may prompt us to be concerned with insurance and with jobs that offer security.

Like biological needs, our safety needs do not dominate our lives except in times of emergency or danger. Nevertheless, many people are seriously concerned with threats to their security. A change in a work routine, even when carefully explained, often causes visible anxiety. The change in environment experienced by college freshmen is often an extreme threat to their safety needs. They may be quite open to persuasion that promises more security in terms of campus organizations, housing, trips home, and friends. The first year of military service is for some a similarly threatening experience. All of us appreciate a certain amount of psychological safety.

Love needs   We may also use the term *belonging* for this group of needs. The assumption underlying the recognition of these needs is that people must be loved and in turn must express their love. Sharing our life with others is important to most of us, and we generally react quickly to even the possibility that this need will be denied. We satisfy our love needs most often through our family and close friends, but they extend beyond this. We desire the approval and acceptance of our classmates, our fellow workers, and the many groups of people with whom we associate and with whom we tend to identify ourselves. We alter our behavior and perhaps even our standards in order to be accepted and loved by our chosen friends and groups. Lonely-hearts clubs owe their existence to this powerful need to give and share love.

Esteem needs When most of our physiological, safety, and love needs are satisfied, our esteem needs become most important. These needs go beyond the more passive needs to belong or be loved to a more active desire for recognition and self-respect. Esteem needs involve self-evaluation. According to Maslow they are of two slightly different types, or sets: "the desire for strength, for achievement, for adequacy, for confidence in the face of the world and for independence and freedom [and] the desire for reputation or prestige (defining it as respect or esteem from other people), recognition, attention, importance, or appreciation."[18]

In our culture esteem needs are very important. Americans are often accused of being self-centered. A threat to our ego or self-esteem, whether real or fancied, often prompts swift reaction. Our radio and television commercials appeal to our esteem needs by emphasizing the prestige attached to a certain expensive car or by suggesting that our status in a group is threatened if we don't buy a particular product.

The satisfaction of esteem needs leads to self-confidence and a feeling of personal worth. Esteem needs are often accompanied by many frustrations and personal conflicts, since people desire not only the recognition and attention of their chosen groups but also the self-respect and status that their moral, social, and religious standards, or constructs, call for. When the chosen groups call for behavior that conflicts with a person's standards, that person must often make heroic choices in order to remain well adjusted. People play many roles in order to satisfy some of the different groups to which they belong.

The esteem needs of some poorly adjusted individuals are so great that they will seek achievement (or what they consider achievement) at the great price of their own self-respect, morals, and ideals. This is not to say that the so-called achievement motive is abnormal.

Self-actualization needs This term refers to what might be called *self-fulfillment* or *self-realization*—our desire to reach the height of our personal abilities and talents. In Maslow's words, "What a man *can* be, he *must* be." This need becomes increasingly important as the previous four needs become satisfied, and in our culture it is very important. The large number of retired or established people who return to college or take courses in art, writing, or drama in order to satisfy creative urges are responding to self-actualization needs. At Wayne State University in Detroit the average age of the student

---

[18]Ibid., p. 382.

body in 1984 was twenty-six. Many students had full-time jobs. One part-time student was eighty-seven; the oldest full-time student was eighty-two.

Maslow describes self-actualized people as having the following characteristics:

1. a more efficient perception of reality and more comfortable relations with it
2. increased acceptance of self, of others, and of nature
3. spontaneity, simplicity, naturalness
4. problem-centered rather than ego-centered
5. increased detachment and desire for privacy
6. ability to be independent of their physical and social environment
7. freshness of appreciation and richness of emotional reaction
8. higher frequency of "peak," mystic, or transcendent experiences
9. increased identification with and feeling for mankind
10. deeper, more profound interpersonal relationships
11. a more democratic character structure
12. strongly ethical; able to distinguish clearly between means and ends
13. a philosophical, unhostile sense of humor
14. a natural, spontaneous creativity
15. ability to detach and resist their culture[19]

Figure 2–2 is our attempt to relate what we call the psycho-environmental prerequisites to the basic-needs system.[20]

The rank and the practical importance of these needs depend on the degree to which each is satisfied. Because this degree of satisfaction is constantly changing, we are well advised to know our audience. Receivers decode in terms of their past experiences, emotions, and attitudes. At one time our need for love may predominate, coloring the meaning we attach to a communication. At another time our need for esteem may be foremost, and our openness to persuasion may be altered.

The degree of satisfaction of these five needs for an average person changes and is therefore hard to pin down. Nevertheless, an estimate, even an old one, gives us a benchmark for discussion. Maslow suggests that the average American probably achieves the degrees of satisfaction represented in Figure 2–3, shown on page 48.

[19]Abraham H. Maslow, *Motivation and Personality*, 2nd ed. (New York: Harper & Row, Pub., 1970), pp. 153–74.

[20]For another attempt, see Frank Goble, *The Third Force* (New York: Grossman, 1970), p. 50.

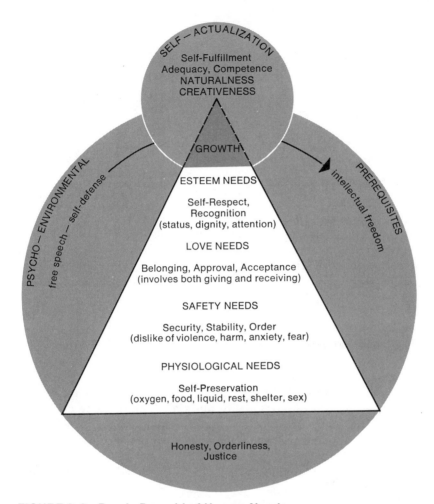

FIGURE 2–2   Ross's Pyramid of Human Needs

Since a satisfied need is not a strong motivator, the smaller figures should indicate the areas in which we are most open to persuasion.

The psycho-environmental prerequisites portrayed in Figure 2–2 are so important to the Maslow explanation of human needs and motivations that they become strong motivators in themselves when denied or endangered. These prerequisites include free speech, intellectual freedom, the right to self-defense, and a desire for justice, honesty, and orderliness.

Motive Terms and Basic Needs

Specific terms describing particular needs can be roughly sorted under the five categories of basic needs:

PHYSIOLOGICAL NEEDS	SAFETY NEEDS	LOVE NEEDS	ESTEEM NEEDS	SELF-ACTUALIZATION NEEDS
1. Bodily comfort	1. Fear	1. Loyalty	1. Pride	1. Creativeness
2. Sex attraction	2. Conformity	2. Family affection	2. Reputation	2. Curiosity
3. Physical exercise	3. Companion-ship	3. Sympathy	3. Power	3. Constructive-ness
4. Hunger	4. Saving	4. Mothering	4. Achievement	4. Ambition
5. Activity	5. Conflict	5. Respect for deity	5. Social distinction	5. Independence
6. Rest and sleep	6. Cleanliness	6. Sentiments	6. Appearance	6. Freedom from restraint

These *motivation terms* are thought to be appeals to the basic human needs. To be effective they must filter their way through the layers of personal abilities and constructs shown in Figure 2–4. Audience motivation through symbolic interaction is terribly complex; we should be wary of "infallible" motive appeals.

SUMMING UP

When biological needs are not being met, even our complex social needs may have to stand aside. The systems of the body (nervous, circulatory, respiratory, digestive, etc.), along with one's biological equipment, are intimately involved in all human behavior and motivation. Homeostasis refers to the body's unceasing and automatic self-regulation efforts designed to maintain a constantly balanced internal environment. When the internal resources are low, homeostasis becomes biological motivation. It is essential

FIGURE 2–3

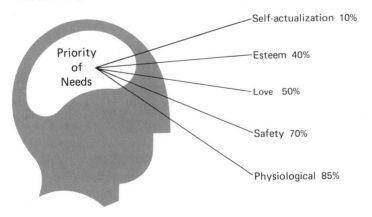

Priority of Needs

Self-actualization 10%

Esteem 40%

Love 50%

Safety 70%

Physiological 85%

FIGURE 2–4 Persuasion Filters

for survival that we have oxygen, food, water, rest, elimination of wastes, and exercise.

Four general human motives are survival and security (deficiency motives) and satisfaction and stimulation (abundancy motives). Deficiency motivation is characterized by the need to avoid danger, threat, disruption, and discomfort. Abundancy motivation is characterized by the desire to grow, discover, create, enjoy, and achieve. Values act as life guides. There are two types of values: *terminal* (e.g. peace, freedom), the ultimate goals which motivate us; and *instrumental* (e.g. honest, responsible), the guidelines which motivate our everyday behavior.

Social tendencies in humans have been called the *affiliation* motive, that is, seeking others for help, encouragement, and sympathy.

It has been found that people with high achievement needs are more realistic about effort and can tolerate negative feedback better than those with low achievement needs. Those with high achievement needs have lower affiliation needs, and are more conservative risk takers than their counterparts. Achieving a standard of excellence is more important to them than gaining monetary or other rewards.

Competence means capacity, fitness, or ability. The sense of competence that one brings to a practical life problem helps shape one's motivation and success in solving the problem.

The Maslow theory of human needs includes five general categories. In order of importance they are: *physiological, safety, love, esteem,* and *self-actualization.* Environmental prerequisites include free speech, intellectual freedom, the right to self-defense, and a desire for justice, honesty, and orderliness.

STUDY PROJECTS
AND TASKS

1. Try some harmless deprivation studies on yourself and report the results.
   a. Skip two or three meals and assess the persuasiveness of some radio or television commercials; repeat the experiment with a full stomach (be sure to include some food commercials).
   b. When you are completely fatigued, test persuasive impact as above.
2. Observe and report cases in which persuasion or communication failed principally because of biological needs and poor timing (for example, your attempt to persuade Dad to help you finance a motorcycle when Dad was tired, irregular, and coming down with a virus).
3. Prepare a one-minute food commercial for (1) a starving audience and (2) a sated audience.
4. Discuss the sex differences in the value rankings shown in Table 2–2. What might they have to do with persuasion? Do your values agree with the composite?
5. Clip advertisements based upon (1) affiliation motives, (2) achievement motives, and (3) competence motives.

6. In one page describe a life situation that supports the fact that misery loves miserable company (for example, students consistently doing poorly may seek one another out).

7. Describe and be prepared to report orally about a person with unusually high achievement needs. Tell how you would motivate that person to support a cause of your choice.

8. Describe and be prepared to report orally about a person with unusually low achievement needs. Tell how you would motivate that person to support a cause of your choice.

9. Report a real case or devise a hypothetical case where a sender's sense of incompetence led to reverse persuasion and/or aggression.

10. Prepare a five-minute persuasive speech that relies on three of the five Maslovian needs (physiological, safety, love, esteem, self-actualization).

11. Clip a magazine, poster, or newspaper advertisement that is built around the hierarchy-of-needs theory. Attach a one-page analysis of the needs and the persuasion sequence used.

12. Make a brief study of the propaganda of a political-action group in terms of the Maslow needs.

13. Write a two- or three-minute commercial or persuasive speech that relies on as many of the human needs or values as possible.

3

Sources of Influence

Credibility
       Definitions and Qualifications
       Personal Characteristics (Attraction)
The Self: Concept and Presentation
       Influences on Self-Concept
       Self-presentation
Summing Up
Study Projects and Tasks

CREDIBILITY

Definitions and Qualifications

The expression "What you are speaks so loudly I can't hear what you're saying" may be more fact than exaggeration. *Credibility* refers to the receiver's acceptance of or disposition toward the source. Aristotle used the term *ethos* to designate the audience's perception of the speaker. In regard to ethical proof, Aristotle set forth the general rule that "there is no proof so effective as that of the character."[1]

Speaker credibility is composed of what Aristotle called good will, good moral character, and good sense, as these are perceived by receivers. In modern times, speaker credibility has been discussed in terms of good intentions, trustworthiness, and competence or expertness. A speaker's credibility is determined by the receivers' perceptions and attitudes of trust and confidence, which are based in part on their beliefs about the intent, position in society, knowledge, and sincerity of the speaker. That the clever actor, the messianic personality, the evil doer can fool us is all too clear. The embezzler, the dictator, the false prophet are successful because they are *perceived* as having credibility. Both reason and research tell us that once they are discovered to be untrustworthy, they will be viewed as a questionable message source, regardless of their other qualities.[2] Receivers should be especially vigilant for sources that have good intentions but use unethical means.

In its 1908 catalogue, Sears, Roebuck used the credibility of its bankers to persuade the customer that the company was respectable and responsible (Figure 3–1).

In a pioneering study by Franklyn Haiman a speech was recorded, then variously attributed to the surgeon general of the United States, the secretary of the American Communist Party, and a university sophomore.[3] The higher credibility of the surgeon general produced more attitude change.

In an early study of written communications, materials were attributed half of the time to trustworthy sources and half of the time to untrustworthy sources.[4] The subjects were asked to evaluate the materials in terms of fairness and justification. The materials attributed to untrustworthy sources produced judgments of "less fair" and "less justified." When the same materials were

[1]Aristotle, *Rhetoric,* 1377b21–1378a19.

[2]Raymond G. Smith, "Source Credibility Context Effects," *Speech Monographs,* 40, no. 4 (1973), 303–9.

[3]Franklyn Haiman, "An Experimental Study of the Effects of Ethos in Public Speaking," *Speech Monographs,* 16 (1949), 190–202.

[4]Carl I. Hovland and Walter Weiss, "The Influence of Source Credibility on Communication Effectiveness," *Public Opinion Quarterly,* 15 (1951), 635–50.

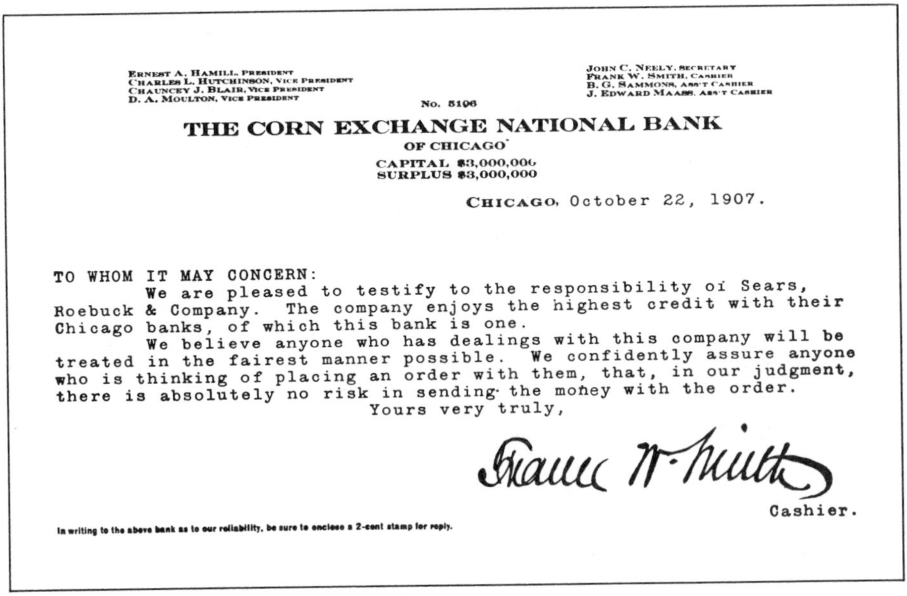

ERNEST A. HAMILL, PRESIDENT
CHARLES L. HUTCHINSON, VICE PRESIDENT
CHAUNCEY J. BLAIR, VICE PRESIDENT
D. A. MOULTON, VICE PRESIDENT

JOHN C. NEELY, SECRETARY
FRANK W. SMITH, CASHIER
B. G. SAMMONS, ASS'T CASHIER
J. EDWARD MAASS, ASS'T CASHIER

No. 5106

THE CORN EXCHANGE NATIONAL BANK
OF CHICAGO
CAPITAL $3,000,000
SURPLUS $3,000,000

CHICAGO, October 22, 1907.

TO WHOM IT MAY CONCERN:
    We are pleased to testify to the responsibility of Sears,
Roebuck & Company. The company enjoys the highest credit with their
Chicago banks, of which this bank is one.
    We believe anyone who has dealings with this company will be
treated in the fairest manner possible. We confidently assure anyone
who is thinking of placing an order with them, that, in our judgment,
there is absolutely no risk in sending the money with the order.
                    Yours very truly,

                    Frank W. Smith

                                        Cashier.

In writing to the above bank as to our reliability, be sure to enclose a 2-cent stamp for reply.

FIGURE 3-1

From Joseph J. Schroeder, Jr., ed., *1908 Sears, Roebuck Catalogue* (Northfield, Ill.: DBI Books), p. 18.

attributed to trustworthy sources, they were judged "more fair" and "more justified."

However, research has not always produced consistent results, and modern theorizers have wisely challenged the general linear notion of credibility.[5] Rather than simply presuming that sources either have or do not have a level of credibility that has a persuasive impact on an audience, we should view credibility as an interactive process among sources, messages, and receivers. Gary Cronkhite and Jo Liska have proposed a model of such a process. It consists of five interacting factors:

1. *Source characteristics.* These include physical and vocal characteristics of the source as well as postures and gestures. Some message elements such as language choice and organization are critical features that reflect on the source.
2. *Attributes inferred about the source.* Audiences actively infer source attributes such as occupation, educational level, knowledge, and organizational ability.
3. *The functions the source performs for the audience.* These functions usually relate to the topic situation. In a speech dealing with drug addiction, a heroin addict may *function* as a very credible source indeed.
4. *The criteria employed by receivers to judge whether a source is suitable to perform a given function.* There appears to be some evidence that people use different criteria for

[5]See, for example, Martin Fishbein and Icek Ajzen, *Belief, Attitude, Intention and Behavior* (Reading, Mass.: Addison-Wesley, 1975), pp. 489-95.

acceptability in different situations. A credible source in one situation may be a disaster in another.

5. *Changes in receiver information processing.* In our earlier discussion of McGuire's principles for analyzing receiver persuasibility, we noted the importance of receiver characteristics. Receiver information processing and organizing characteristics may change from situation to situation. The way a receiver organizes a message may influence the credibility he or she perceives in the source.[6]

Clearly many conditions affect people's perceptions of credibility. Although a convicted hard-core car thief may not meet the classical tests of credibility (good will, good moral character, good sense), if he were to speak (or write) about the secrets of his trade, he might indeed be perceived as having a certain credibility. After all, he is an expert! Characteristics that we infer about a source may cancel all or some credibility. Jesse Delia hypothesizes that "many persons hearing a militant speaker openly and explicitly advocate an abhorrent position on an issue important to them would make with equal certainty the attributions that the speaker is honest and forthright, but also very misguided and unsafe."[7]

The receiver's perception of a sender's intent appears to influence credibility. In one study a persuasive message was prepared on the topic of raising the minimum driving age. The same speech was given to two groups of teenagers. One group was told that the purpose of the program was to study the speaker's personality. The other group was told that the speaker considered teenage drivers a menace. In the first group the speaker's intent to persuade is blunted; in the second it is made abundantly clear. The second group perceived the communicator to be more biased, as might be expected. The first group reflected a greater attitude change in the direction advocated.[8]

In a study designed to persuade eighth graders to take a more conservative attitude about drugs, a law-enforcement officer was found to be less successful than others.[9] Perhaps his intent, as perceived by the students, injured his credibility. His presentation may have been too threatening for his audience. Or perhaps his status as a law officer didn't carry over to his expertise (if he had any) about drugs.

People's status may also vary with the issue. We may have high status in

[6]Gary Cronkhite and Jo Liska, "A Critique of Factor Analytic Approaches to the Study of Credibility," *Communication Monographs,* 43, no. 2 (June 1976), 91–107. See also Dominic A. Infante, Kenneth R. Parker, Christopher H. Clarke, Laverne Wilson, and Indrani A. Nathu, "A Comparison of Factor and Functional Approaches to Source Credibility," *Communication Quarterly,* 31, no. 1 (Winter 1983), 43–48.

[7]Jesse G. Delia, "A Constructivist Analysis of the Concept of Credibility," *Quarterly Journal of Speech,* 62, no. 4 (December 1976), 361–75.

[8]Jane Allyn and Leon Festinger, "The Effectiveness of Unanticipated Persuasive Communications," *Journal of Abnormal and Social Psychology,* 62 (1961), 35–40.

[9]James E. McCleaf and Margaret A. Colby, "The Effects of Students' Perceptions of a Speaker's Role on Their Recall of Drug Facts and Their Opinions and Attitudes About Drugs," *Journal of Educational Research,* 68 (July 1975), 382–86.

one role and low status in another. Dr. Spock may have high status as a baby doctor for some people but low status as a politician.

Apparently people's general impression of a sender's credibility is based on a wide array of variables; intent, trust, and competence are only the beginning. It is no wonder that some of the research evidence on credibility is sometimes inconsistent. However, when high source credibility is perceived and when it is relevant to the message and the situation, it generally produces more attitude change in the receivers.

Personal Characteristics (Attraction)

Part of the sender's credibility and attraction is established or reinforced by his or her personal characteristics (as perceived by the audience) and behavior during the sending of the message. Aristotle called this *ethical proof*. In its most general sense, ethical proof refers to the audience's impressions of the honesty, character, wisdom, and good will of the speaker. It is, in Erving Goffman's words, "impression management." It is part of how the speaker presents himself or herself to the receivers.[10]

Receivers are attracted and thought to be persuaded by perceptions of the following, more specific characteristics: perceived attitude similarity, social adjustment, status and recognition, dynamism, use of evidence and information, physical characteristics, and communication skills. Discussions of these follow. We will then consider how we manage impressions in order to present our best self for each audience and context.

Attitude similarity and common ground   A recent convention of Air Force aces brought together a group of people who had some very special experiences in common. They also held in common attitudes about some things, but not about everything. Some of their postmilitary experiences were not at all similar. Relating the issue at hand to these common experiences is not always simple or even possible for the persuader. But if he or she can achieve this and be perceived by the receivers as having related experiences and attitudes, then he or she can likely influence them.

Although they may foster attraction, similarities between receivers and sender do not always carry influence.[11] For example, a black person speaking against discrimination to a white audience might find that the dissimilarity in race enhances his credibility. However, if his audience were the Ku Klux Klan, he'd find his credibility, among other things, in jeopardy. The tax expert may be more persuasive with lawyers if they perceive him or her as different—as

[10]Erving Goffman, *The Presentation of Self in Everyday Life* (Garden City, N.Y.: Doubleday, 1959), p. 208.

[11]Michael Sunnafrank, "Attitude Similarity and Interpersonal Attraction in Communication Processes: In pursuit of an Ephemeral Influence," *Communication Monographs,* 50 (December 1983), 273–84.

having more competence and expertise in this area than they. When our *uncertainty* can be reduced by a dissimilar other, we may respond more positively.[12]

Age, sex, role, status, race, and especially experience—all are important similarities. However, it is the perceived attitude toward the topic that is the critical similarity. The others, for the most part, are important persuasively only when they are clearly related to the topic.[13]

Social adjustment   There is good evidence that we find well-adjusted people with a healthy self-concept more attractive than poorly adjusted people.[14] *Adjustment* is, however, a relative phenomenon. A poorly adjusted or artificially stimulated group of receivers may perceive even a demagogue as well adjusted. Perhaps when one is completely lost in a cause, the degree of adjustment shown by the leader becomes irrelevant. Centuries of cult phenomena pay witness to this possibility. On the other hand, a normal, healthy, socially well adjusted individual may be caught up in a moment of weakness or unusual social or physical pressure. We all lose control once in a while.

Those who exhibit personality extremes, painful exceptions to the contrary, are not perceived as having good social adjustment by most receivers. One extreme is an attitude of superiority, exhibited by aggression, sarcasm, and boastfulness. Another is that of inferiority, as shown by dependence, depression, and listlessness. Either extreme can lead to defensive behavior from receivers.

Some behaviors exhibited by senders are thought to improve receivers' perceptions of their social adjustment. These include establishing rapport easily and showing fairness. Anger is occasionally effective, but only if directed toward those who "should know better." Other things being equal, people who exhibit these traits are thought to be sociable and involved.

Status and recognition   We usually enjoy being associated with people of high status or position because they offer us some reflected status. "I shook hands with the president," we say with pride. High-status people generally enjoy the recognition they get. Superstars seem to thrive on cheering audiences. We all tend to enjoy being with people who provide us with status, praise, and recognition, those who laugh at our jokes, beg us to tell a story, or flatter us for some quality. All of these qualities are thought to contribute to the attraction we feel toward a person.

[12]Benjamin J. Broome, "The Attraction Paradigm Revisited: Responses to Dissimilar Others," *Human Communication Research,* 10, no. 1 (Fall 1983), 137–51.

[13]See Dominic A. Infante, "Similarity Between Advocate and Receiver: The Role of Instrumentality," *Central States Speech Journal,* 29, no. 3 (Fall 1978), 187–93.

[14]James McCroskey and others, "The Effects of Communication Apprehension on Interpersonal Attraction," *Human Communication Research,* 2, no. 1 (Fall 1975), 51–65.

We tend to be persuaded by those who offer us sincere status and recognition. Those who resort to phony praise usually see their persuasion backfire when they are found out. Those who ignore us are almost always perceived as unattractive and not very persuasive.

Dynamism and humor   Receivers are thought—again, other things being equal—to find active, energetic senders more persuasive than dull, lethargic ones. This dimension is usually based on oral delivery. A boring, dull, inactive delivery decreases the persuasiveness of even the most credible of senders. A little showmanship helps convince an audience. Unfortunately, for some mesmerized audiences a dynamic delivery may outweigh any other dimensions of ethical proof.

If you feel you do not tell a joke well, or if you find it difficult to be a humorous speaker, you need not be too concerned. Research on the impact of humor on an audience seems to indicate that at least in persuasive speeches humor makes little difference. A study by P. E. Lull found that audiences listening to humorous and nonhumorous speeches on socialized medicine were equally persuaded by both speeches.[15] Donald Kilpela obtained the same results in a more recent study that used government health insurance as the topic.[16] Both methods were effective, but they did not vary significantly in effectiveness. A series of studies by Charles Gruner produced similar results, except that humor seemed to improve the character ratings of the speaker.[17] A study by Allan Kennedy found that "subjects viewed the humorous introductory speech as significantly more effective, enjoyable, and interesting."[18] A study by J. Douglas Gibb comparing humorous and nonhumorous information lectures showed significantly better student retention of the humorous lecture.[19] Two other researchers found that information recall was better over time (six weeks) when enhanced with humor.[20] Lull and Kilpela were quick to point out, however, that the type of humor in their studies may not have been very professional. In other words, a Don Rickles or a Bill Cosby might have produced significant persuasive results.

Remember that humor can work against you if it is offensive, confuses the

---

[15]P. E. Lull, "The Effectiveness of Humor in Persuasive Speeches," *Speech Monographs,* 7 (1940), 26–40.

[16]Donald Kilpela, "An Experimental Study of the Effects of Humor on Persuasion" (M.A. thesis, Wayne State University, 1961). See also D. Markiewicz, "Effects of Humor on Persuasion," *Sociometry,* 34 (1974), 407–22.

[17]Charles Gruner, "Effect of Humor on Speaker Ethos and Audience Information Gain," *Journal of Communication,* 17, no. 3 (1967), 228–33.

[18]Allan J. Kennedy, "The Effect of Humor Upon Source Credibility," *Speech Communication Association Abstracts,* 1972, p. 10.

[19]J. Douglas Gibb, "An Experimental Comparison of the Humorous Lecture and the Nonhumorous Lecture in Informative Speaking" (M.A. thesis, University of Utah, 1964).

[20]R. M. Kaplan and G. C. Pascoe, "Humorous Lectures and Humorous Examples: Some Effects Upon Comprehension and Retention," *Journal of Educational Psychology,* 69 (1977), 61–65.

mood, or in some other way distracts from the message. Related, funny anecdotes (if told well and in good taste) have probably helped hold attention for many an otherwise dull speaker, subject, or audience.[21]

Evidence and information   Even highly credible sources lose some of their ethical proof or effect over time. "You're only as good as your last show," as one wag put it. This means that there is a limit to how long you can simply assert things without citing evidence or information. Sometimes we're only as good as our information: the only navigator in a ship lost at sea, the only person with the knowledge to handle an emergency—both are examples in which *information* leads to power and influence.

The effect on source credibility of the source's use of *evidence* is a more complicated question. If one interprets early studies on the effects of evidence as McCroskey does in an excellent summary of such research,[22] one discovers a lack of close control for the variable of perceived source credibility. As we have stated so many times before, the question of what the receiver thinks, expects, and perceives is still the crux of human communication. Although McCroskey's conclusions were mixed, they did lead to the tentative conclusion that evidence had at least some impact on credibility.[23]

An updating and rearranging of the conclusions of McCroskey's 1969 study and an accounting for the variable of perceived source credibility lead to the following generalizations:

1. Including good evidence may significantly increase immediate audience attitude change and source credibility when the source is initially perceived to be moderate-to-low credible, when the message is well delivered, and when the audience has little or no prior familiarity with the evidence included or similar evidence.

2. Including good evidence may significantly increase sustained audience attitude change regardless of the source's initial credibility, the quality of the delivery of the message, or the medium by which the message is transmitted.

3. Evidence appears to serve as an inhibitor to counterpersuasion.

4. The medium of transmission of a message has little if any effect on the functioning of evidence in persuasive communication.

5. Including good evidence has little if any impact on immediate audience attitude change or source credibility if:
   a. the source of the message is initially perceived to be high-credible;

[21]D. Zillmann, B. R. Williams, J. Bryant, K. R. Boynton, and M. A. Wulf, "Acquisition of Information From Educational Television Programs as a Function of Differently Placed Humorous Inserts," *Journal of Educational Psychology*, 72 (1980), 170–80.

[22]James C. McCroskey, "A Summary of Experimental Research on the Effects of Evidence in Persuasive Communication," *Quarterly Journal of Speech*, 55 (1969), 169–76.

[23]See especially Robert S. Cathcart, "An Experimental Study of the Relative Effectiveness of Four Methods of Presenting Evidence," *Speech Monographs*, 22 (1955), 226–33.

b. the message (when oral) is delivered poorly;

c. the audience is familiar with the evidence prior to exposure to the source's message.[24]

Physical characteristics When we first see another person we are affected by our own biases about what we see (or think we see) even before the person communicates orally. Large, fat, sloppy, handsome, beautiful, cool, or whatever, each characteristic will attract or repel us. Physical characteristics engender more attributions than just physical attractiveness, although in an initial or brief meeting, we may start there, especially if the other person's face or body is unusually striking.

In a "computer dance" study individuals were randomly paired with one another. The participants were surveyed as to how much they liked their partner, how much they wanted to date their partner again, and how often they did in fact date their partner again. None of the personality and scholastic-aptitude characteristics tested predicted couple compatibility; the largest determinant of a participant's liking for his or her date was physical attractiveness.[25] In an initial or short-term encounter in a predominantly similar group this factor must be worth something; in more serious, long-term relationships it is probably less important.

There are sharp cultural differences of opinion about what constitutes physical beauty. Our male students from the Middle East consider our lean model stereotypes less attractive than their chunkier sisters. There are also *individual* differences about these matters in all cultures.

Western art and media have perpetuated our stereotype attributions. We tend (unfortunately sometimes) to attribute less competence, less status, and less credibility to the less physically attractive. Physical attractiveness, however, should include the total physical makeup of an individual. This includes environmental causes of appearance, such as diet, drugs, and climate, as well as hereditary factors. People vary physically in their reaction time, energy level, and rate of learning. They also vary in hearing, sight, color, size, shape, and so on, all of which add up to and influence total personality as well as physical attractiveness. After all, beauty is skin-deep only in the superficial sense. The feedback we decode over time from society about our physical makeup and the way we accommodate that feedback probably affect our attractiveness more than our superficial physical characteristics do.

Other things being equal, well-adjusted, smart young people are perceived as more attractive than those who do not possess these characteristics. There is some evidence that physical attractiveness is more important between

[24]James C. McCroskey, "The Effects of Evidence as an Inhibitor of Counterpersuasion," *Speech Monographs,* 37 (1970), 188–94; conclusion 3 from McCroskey, "Summary of Experimental Research," 175.

[25]Elaine Walster and others, "Importance of Physical Attractiveness in Dating Behavior," *Journal of Personality and Social Psychology,* 4 (1966), 508–16.

the sexes than within each sex. That is, women tend to care more about what their men friends look like than what their women friends look like (and vice versa).

The role of clothing, cosmetics, calorie counting, surgery, and other possible means of improving our appearance becomes critical when these are added to what nature gave us. Research suggests that individuals who appear attractive to the receivers of communication are more successful. In one clever study a young woman was dressed and made up attractively for one group of receivers and was then dressed and made up to look unattractive to a similar audience. The young woman was judged to be more believable and was generally found to be more persuasive and more desirable when presented attractively.[26]

We cannot change everything about our physical appearance through clothing, grooming, and accessories such as rings, wigs, eyeglasses, girdles, flowers, lipstick, and aftershaves. We can do a lot, but the distance from appropriate to inappropriate is sometimes short.

Right or wrong, many stereotypes are associated with clothes and accessories. Research helps us define even these. Persons who wear bizarre clothes are considered more radical, more activist, and more likely to experiment with drugs. People who wear more conventional dress are associated with everyday jobs and "traditional fun."[27] The problem is in knowing what kind of clothes and accessories are conventional, in fashion, or expected of us.

The nonverbals of clothes and accessories make a big difference in the way we are seen totally—socially, vocationally, sexually, and so on. The key word is *appropriate*. We usually do not wish to stand out in a crowd. Yet we want to be fashionable and appropriate to what is expected of us at any given time or in any particular situation.

Communication skills   Our use of voice and language affects our credibility. Studies show that people who exhibit a greater linguistic diversity in terms of verb tenses, adjectives, adverbs, and connectives are perceived as more credible. Inarticulate people are rated low in competence, dynamism, and social status.[28] Of course a showy display of language can work against a speaker, hurting not only credibility but also clarity. On the other hand,

[26]J. Mills and E. Aronson, "Opinion Change as a Function of the Communicator's Attractiveness and Desire to Influence," *Journal of Personality and Social Psychology*, 1 (1965), 73–77. See also R. N. Widgery and B. Webster, "The Effects of Physical Attractiveness Upon Perceived Initial Credibility," *Michigan Speech Journal*, 4 (1969), 4–15.

[27]For more on these matters, see Mark L. Knapp, *Nonverbal Communication in Human Interaction* (New York: Holt, Rinehart & Winston, 1978).

[28]James J. Bradac, Catherine W. Konsky, and Robert A. Davies, "Two Studies of the Effects of Linguistic Diversity Upon the Judgments of Communicator Attributes and Message Effectiveness," *Communication Monographs*, 43 (March 1976), 70–79.

nonfluent, inarticulate language generally decreases one's credibility.[29] The same can be said of poor use of voice. It has been found that receivers can detect a person's social status from voice cues alone.[30] You must determine what is *appropriate* language and voice for your receivers in specific situations. Other communication skills, such as analyzing audiences, organizing messages, and reading feedback cues, are of course critical, and indeed are the heart of this book.

THE SELF: CONCEPT AND PRESENTATION

How we perceive ourselves is important because it helps control our actions. It partially determines how an individual will behave and then perceive and evaluate that behavior. For example, if an individual perceives himself or herself to be uncoordinated, then that individual's behavior will reflect that belief. The individual will shun or at least avoid athletics and may even resent physical education. In contrast, an individual with similar physical coordination who perceives himself or herself to be adequately coordinated will be more likely to enjoy athletics and display greater athletic prowess. Thus, self-concept can affect performance, and although the two individuals possess similar ability, the second individual may appear more coordinated. Self-concept can also affect one's attitude and achievement.[31]

Rules theorists who view self-concept as a personal construct expect "the structure and strength of individual self-concepts to exert a necessary and substantial influence on message comprehension, message adaptation, and message effectiveness in controlling our own and other's behaviors."[32]

Self-concept has been defined as "the sum total of the view which an individual has of himself. . . . a unique set of perceptions, ideas, and atti-

[29]Eldon E. Baker, "The Immediate Effects of Perceived Speaker Disorganization on Speaker Credibility and Audience-attitude Change in Persuasive Speaking," *Western Speech,* 29 (1965), 148–61; and Gerald R. Miller and Murray A. Hewgill, "The Effect of Variations in Nonfluency on Audience Ratings of Source Credibility," *Quarterly Journal of Speech,* 50 (1964), 36–44. See also Anthony Mulac, "Evaluation of the Speech Dialect Attitudinal Scale," *Speech Monographs,* 42 (1975), 184–89; and Tamara Carbone, "Stylistic Variables as Related to Source Credibility: A Content Analysis Approach," *Speech Monographs,* 42 (1975), 99–106.

[30]James D. Moe, "Listener Judgments of Status Cues in Speech: A Replication and Extension," *Speech Monographs,* 39 (1972), 144–47. See also William Goldman and Philip Lewis, "Beautiful is Good: Evidence That the Physically Attractive Are More Socially Skillful," *Journal of Experimental Social Psychology,* 13 (1977), 125–30.

[31]See Shirley C. Samuels, *Enhancing Self-Concept in Early Childhood* (New York: Human Science Press, 1977), p. 36.

[32]Donald P. Cushman, Barry Valentinsen, and David Dietrich, "A Rules Theory of Interpersonal Relationships," in Frank E. X. Dance, *Human Communication Theory* (New York: Harper & Row, Pub., 1982), p. 100.

tudes. . . ."[33] It is both conscious and unconscious, and it changes with our most recent experiences and self-perceptions. We use words such as *self-percept, self-concept,* and *self-identity* to talk about one's notion of oneself.[34] However, words such as *self-esteem, self-valuation,* and *self-regard* are of a slightly different order. We tend to think of these as positive or negative traits. A related term is *self-acceptance.* A person with high self-acceptance exhibits a willingness to accept both positive and negative notions as a part of his or her total self-concept.

For the most part we try to be consistent in our self-concept. However, when we are extremely frustrated, perhaps by too positive or too negative a self-concept, we may resort to various unrelated behaviors to compensate for our frustration. For example, we may become overtalkative when insecure. A realistic self-image can be a critical part of communication and perception as well as of motivation in general. Every person is the center of his or her own field of experience, and the way one perceives and responds to that field is one's own reality.

Research suggests that an unreasonable or unrealistic self-concept, particularly one low in self-esteem, may contribute to failure, thereby acting as a kind of self-fulfilling prophecy. A student who will not even discuss a math course because his or her self-concept says that he or she is mathematically illiterate is not apt to do well in a math course. This is tragic when *only* a student's poor opinion of himself or herself stands in the way of success. However, suppose a student really has little or no math aptitude. Were this person to develop an unrealistically positive conception of his or her mathematical ability, then he or she would obviously be headed for frustration and ultimately an even poorer self-concept than the original one.

The point is that your self-concept, whether good or bad, high or low, should be within the realm of physical or social reality. Knowing what is *realistic* as well as what is unique is, of course, the eternal problem. A discussion of some of the major influences on self-concept follows.

Influences on Self-Concept

Significant others   A large portion of our self-concept is shaped by interactions and social comparisons with others, competence, judgments, and feelings from the clues we observe or infer from others—a word or look of approval, an honest criticism, even the appearance of another. We thus develop concepts of our physical, emotional, and social selves, and to a considerable extent we tend to use this complex self-image when we perceive, respond, act, and communicate.

People who are significant to us form no small part of our self-concept. *Group memberships* are an important influence on us. Our self-concept reflects the society in which we live. Our family, school, church, and temple are all

---

[33]Donald W. Felker, *Building Positive Self-Concepts* (Minneapolis: Burgess, 1974), p. 2.
[34]John J. Sherwood, "Self Identity and Referent Others," *Sociometry,* 28 (1965), 66–81.

thought to greatly influence our self-concept. This is not to suggest that we are all carbon copies of those having backgrounds similar to our own. Even the culture in which we live determines only what we learn as a member of a group, not what we learn as an individual. This explains in part why humans alter their behavior in what seem to be the most inconsistent ways. Living in a society requires meeting certain standards or fitting into certain patterns that are roughly agreed on by the members of that group. Much nonstandard individual behavior is *sublimated*—expressed in constructive, socially acceptable forms in deference to these group codes. The *valuation, regard,* and *acceptance* individuals have of their total group—and their conceptions of the group's valuation, regard, and acceptance of them—are critical to the development of their self-concept. How others feel about us, or at least how we think they feel about us, particularly if they are significant others—whether reference groups, respected friends, or even those whose roles are ill defined—is probably the most important part of self-concept. What these others expect of us, how they react to us, and how socially realistic we are in evaluating these expectations and reactions form another large part of our self-concept.

Competence   Your sense of *competence* is also related to your self-concept. "Competence means capacity, fitness, or ability. The competence of a living organism means its fitness or ability to carry on those transactions with the environment which result in its maintaining itself, growing and flour-ishing."[35] A self-concept that includes a feeling of incompetence may leave you in a state of helplessness and inertia and promote a sense of inferiority. You must build realistic confidence as well as competence into your self-concept. A persistent challenge to your sense of personal and social competence is a prime contributor toward frustration and, not infrequently, aggression. Your sense of competence is important to your communication with others. As we explained in Chapter 2, competence is an important source of motivation for both senders and receivers of persuasive messages.

Role   *Role* pertains in part to a more specific aspect of group member-ship and is also thought to have a strong influence on self-concept. Some roles are cast upon us by society because of our age, our sex, even our size, and, unfortunately, sometimes our race. Some roles we assign ourselves on the basis of our life goals, and some are really disguises of our private personalities, disguises that we create in order to be accepted by certain groups. In its most important sense a role is that part we cast for ourselves on the stage of life. We may portray many roles to the world, but each of us determines, with the aid of society and its subgroups, what our particular role will be. Our self-concept is influenced by that decision. Occupational roles are often stereotyped, and we

---

[35]Robert W. White assisted by Katherine F. Bruner, eds., *The Study of Lives* (New York: Atherton, 1966), p. 74.

learn to expect (if not always approve) certain roles from supervisors, police officers, teachers, lawyers, doctors, and so forth. Professors who do not act like professors are often enigmas to society. The doctor who does not play the role patients expect had better develop an interest in research. A persuader needs to know not only his or her own role but that role as it is perceived by the audience. More will be said of role under the heading of self-presentation.

Context and situation   The *situational* influences upon our self-concept and our total personality include those exceptional, unpredictable, and often accidental events that happen to all of us. These are events that can alter our lives, casting us into roles that may profoundly affect our self-concept—a jail sentence, a lost love, a scholarship, a riot, an insight or perspective suddenly and never before achieved. A really good teacher probably alters the lives and careers of many unsuspecting students. An unexpected failing grade or a hard-won A from such a teacher can either shake or make our self-concept.

To review, self-concept is a major part of one's personality. We may consider personality to be the sum of a person's knowledge, motives, values, beliefs, and goal-seeking patterns.

Persuasion is affected by self-concept in several interesting ways. In general, we can expect others to perceive and react to us and the rest of the world in ways that are as consistent with their self-concepts as possible. Trying to "see" and understand others by understanding what their self-concept is thus becomes a characteristic of sensitive human communication. We all should occasionally reevaluate how realistic our *own* self-concept is. Sometimes we either downgrade ourselves or take ourselves too seriously.

If the *self-regard* part of our self-concept is unusually negative, we might very well become difficult, negative, or even sullen communicators. An unrealistically positive *self-valuation* can, of course, make us different but equally painful communicators. Other things being equal, a healthy, reality-centered, positive self-concept should make us better and more confident communicators. Most important, it should include some willingness to accommodate change.

Ideally, a good self-concept is objective, realistic, positive, and yet self-accepting; it can live with negative notions, too. A healthy self-concept should include some willingness to change, a tolerance for confusion, patience with disagreement, and empathy for other self-concepts. If you are a significant other for someone, if only for a moment, you have a special communication responsibility, for we are reasonably sure that such individuals are a key to the development of one's self-concept.

Self-presentation

The creative sociologist Erving Goffman suggests that in our efforts to present our best and most persuasive self, we try to give appropriate performances on the stage of life. Consider a college senior preparing for an employment interview. He or she may attempt to present an impression of maturity, self-confidence, knowledgeability, and dependability. This can be done in the following general ways: an appropriate front, dramatic realization, and mystification.[36]

An appropriate front   This is general behavior designed (if not natural) to better define (persuasively, you hope) who you are. Your personal front includes things over which you have only limited control, such as sex, age, and size. It also includes more modifiable dimensions: your clothes, posture, gestures, facial expressions, and language patterns. Should our hero appear in dirty shorts, needing a haircut, and using profanity—quite a different front, isn't it?

Dramatic realization   According to Goffman, we must clearly realize the role expected of us and work it into the performance. We may have to be talented performers to hide our lack of confidence. If the role calls for attentiveness, our college student had better give such an impression. To be paying attention but not be perceived that way is unfortunate impression management. A flip physician who writes a fast prescription, however accurate the quick diagnosis, may be viewed suspiciously by the patient.

Mystification   This aspect of impression management refers to the perception of social distances between the actor and the audience. Our flip physician is more apt to be concerned with this kind of impression than our interviewee. That is, the physician must not become too folksy lest he or she lose some of the mystery in the medical role. Our college student, however, must accommodate the real or fancied social distance in the theater in which he or she is located.

For all of the superficial aspects of self-presentation, we do present ourselves to others and they do draw impressions—good, bad, and indifferent. If as students of persuasion we learn to better understand this dramaturgical model, we should be better equipped to deal with impression management—good, bad, and indifferent.

The important lesson of this chapter is that influence involves impressions of trust and confidence based on the perceived intent, position, knowledge, and sincerity of the source.

[36]These three concepts are discussed in Goffman, *Presentation of Self,* pp. 22, 30, 67.

SUMMING UP

Credibility refers to the receiver's acceptance of or disposition toward the source. "There is no proof so effective as that of the character." (Aristotle) Credibility should be viewed as an interactive process between sources, messages, and receivers. Credibility is related to notions of good intentions, trustworthiness, and competence or expertise. These are based, in part, on perceptions of intent, position in society, knowledge, and sincerity of the speaker. Part of one's credibility and attraction (ethical proof) is established or reinforced by the sender's personal characteristics and behavior during the sending of the message. How you present yourself is called *impression management*. Receivers are attracted and thought to be persuaded by perceptions of: attitude similarity, social adjustment, status and recognition, dynamism, use of evidence and information, physical characteristics, and communication skills.

Self-concept is the sum total of the view which one has of one's self. It is both conscious and unconscious and it changes with our most recent experiences and self-perceptions. Some of the major influences upon our self-concepts are: significant others, competence, role, group memberships, and situational events.

Self-presentations are the performances we give on the stage of life. Three dimensions of your presentation are: *front* (appearance and manner), *dramatic realization* (playing our roles), and *mystification* (social distancing).

Social influence almost always involves impressions of trust and confidence based on the perceived intent, position, knowledge, and sincerity of the source.

STUDY PROJECTS
AND TASKS

1. Find a persuasive message (such as an article, book, speech, or recording), and then systematically analyze it in terms of the source's (1) intention, (2) trustworthiness, (3) competence or expertness, (4) evidence.
2. Find an example of short-term persuasion that failed in the long run because the person or persons lacked enough good sense, good moral character, and good will (for example, unscrupulous land dealers, zealots for radical causes, sellers of illegal goods).
3. Form a three-to-five-person discussion group. Examine the project above and seek explanations for the apparent exceptions so often found in society (some examples: the Mafia, pushers, pimps, some radical groups, purchased term papers).
4. Prepare a speech in which you introduce a classmate who will speak on a topic with which he or she has at least some competence or expertness. Your purpose is to enhance the speaker's credibility. Interview the speaker before preparing your introduction. (Some possibilities: a speech on skiing in Colorado by the captain of

the ski team, who has been there; a speech on backpacking by an experienced eagle scout; a speech on person-to-person combat by a Grenada veteran.) The main speech may or may not be given, but introduce the speaker as if he or she were actually about to speak. Make your speech true to the facts, but attempt to enhance the person's credibility on the topic.

5. Prepare a three-to-five-minute persuasive speech on a topic of your choice in which you attempt to subtly enhance your own *ethos* or credibility through the use of ethical proof (for example, similarity, status, voice and language, dynamism, evidence).

6. You most likely formed an initial impression of your instructor. Impression formation is quite normal and sometimes aids us in our general persuasive stance. However, our first impressions do not always guide us correctly.

    Develop and write a 100-word first impression of your instructor. Be sure to include an analysis of variables such as his or her motives, traits, and personality attributes. You may want to share these first impressions with your instructor and others in the class. You may be surprised!

7. Select a person who attracts you, and assess your evaluation of that person in terms of the elements of attraction discussed in this chapter. (Or do the same for a person whom you find unattractive.) Be prepared to discuss assessment in class.

8. "All the world's a stage, and all the men and women merely players." (Shakespeare)

    We all attempt to manage other's impressions of us. Analyze the impression management conducted by one of your instructors, in terms of his or her front, dramatic realization, and mystification.

9. Research either a really good or really bad example of impression management. Consider and describe how the person or organization developed a *front,* attempted *dramatic realization,* and used *mystification.* (Possible examples: a doctor's office, the dean's office, a fancy party, a police officer, a rock group or singer, a teacher.)

4
Theories
of Persuasion

Classical Rhetoric
        The Canons of Rhetoric
        Forerunners of Modern Rhetoric
Consistency Theories
        Balance Theory
        Congruity Theory
        Dissonance Theory
        Cognitive-response Theory
Theories of Behavioral Perception
        Social-judgment Theory
        Self-perception Theory
        Attribution Theory
Summing Up
Study Projects and Tasks

A theory allows us to *make sense* of information, events, and observations. For George Kelly it is "a way of highlighting events so they may be viewed in some kind of perspective."[1] No matter how elegant the theory, no matter how clearly it explains events, Kelly cautions, "it is quite unreasonable to hope they [events] ever can be so completely revealed there will be nothing left to look for. The best one can ever expect of a theory is that it will enable him to see what he has never seen before, and that it will be succeeded in time by another theory which will disclose some of what still remains hidden."[2]

Even the sciences refine and sometimes change long-standing theories (such as matter and energy). Mathematics, with all of its predictive power, concedes that it does not know if it is free of contradictions. Is Euclidean geometry as consistent or inconsistent as the arithmetic of real numbers? There are, of course, practical, common-sense predictions from geometry that we live by—navigators, engineers, and architects certainly do. Sometimes the "wrong" rules turn out to work as well as the "right" ones. A city planner laying out a rectangular pattern for the streets of a town would find that spherical-geometry rules *worked* as well as those of plane geometry. The arcs would be so great that they would *act* like straight lines.

Theories of social influence have similar problems: the elegant, broad-range theories of the 1960s and 1970s need refinement, certainly more quali-fications, and perhaps even reconceptualization. Persuasive messages are interpreted by people and the important meanings constructed out of their knowledge, emotions, and past experiences. Messages are also real: some act like causes, and some *work* better than others. Advertisers, campaigners, professional speakers know very well the loose, causal connections between theory and response; students may not. Mary John Smith's suggestion is a good one: "persuasion theories should be reconceptualized as generalizations describing probable covariations between persuasive strategies and purposive responses, given the nature of the contextually relevant rules in operation."[3]

Since our interest lies mainly in one-to-many persuasion, our pragmatic, multidisciplinary framework is easier for us to live with than it is for those interested primarily in interpersonal influence or research methodology. All theories are imperfect, all have detractors (as a rule)—even classical rhetoric and, within it, the *canons* of rhetoric.

---

[1]George A. Kelly, "A Brief Introduction to Personal Construct Theory," in *Perspectives in Personal Construct Theory*, ed. D. Bannister (London: Academic Press, 1970), p. 260.

[2]Ibid.

[3]Mary John Smith, *Persuasion and Human Action* (Belmont, Calif.: Wadsworth, 1982), p. 315.

CLASSICAL RHETORIC

Aristotle defined rhetoric as "the faculty of observing in any given case the available means of persuasion."[4] The classical period of rhetoric extended from the seventh century B.C. to the fifth century A.D. In addition to Aristotle the major early rhetoricians were Plato, Isocrates, Cicero, and Quintilian. They were interested mainly in specific occasions calling for primarily oral communication. These occasions were categorized as follows:

1. *forensic:* situations such as courtroom appeals, where one dealt with past facts
2. *epideictic:* ceremonial occasions where one dealt with present facts
3. *deliberative:* political speaking in which one dealt with future facts

Pragmatic in approach, the classicists named the speech parts, classified the principles and patterns of organization, and specified the tasks of preparation. One customary pattern consisted of (1) exordium (introduction), (2) narration (the facts of the case), (3) confirmation (proofs), (4) refutation, and (5) peroration (conclusion).[5] The most famous set of tasks were called *canons*, and we will turn to them shortly. Classical teachers of rhetoric separated rhetoric from grammar, logic, and poetics. Rhetoric was primarily a strategy and an art of persuasion.

Aristotle's emphasis was, of course, on public speaking, since that was the primary communication mode of his time. Recent rhetorical thinkers have broadened that focus to include modern communication situations and channels, and more sophisticated notions of how attitudes change.[6]

Aristotle's *Rhetoric* is based on four fundamental assumptions. First rhetoric is a functional art. It is "a useful art operating in the social medium for the purpose of *doing* something. . . . speech is an instrument of social adaptation."[7] Second, rhetoric can be taught. Aristotle believed "rhetoric was composed of a body of material yielding to systematic treatment and . . . it was possible through practice to develop speaking skills."[8] Third, rhetorical theory is based on the doctrine of the *mean.* "This standard . . . makes balance, proportion, and freedom from extremes the ideal toward which practice and instruction should lead."[9] The mean is relative rather than mathematical and

[4]Aristotle, *Rhetoric and Poetics,* trans. W. Rhys Roberts (New York: Modern Library, 1954), p. 24.

[5]See Douglas Ehninger, "Campbell, Blair, and Whately Revisited," *Southern Speech Journal,* 28 (1963), 169–82.

[6]See, for example, Wayne Brockriede, "Dimensions of the Concept of Rhetoric," *Quarterly Journal of Speech,* 54 (1968), 1–12. See also Wayne Brockriede, "Toward a Contemporary Aristotelian Theory of Rhetoric," *Quarterly Journal of Speech,* 52 (1966), 33–40.

[7]Lester Thonssen and A. Craig Baird, *Speech Criticism* (New York: Ronald Press, 1948), pp. 70–71.

[8]Ibid., p. 71.

[9]Ibid., p. 73.

depends upon the circumstances. Fourth, rhetoric is the method of "giving effectiveness to truth"[10] within the body politic. Consequently, Aristotle gives primary emphasis to logical modes of persuasion and the means for seeing that "truth will out."[11]

Our discussion in Chapter 1 of socially imperative reasons for studying persuasion reflects the first assumption (speech is an instrument of social adaptation). The second assumption (rhetoric can be taught) is the reason for this book and the course you're taking. The third assumption, regarding the doctrine of the mean, will be reflected in subsequent chapters. Intelligent people can be expected to hold different views about the wide range of controversial topics available today, and persuasion allows us the opportunity to see both sides of such issues. The fourth assumption suggests that skillful persuasion helps assure that truth will win out. Humans find truth and justice easier to accept than their opposites.

It was Aristotle's view that a knowledge of persuasion also gives us a better chance to defend ourselves from the unscrupulous. Today this knowledge becomes a form of consumer protection.

The Canons of Rhetoric

Aristotle and other classical rhetoricians advocated the completion of five basic, interrelated tasks in the preparation and delivery of a persuasive message. These tasks are referred to as the five *canons*. Although *canon* has the ring of *law*, in modern times we should view canons as rules.

Invention (inventio)   This is the task of investigating the message and the audience in order to discover the available means of persuasion. It includes narrowing the purpose and gathering and analyzing facts and evidence on the issues that are found, particularly as they relate to the receiver's needs—a reminder that audience analysis and adaptation are critical. This canon would also have us examine a list of twenty-eight common topics (*topoi*) that can suggest lines of argument—for example, possible-impossible, good-evil, honor-disgrace, and justice-injustice. This canon also recommends appealing to things desired by all people, such as happiness, justice, courage, temperance, health, wealth, friendship, reputation, and life itself.

Aristotle defined three modes or means of persuasion that, when used to investigate a specific message and audience, become sources of persuasion. "The first kind depends on the personal characteristics of the speaker ETHOS; the second on putting the audience into a certain frame of mind PATHOS; the third on the proof or apparent proof provided by the words of the speech itself LOGOS."[12] *Ethos* is identical to the concept of source credibility discussed in

10Ibid., p. 74.
11For more on the classical period of rhetoric, see Gary Cronkhite, *Persuasion: Speech and Behavioral Change* (Indianapolis: Bobbs-Merrill, 1969), pp. 18–48.
12Aristotle, *Rhetoric and Poetics*, pp. 24–25.

Chapter 3. *Pathos* refers to emotional appeals similar to those used today (see Chapter 2). *Logos* refers to logical appeals through reasoned discourse (see Chapter 7).

Other tools provided by Aristotle in the *Rhetoric* to assist in the invention process include the *enthymeme,* "a kind of imperfect syllogism, which produces, not the conclusive demonstration that we get in science and logic, but belief or persuasion," and the *example,* a specific verifiable phenomenon used as the basis for inductive reasoning.[13]

Arrangement (disposito)   This canon is concerned with the organization of the speech or message. Aristotle used the Greek word *taxis,* denoting division or arrangement, to explain what he thought was the most obvious and logical arrangement of the parts of a speech, particularly a persuasive one. He felt that the following elements were related most closely to the thinking habits of humans: proem (introduction), statement, argument, and epilogue (conclusion).[14] The purpose of the proem is most interesting to modern students of persuasion. For Aristotle, the proem (when necessary) involved gaining attention, establishing speaker credibility (ethos), and stating the purpose. More will be said of arrangement in Chapter 6.

Style (elocutio)   This canon involves the kinds of words and language in which one clothes the message. It advises one to use acceptable, correct, appropriate language; make the language clear and direct; make it polished, noble, and vivid; and adjust it to the message, audience, and speaker. Style involves selecting words that arouse the appropriate emotional response in the audience and help establish the proper ethical image for the speaker.[15] Style was described by Cicero in terms of level—a grand or superelevated style; a moderate style; and a plain or simple style.

Memory (memoria)   This canon refers to a speaker's retention and grasp of the content in some kind of sequential order. The idea of associating your main points with other natural sequences of events as a mnemonic device was suggested by the ancients. Of the five canons, Aristotle had the least to say about memory. Modern writers also say little of this canon, although Ross in a 1983 text developed the idea that the key word for memory protection is *system.*[16]

Delivery (pronunciatio)   This canon refers to the art of sending the oral message. Its main elements are voice and body action. The ancients

[13]Edward P. J. Corbett, *Classical Rhetoric for the Modern Student* (New York: Oxford University Press, 1965), p. 68.

[14]Lane Cooper, *The Rhetoric of Aristotle* (New York: Appleton-Century-Crofts, 1932), p. 220.

[15]Corbett, *Classical Rhetoric for the Modern Student,* p. 375.

[16]Raymond S. Ross, *Speech Communication,* 6th ed. (Englewood Cliffs, N.J.: Prentice-Hall, 1983), pp. 196–97.

warned of vocal monotony, improper rate of delivery, bad posture, and excessive random gestures and movements. The nonverbal aspects of communication were considered even then.

There was a strong *ethical* character to the ancient theory of rhetoric. For Plato, the purpose of rhetoric was to make known the will of God. Aristotle said that a major purpose of rhetoric was to make truth and justice prevail. Quintilian's definition of a successful orator as a *good man* skilled in speaking sums up the point.

Concerns over pretheoretical orientations are not new. Richard Jebb makes this cogent comment about the canons and Aristotle's *Rhetoric:*

> Complex, lucid, seminal, Aristotle's work has had both beneficial and harmful influences on the study of rhetoric. On the one hand, it supplies the basis for opening up the compositional and theoretical possibilities in a rhetorical situation; on the other, it is so persuasive that it has closed many theorists into an ingrown and mechanical system. Aristotle himself has avoided the dilemma by creating a work at once systematic and open-ended.[17]

Forerunners of Modern Rhetoric

James A. Winans was one of the most important contributors to rhetorical theory and one of the most important bridges to modern speech-communication approaches to human persuasion. His book *Public Speaking,* published in 1917, was the first to apply the popular Jamesian-Tichenerian psychology of the times to oral persuasion.[18] Following James's notion that *what holds attention determines action,* Winans defined persuasion as "the process of inducing others to give fair, favorable, or undivided attention to propositions."[19] He, like his psychologist contemporaries, recognized the importance of emotion and recommended "arousing emotion to fix attention by awaking desire for the end sought."[20] Desire could be awakened through an appeal to the psychological motives of personal interest, social duty, and religious duty couched in logical, emotional, and ethical types of proof.

Winans emphasized spoken persuasion; his distinctions between conversational style and conversational quality were pioneering. He believed that the public speaker should exhibit the best qualities and moods of conversation rather than a stylized version.[21] His entire discussion of the canon of delivery is of historic importance.

---

[17]Richard Cloverhouse Jebb, trans., "Aristotle: The Rhetoric," in *Readings in Classical Rhetoric,* ed. Thomas W. Benson and Michael H. Prosser (Boston: Allyn & Bacon, 1969), p. 53.

[18]William James and E. B. Tichener.

[19]James A. Winans, *Public Speaking* (New York: Century, 1917), p. 194.

[20]Ibid., p. 196.

[21]James A. Winans, *Speech Making* (New York: Appleton-Century-Crofts, 1938), p. 17.

Winans was one of the founders of the Speech Communication Association (1915), and his influence is still felt in the organization. His uniting of rhetoric and psychology set a pattern for others to follow in the area of human thought and behavior influence.[22]

Charles Henry Woolbert was another founder of the Speech Communication Association. Woolbert was the first to view speech communication as a behavioral science. He felt that to understand persuasion one had to study human nature behaviorally and minutely. He was profoundly influenced by the psychologist John B. Watson, the founder of behaviorism. Woolbert's philosophy is clearly shown in the 1920 preface to his book *The Fundamentals of Speech:*

> It is frankly psychological in foundation, and of psychologies is outspokenly behavioristic—that is to say, it insists that speech is a matter of the whole man, the cooperative activity of the entire organism; that it is a revelation of personality, but that the true definition of personality gives a picture compounded of thinking apparatus, emotional machinery, muscular activity, and body-wide participating parts—voice, brain, muscles, trunk, and limbs. Its essential thesis is that no speaking is good speaking which is not of the whole machine and which does not establish the desired relationship between the one speaking and the one listening.[23]

For all his positivism and behaviorism, Woolbert understood the *process* notion of communication—he was different from psychologists of his time.

His bias toward oral persuasion is also clear: "The spoken word is still supreme . . . always speech must precede [reading and writing] . . . men speak twenty times to once that they write. . . . The page is impersonal, but the speaker is a living personality."[24]

Woolbert felt that a good system of logic was the primary basis of persuasion.[25] He counseled would-be persuaders to be understood, acceptable, plausible.[26] In terms of preparation he had this to say: "The entire need [to be logical] is served by (1) studying the purpose, (2) knowing the audience and the peculiar occasion . . . , (3) framing a specific proposition to suit the *specific* audience and the occasion, and then (4) selecting logically connected topic sentences that support this proposition."[27]

In discussing the conciliatory method of topic development, Woolbert anticipated the findings of Hovland and others on "both-sides" persuasion.[28]

[22]See Karl R. Wallace, ed., *History of Speech Education in America* (New York: Appleton-Century-Crofts, 1954).

[23]Charles Woolbert, *The Fundamentals of Speech* (New York: Harper & Brothers, 1920).

[24]Ibid., pp. 1–2.

[25]Charles H. Woolbert, "The Place of Logic in a System of Persuasion," *Quarterly Journal of Speech Education,* 4, no. 1 (January 1918), 19–39.

[26]Woolbert, *The Fundamentals of Speech,* p. 24.

[27]Ibid., p. 303.

[28]Ibid., p. 357.

Woolbert is also remembered for challenging the long-standing theory of the duality of conviction and persuasion. This theory, also known as the faculty-psychology approach to communication, had defined conviction as an appeal to reason and persuasion as an appeal to the emotions.[29] Woolbert took a more holistic or comprehensive position arguing that all verbal communication sought to achieve action and response. He referred to inner and outer stimulators in much the same way that this book refers to biological and social-psychological springboards of motivation. For a short while, before Woolbert's untimely death, the speech communication field was ahead of psychology in empirical theorizing about oral persuasion.

William Norwood Brigance was an innovative modern theorist of persuasion. He wrote:

> Anyone with common sense recognizes the truth of Oliver Wendell Holmes' statement, written after nearly 30 years on the Supreme Court: "As I grow older I realize how limited a part reason has played in the conduct of men. They believe what they want to".... "Belief is rarely the result of reasoning.... We tend to believe what arouses our desires, our fears, and our emotions." Persuasion is largely a matter of making others want to believe.[30]

His differences with Woolbert are evident.

Brigance's message was "persuade or perish." In the mid 1930s he indicated deep concern that the Europeans still outsold the Americans, not because their goods were better, but because they were better salesmen, more professional, sophisticated persuaders. And in the 1950s it was Brigance who boldly stated that people have only two methods for settling differences—to shoot it out or to talk it out! Both require skill, discipline, and training. If society would be free, it must develop leaders who can talk it out.[31]

Building on the Winans-James theory of persuasion, Brigance reaffirmed the importance of the attention factor but suggested that newer findings indicated *desire* to be the most important element of persuasion. He defined persuasion as follows:

> (1)   Where the aim is to rouse from indifference, to inspire, or to stimulate lagging enthusiasm and faiths, *persuasion is a process of vitalizing old desires, purposes, or ideals.*

[29]Charles Woolbert, "Conviction and Persuasion: Some Considerations of Theory," *Quarterly Journal of Public Speaking,* 3 (1917), 249–64. See also Edward Z. Rowell, "The Conviction-Persuasion Duality," *Quarterly Journal of Speech,* 20 (1934), 469–82; and Mary Yost, "Argument From the Point-of-View of Sociology," *Quarterly Journal of Public Speaking,* 3 (1917), 109–27.

[30]William N. Brigance, *Speech Communication* (New York: Appleton-Century-Crofts, 1955), p. 115.

[31]William N. Brigance, *Speech Composition,* 2nd ed. (New York: Appleton-Century-Crofts, 1952), p. ix.

(2)   Where the aim is to secure the acceptance of new beliefs or courses of action, *persuasion is a process of substituting new desires, purposes, or ideals in place of old ones.*[32]

Persuasion as a matter of making others desire to believe involved four components: (1) holding the listeners' attention; (2) getting the listeners to accept one's competence and character; (3) resting reason on impelling wants, which he defined as survival, security, recognition, dignity, and self-respect, on wanting to belong to something worthwhile, and on reverence for something higher than oneself; and (4) developing each idea according to the listeners' attitude.[33]

Perhaps the most controversial part of Brigance's theory of persuasion was called the *genetic* approach. It rests on what he called the three modes of persuasion in the human race:

(1)   The acceptance of ideas borrowed and ready made, which we call Authority, is the oldest mode. . . . It is still the most potent with primitive man: still highly potent with the masses; and becomes less effective as we go up the educational and intellectual scale. . . .

(2)   The second mode of persuasion acquired in the human race was the acceptance of ideas that fit into organized and ordered Experience. It is potent at all levels of society.

(3)   The most recently acquired mode of persuasion in the race is Reason. It is the newest, therefore the weakest. It is ineffective among primitive peoples; almost equally ineffective among the lowest stratum of civilized peoples. It is safe for the common man only upon familiar ground.[34]

By reason of his more recent training, Alan H. Monroe probably had a better academic grasp of psychology than the three forerunners mentioned thus far. He was well acquainted with the theories of his time and evidences of James, Titchener, Kohler, Watson, McDougall, Hollingworth, and other prominent early psychologists are found in his books. He knew the various schools of psychology and taught them to many students during his long tenure at Purdue University. Beginning in the mid 1920s Monroe's staff worked on a fresh idea in rhetorical persuasion, which they referred to as the *motivating process.* One of those staff members, John A. McGee, put the process in print.[35] According to McGee, the process consisted of (1) attention, (2) problem, (3) situation, (4) visualization, and (5) action. It was not until 1935, however, that the final version of this idea, which Monroe called the *motivated*

[32]William N. Brigance, "Can We Re-define the James-Winans Theory of Persuasion?" *Quarterly Journal of Speech,* 21 (February 1935), 19–26. See also William N. Brigance, *Speech Composition* (New York: Appleton-Century-Crofts, 1937), p. 139.

[33]Brigance, *Speech Communication,* pp. 115–28.

[34]William N. Brigance, "A Genetic Approach to Persuasion," *Quarterly Journal of Speech,* 17 (June 1931), 329–39.

[35]John A. McGee, *Persuasive Speaking* (New York: Scribner's, 1929).

sequence, was brought to widespread public attention, in the first edition of his very popular book *Principles and Types of Speech.* Monroe's contribution to rhetoric is really one of message organization. His motivated sequence, he argued, was based on the normal thinking process. He reasoned that

> the mental process of the listener as applied to the various general ends of speech is not different, but cumulative, [and] this normal process of human thinking is sufficiently uniform that . . . we can outline a form of speech structure that will conform to it rather closely on nearly all occasions. This form of speech structure we shall call *the motivated sequence: the sequence of ideas which, by following the normal process of thinking, motivates the audience to respond to the speaker's purpose.*[36]

The steps in this sequence are: (1) attention, (2) need, (3) satisfaction, (4) visualization, and (5) action. More will be said of this and other theoretical sequences of persuasion in Chapter 6.

Monroe believed there were four primary motives that influenced human beings. "Behind every act, belief or emotion," he wrote, "will be found one or more of these basic desires:"

1. Self-preservation and the desire for physical well being.
2. Freedom from external restraint.
3. Preservation and increase of self-esteem (ego expansion).
4. Preservation of the human race.[37]

Monroe also wrote of *motive appeals,* which he defined as appeals to some sentiment, emotion, or desire by which the speaker might set the primary motives into action. Similar appeals were presented in Chapter 2.

There are other scholars of speech and rhetoric who deserve to be classed as forerunners of modern rhetoric. Certainly A. E. Phillips was among the earliest to incorporate a psychological and very practical use of *impelling* motives.[38] Winston Brembeck and William Howell gave us what is probably the first truly eclectic approach to the subject by speech professors.[39] Another who contributed to a theory of rhetorical communication was Robert T. Oliver.[40] Franklin Knower deserves mention as the speech psychologist who first demonstrated empirically that *oral* persuasion can change attitudes.[41]

Pretheoretical differences of opinion about persuasion still abound today, especially in the newer area (for communicologists) of interpersonal

---

[36]Alan H. Monroe, *Principles and Types of Speech,* 3rd ed. (Glenview, Ill.: Scott, Foresman, 1949), pp. 308–9.

[37]Ibid., p. 194.

[38]See A. E. Phillips, *Effective Speaking* (Chicago: Newton, 1908).

[39]Winston L. Brembeck and William S. Howell, *Persuasion: A Means of Social Control* (Englewood Cliffs, N. J.: Prentice-Hall, 1952).

[40]Robert T. Oliver, *The Psychology of Persuasive Speech* (New York: Longmans, Green, 1942).

[41]Franklin H. Knower, "Experimental Studies of Changes in Attitudes: I. A Study of the Effect of Oral Argument on Changes of Attitude," *Journal of Social Psychology,* 6 (1935), 315–47.

influence. Our communication scholars and writers are divided about this subject: Are we to be behaviorally oriented or action-oriented? Will we teach laws or rules? Should we think of rhetorical communication as a multidisciplinary framework?[42]

A popular text by Erwin Bettinghaus is clearly a straight-line *behavioral* approach.[43] So are most of the social-psychology texts. A text by Mary John Smith takes an *action* approach and aims to set guidelines for a *rules-based* conceptualization of persuasive communication.[44] A text by Charles Larson is written almost entirely from the perspective of the *receiver* and is both behavioral and rhetorical in orientation.[45] Other texts, while still behavioral, have modified their explanations considerably.[46] A serious effort to borrow eclectically from behaviorally oriented as well as humanistically oriented social scientists has been provided by Herbert Simons.[47]

Can we take advantage of the exciting, new, projectionist, rules-based research and speculation without completely abandoning laws and philosophical positivism? Two contemporary scholars, Gerald Miller and Charles Berger, think so.[48] Logical mechanistic positivism has been obsolete for twenty-five years. Positivism now accepts laws as generalizations about how people will probably respond—and then only when the context is specified. Moreover, these generalizations need not always be thought of as causal; they can be viewed rather as correlations between messages and their effects. Behavioral theorists holding this modified view have less trouble with more action-oriented speculation. Confirmed rules theorists may disagree. In our pragmatic view, the truth "is" what experience shows it to be. As William James put it, "Truth is what works." We shall therefore cheerfully try to explain consistency theory.

[42]See Stephen W. Littlejohn, "An Overview of Contributions to Human Communication Theory From Other Disciplines," in Frank E. X. Dance, *Human Communication Theory* (New York: Harper & Row, Pub., 1982), pp. 243–85. See also Stephen W. Littlejohn, *Theories of Human Communication* (Columbus, Ohio: Chas. E. Merrill, 1978).

[43]Erwin P. Bettinghaus, *Persuasive Communication,* 3rd ed. (Holt, Rinehart & Winston, 1980).

[44]Smith, *Persuasion and Human Action,* p. 62. See also Kathleen K. Reardon, *Persuasion Theory and Context* (Beverly Hills, Calif.: Sage Publications, Inc., 1981), pp. 81–90.

[45]Charles U. Larson, *Persuasion: Reception and Responsibility* (Belmont, Calif.: Wadsworth, 1983).

[46]For example, Robert N. Bostrom, *Persuasion* (Englewood Cliffs, N.J.: Prentice-Hall, 1983). See also Winston L. Brembeck and William S. Howell, *Persuasion: A Means of Social Influence* (Englewood Cliffs, N.J.: Prentice-Hall, 1976); and Kenneth E. Anderson, *Persuasion Theory and Practice* (Boston: Allyn & Bacon, 1978).

[47]Herbert W. Simons, *Persuasion: Understanding, Practice and Analysis* (Reading, Mass.: Addison-Wesley, 1976). See also Raymond S. Ross, *Persuasion: Communication and Interpersonal Relations* (Englewood Cliffs, N.J.: Prentice-Hall, 1974).

[48]See Gerald R. Miller and Charles R. Berger, "On Keeping the Faith in Matters Scientific," *Western Journal of Speech Communication,* 42 (1978), 44–50. See also Michael E. Roloff and Gerald R. Miller, eds., *Persuasion: New Directions in Theory and Research* (Beverly Hills, Calif.: Sage Publications, Inc., 1980).

> "... to say that human beings, as a whole, are marvelously complex does not imply that *none* of their important communicative behaviors can be explained by recourse to relatively simple antecedent mechanisms."
>
> Gerald R. Miller
> *Journal of Communication,* 33, no. 3 (Summer 1983), 34.

CONSISTENCY THEORIES

When our attitudes no longer adequately reference new and changing situations—when we find old attitudes in conflict with new information—we tend to feel out of phase, off balance, *inconsistent.* Cognitive-consistency theory supplies us with many useful coping and persuasion principles.

Cognitive consistency is mental agreement between a person's notions about some object or event and some *new* information about that same object or event. *Cognition* is the mental process or faculty by which knowledge is both acquired and known. However, it is more than a search for meaning. It denotes the attitudes and images we hold of the world. The assumption underlying cognitive-consistency theory is that when new information is contradictory or inconsistent with a person's attitudes, it will lead to some confusion and tension. This tension motivates a person to alter or adjust his or her attitudes or behavior. We seek a harmonious, agreeable, balanced, *consistent* set of relationships between our notions of the world and our latest perception of it. In some respects these theories might better be called *inconsistency* theories since it is the inconsistency that causes the tension that causes the motivation that may cause a change in attitude or behavior.

A review of the major consistency theories follows. Cognitive-response theory is included here because it also helps explain how we process our existing notions and information as we attempt to evaluate persuasive messages and relate, adjust, and respond to them.

Balance Theory

Fritz Heider pioneered this early cognitive-consistency theory.[49] Heider's theory is primarily interpersonal in that he considers only the interaction between two persons and an event or object of mutual concern. According to Heider, when two persons interact in relation to an event or object of mutual concern, the intrapersonal and interpersonal situations are cognitively balanced or unbalanced. Unbalanced situations produce a tension that motivates a change in attitudes (to restore balance). It should be clear that

---

[49]Fritz Heider, "Attitudinal and Cognitive Organization," *Journal of Psychology,* 21 (1946), 107–12. See also Fritz Heider, *Psychology of Interpersonal Relations* (New York: John Wiley, 1958).

persuasion can operate only after some "felt tension" (an unbalanced situation). If the relationship is balanced, little motivation to change is present and persuasion is doubtful.

Suppose, for example, that John and George are talking about Chevrolets. There are eight possible relationships that can exist. Four are considered balanced and four unbalanced. Figure 4–1 presents the balanced states. In any of these states little tension exists, and hence the probability of attitude change is very low.

Attitude change is possible in unbalanced states, according to Heider, for people are motivated to balance their cognitions. Figure 4–2 represents the four possible unbalanced states. In all of these situations the inherent tension allows for the possibility of persuasion.

These are Heider's classic models, tortured a little for clarity. The basic point is that unbalanced states exist if an odd number of the three relationships is negative. (One *hate* and two *likes* or three *hates* is unbalanced.) An unbalanced state produces tension in a person's life that motivates him or her to restore the balance.

Despite adages to the contrary, Heider argues that comparable personalities attract and that, other things being equal, familiarity breeds attraction, not contempt. "With similar attitudes proximity will increase the degree of positive sentiment; with slight dissimilarity of attitudes a mutual assimilation might be produced, and with it an increase in friendliness; with strong dissimilarities the hostility will be increased."[50]

A number of theorists have built upon Heider's basic model.[51] Among

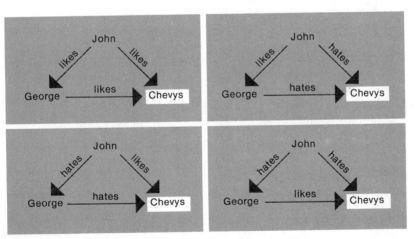

FIGURE 4–1   Balanced States

[50]Heider, *Psychology of Interpersonal Relations,* p. 190.

[51]See, for example, Dorwin Cartwright and F. Harary, "Structural Balance: A Generalization of Heider's Theory," *Psychological Review,* 63 (1956), 277–93; and N. Feather, "A Structural Balance Approach to the Analysis of Communication Effects," in *Advances in Experimental Psychology,* ed. Leonard Berkowitz (New York: Academic Press, 1967), vol. 3, pp. 100–166.

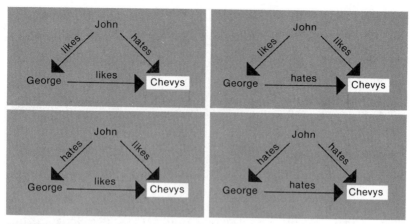

FIGURE 4–2   Unbalanced States

the most noteworthy are Milton Rosenberg and Robert Abelson.[52] According to their theory, attitudes consist of two elements, the affective (feelings) and the cognitive (beliefs), and people seek balance or consistency between them. Persuasion is thus possible if one modifies *either* the affective or the cognitive. The model presumes an imbalanced or unstable state when a person's feelings and beliefs about an object suddenly do not agree. If long-time Representative Jones is suddenly discovered getting kickbacks from his staff after their salaries have been padded, you may suffer considerable dissonance (or inconsistency) in supporting him. Your new information (he's dishonest) is inconsistent with your longtime affection for Jones the man..

To achieve consistency in this dilemma, you can do one of three things: (1) *reject* the data and communication that brought about the difficulty: "I simply don't believe it"; (2) *fragment* the original attitude by trying to isolate the affective and cognitive elements: "Others do it. He just got caught," or "The good he's done outweighs the bad"; or (3) *change* your attitude by accommodating the dilemma in such a way that your feelings and beliefs are consistent: "I'll not vote for him. My feelings have changed. I don't believe in dishonesty."[53] Presumably you could also escape by trying not to think about the inconsistency.

Congruity Theory

The principle of congruity is an attempt to explain attitudes mathematically.[54] Congruity is a state of agreement, correspondence, or harmony between attitudes about things, people, or objects. According to this

[52]Milton Rosenberg and Robert Abelson, "An Analysis of Cognitive Balancing," in *Attitude Organization and Change*, eds. Carl Hovland and Milton Rosenberg (New Haven: Yale University Press, 1960), pp. 112–63. See also Milton Rosenberg, "An Analysis of Affective-Cognitive Consistency," in *Attitude Organization and Change*, eds. Hovland and Rosenberg, pp. 15–64.

[53]Milton Rosenberg, "A Structural Theory of Attitude Dynamics," *Public Opinion Quarterly*, 24 (1960), 322.

principle, when a person encounters a lack of agreement between two attitudes, he or she tends to strike a balance between them. The point of balance varies with the intensity or weight of the attitudes. For example, if one has a positive attitude toward Jane Fonda and a positive attitude toward nuclear power and Jane Fonda speaks out against nuclear power, one may find the message *incongruous*. The theory suggests that the receiver must either reduce the positive attitude toward Fonda, become less favorable toward nuclear power, or both. "When change in evaluation or attitude occurs, it always is in the direction of increased congruity with the existing frame of reference."[55] In another sense, we assume our heroes should always denounce propositions we oppose and speak out for propositions we support.

This theory suggests that attitudes tend toward maximal simplicity or polarization. It is more convenient to be left or right, good or bad, for or against. However, it should be made clear that extreme positions are usually associated with immaturity and a lack of education and are usually shorter-lived. The theory of congruity illustrates that people with similar pro or con attitudes may have arrived at their positions for quite different reasons. Some people feel that the United Nations is *weak* and *impotent*; others feel it is too *strong* and *active*. Both groups of people may respond negatively to the United Nations for different reasons.

One may have incompatible attitudes toward objects or events with no resultant tension if there is no apparent relationship or association between them. For instance, we could be favorably disposed toward President Reagan and dislike the idea of moving the Washington Redskins football team to Indiana. Should some reasonable association be made to link the president and the move (he's for it), then incongruity emerges, and we struggle for internal consistency. Persuasion, according to this theory, is the result of pressure to reduce incongruity.

When incongruence is so gross as to be unbelievable, then it may actually inhibit persuasion and attitude change. During World War II our production of ships was so high that American propaganda reduced the actual figures for fear the enemy would be incredulous and therefore less likely to surrender.

When incongruence is based on a neutral attitude toward a concept and a favorable polar position toward a source—the president of Ohio State University (neutral) is paid a sincere compliment by Ohio's governor (positive assertion)—then the pressure for congruency causes us to feel more positive toward the president of Ohio State University (Figure 4–3).

We strive to make our attitudes congruent. According to congruity theory, when we know beforehand the various strengths or weights of attitudes that are about to become associated, theoretically we can predict where on a numerical scale the attitudes will balance or average out.

---

[54]Charles E. Osgood and Percy H. Tannenbaum, "The Principle of Congruity in the Prediction of Attitude Change," *Psychological Review*, 62, no. 1 (1955), 43.

[55]Ibid.

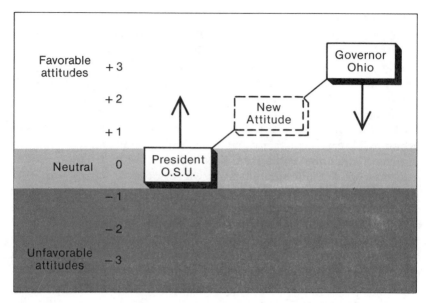

FIGURE 4-3

Dissonance Theory

Cognitive dissonance is another aspect of consistency theory. *Cognitive* describes "any knowledge, opinion, or belief about the environment, about oneself, or about one's behavior."[56] The word *dissonance* replaces the word *inconsistency,* used previously; *consonance* means *consistency.* One can substitute *frustration* or *disequilibrium* for *dissonance.* The essential notion of dissonance theory is that people have a strong need for agreement (consonance or consistency) among their beliefs and actions. According to Leon Festinger, chief architect of this theory, the basic hypotheses are as follows:

1. The existence of dissonance, being psychologically uncomfortable, will motivate the person to try to reduce the dissonance and achieve consonance.
2. When dissonance is present, in addition to trying to reduce it, the person will actively avoid situations and information which would likely increase the dissonance.[57]

Motivation springs from the tension caused by the existence of nonfitting relations among cognitions, a practically unavoidable condition in a wide variety of situations.

Festinger suggests some typical sources of dissonance between two cognitions: they lack logical consistency; they represent different cultural

[56]Leon Festinger, *A Theory of Cognitive Dissonance* (Stanford, Calif.: Stanford University Press, 1957), p. 3.
    [57]Ibid.

mores; they contradict past experience; and they include by definition one specific opinion in a more general opinion (for example, Democrats aren't supposed to favor a Republican candidate for office).[58]

Dissonance theory clearly postulates that one's own behavior can cause persuasion. Many very creative researchers support this point and provide implications for how personal involvement, even contrary behavior, may cause self-persuasion.

For example, in a study of arguing against one's own point of view (as college debaters must often do), Irving Janis and Bert King found that the speakers changed their attitudes more than the listeners. This kind of behavior apparently creates dissonance and consequent self-persuasion. It also indicates the possible influence of role playing on opinion change.[59]

Harvey and Beverly found similar results in a study of written advocacy.[60] Students from a dry college were given a proalcohol message and asked to write down the principal arguments. Half of the group were then asked to write out an affirmative speech that could be used in a college debate. Analysis before and after indicated that the latter students—those playing a role, as it were—had a significantly greater attitude shift in favor of alcohol than those not so involved.

Arthur Cohen reported a most creative and convincing study relating behavior and dissonance theory.[61] After a student riot at Yale in which the New Haven police were called, Cohen and a class of students went into action. The police had been accused of brutality, and the prevailing student attitude toward the police actions was negative, to say the least. Yale students were contacted and asked to write strong essays *justifying* the police actions. This study of counterattitudinal advocacy was further enriched with an incentive for compliance: students were divided into groups and, according to which group they were in, were paid ten dollars, five dollars, one dollar, or fifty cents. Each participant was also asked to indicate their actual opinion regarding the police actions *after* they had finished their essay. Upon completion of the essay, those who had been paid ten dollars and five dollars still held the same attitudes as students who had not written the counterattitudinal essays. They still felt negative about the police actions. However, those who had been paid one dollar revised their attitudes significantly in favor of the police actions. Those

[58]Ibid., p. 14.

[59]Irving Janis and Bert King, "The Influence of Role-playing on Opinion Change," *Journal of Abnormal Social Psychology*, 49 (1954), 211–18. See also Gary Hobbs, "The Influence of Counter-attitudinal Acting on the Attitudes of Actors," *Speech Teacher*, 24, no. 4 (November 1975), 328–34.

[60]O. J. Harvey and G. Beverly, "Some Personality Correlates of Concept Change Through Role Playing," *Journal of Abnormal Social Psychology*, 63 (1961), 125–30.

[61]Arthur R. Cohen, "An Experiment of Small Rewards for Discrepant Compliance and Attitude Change," in *Explorations in Cognitive Dissonance*, Jack W. Brehm and Arthur R. Cohen (New York: John Wiley, 1962), pp. 73–78. For additional support, see Eliot Aronson and Judson Mills, "The Effect of Severity of Initiation on Liking for a Group," *Journal of Abnormal and Social Psychology*, 59 (1959), 177–81.

paid fifty cents made even greater attitude shifts. Self-persuasion appeared to work best when the pay was the least.

These results, of course, constitute strong support for dissonance theory if one assumes that it is inconsistency that causes persuasion. The larger amounts of money reduced inconsistency by giving students a justification for writing the essay. By the same logic, when the value of money was significantly decreased, the essay writers lost their justification—or perhaps excuse is more appropriate—and suffered the pangs of dissonance. If one is to escape these pangs, one must change one's attitude so that it agrees more closely with one's behavior.

Festinger's second hypothesis—that we actively avoid information and situations that might increase rather than reduce dissonance—also has much relevance to persuasion. The way a message is prepared as well as the media used to transmit it become very important. To begin a message with dissonant information or arguments may sound like a logical way to get the attention of people already suffering dissonance, but it may be just the opposite if it causes your audience to tune out.

When dissonance or perhaps hostility already exists, media that are easier to tune out may have to be used very subtly as persuasive tools. *Fear* of dissonance should be of great interest to salespeople because it may very well make people reluctant to commit themselves to action.

Despite charges that theories of cognitive consistency are oversimplified and limited,[62] it does seem reasonable to believe that our cognitive systems seek harmony, agreement, balance, and *consistency* between our notions of the world and our latest perception of it.[63]

In review, the assumption of cognitive-consistency theories is that when new information is contradictory or inconsistent with a person's notions and attitudes, it will lead to some psychological confusion and tension. This tension motivates the person to alter his or her attitudes or behavior in order to reduce the inconsistency. Theories of cognitive consistency provide us with many practical and reasonable postulates for persuasion.

Cognitive-response Theory

This approach emphasizes the *thoughts* people have while listening to persuasive messages. The basic sender strategy, according to this theory, is

[62]Natalie P. Chapanis and Alphonse Chapanis, "Cognitive Dissonance: Five Years Later," *Psychological Bulletin,* 61 (1964), 1–22. See also Smith, *Persuasion and Human Action,* p. 128.

[63]See Robert P. Abelson, Eliot Aronson, William J. McGuire, Theodore M. Newcomb, Milton J. Rosenberg, and Percy H. Tannenbaum, eds., *Theories of Coignitive Consistency: A Sourcebook* (Skokie, Ill.: Rand McNally, 1968).

for speakers to develop communications that are sufficiently persuasive to (1) evoke favorable thoughts from people and (2) induce people to rehearse and remember these favorable thoughts.[64] This familiar notion of communication as a process suggests that listeners in their decoding sort, select, and elicit from their storehouse of knowledge, attitudes, emotions, and so forth, those things they feel relate best to the message elements.[65] This theory helps show how people may evoke persuasive materials (thoughts) from their storehouses that may not be in the message sent. If these "cognitive responses" (thoughts) agree with the persuader's purpose, they should promote attitude change in the desired direction. If, on the other hand, the message somehow backfires and evokes unfavorable or disagreeing thoughts, the sender's purpose may be defeated or at least inhibited attitudinally.

Cognitive-response theory suggests that just as personal growth and development are often considered to be really *self*-growth and *self*-development (or that learning is in the final analysis self-generated), we really persuade ourselves through these cognitive reevaluations. This does not mean that the message is unimportant, at least not in all cases. However, this theory helps explain that the receivers of highly polarized attitudes are sometimes so busy processing, repeating, and rehearsing their own thoughts and views that they really cannot hear the message. Our decisions about message strategy, if unconstrained by this rigid attitude set, are critical. Analyzing an audience's cognitive response should help us better decide the ordering and length of arguments so that we can let receivers "self-generate" responses.

Enthymematic persuasion seems a logical extension of the strategy implicit in cognitive-response theory. Enthymemes are syllogistic arguments with unstated premises. Their rhetorical function is to let the audience supply the missing premises. Like cognitive-response theory, enthymematic persuasion assumes that thoughts are often more influential if they are our *own* than if they were explicitly stated in the message. More will be said about enthymemes in Chapter 7. Applications of cognitive-response theory were noted in Chapter 3 in our examination of credibility, self-concept, and elsewhere, and will be discussed further when we turn to social judgment theory, later in this chapter, and message organization (Chapter 6).

[64]Richard M. Perloff and Timothy C. Brock, ". . . 'And Thinking Makes It So': Cognitive Responses to Persuasion," in *Persuasion: New Directions in Theory and Research,* eds. Michael E. Roloff and Gerald R. Miller (Beverly Hills, Calif.: Sage Publications, Inc., 1980), p. 90. See also Anthony Greenwald, "Cognitive Learning, Cognitive Response to Persuasion, and Attitude Change," in *Psychological Foundations of Attitudes,* eds. Anthony G. Greenwald, Timothy C. Brock, and Thomas M. Ostrom (New York: Academic Press, 1968), pp. 147–70.

[65]See David K. Berlo, *The Process of Communication* (New York: Holt, Rinehart & Winston, 1960). See also Ross, *Speech Communication,* 1965–1983.

THEORIES OF
BEHAVIORAL PERCEPTION

Social-judgment Theory

Personal involvement and attitudes   "I feel very strongly that there are over one hundred beans in that jar." Although this attitude statement is quite strong, the person who made it would probably not be very upset if he or she were wrong, for this statement is not underlain by a deeply rooted belief system. A lightly held attitude such as a preference for one brand of coffee over another suggests only a modest personal involvement. A commitment to one's religion, family, country, or life-style may be quite another matter. Attitudes about these may be the result of a much more deeply engaged belief system. These attitudes may involve us very personally. They help define our self-concept. They involve our ego. The point is that attitudes are seldom best represented by a single point on a numerical scale. The degree of involvement, or belief-system engagement, is difficult to ascertain from such a point. Consistency theories give us a conceptual understanding of attitudes, but their actual measurement of them could be more sensitive. Clearly, attitudes represent different strengths or weights. They also represent different *ranges* of acceptance. Social-judgment theory adds to consistency theory by providing us with an explanation of the notion of range or latitude of attitude. Recall the attitudes toward the smoking that we used as examples in Chapter 1.

The proponents of this theory offer the following generalizations about latitudes of attitude:

1. In proportion to the extremeness of an individual's stand on an issue, the latitude of rejection is greater than the latitude of acceptance and noncommitment approaches zero.
2. Proportional to the moderateness of the individual's position on an issue, the size of his latitudes of acceptance and rejection approaches equality.
3. As a result, the latitude of rejection of a person with an extreme stand is greater than that of a person taking a moderate position on the issue and his latitude of noncommitment is smaller.

. . . we postulate on the basis of research findings that size of latitudes of rejection *increases* and size of latitudes of noncommitment *decreases* in proportion to degree of involvement in the issue, regardless of extremeness of the most acceptable position. On this basis, we have suggested the average frequency of noncommitment (failure to endorse or reject positions) as a general measure of involvement in an issue or lack of it. More frequent noncommitment would be expected on issues not high in the concerns of the persons and fewer noncommittal positions on issues more involving for them.[66]

[66]Carolyn Sherif, Muzafer Sherif, and Roger Nebergall, *Attitude and Attitude Change* (Philadelphia: Saunders, 1965), pp. 233–34. For another viewpoint see M. S. Pallak, M. Mueller, K. Dollar, and J. Pallak, "Effect of Commitment on Responsiveness to an Extreme Consonant Communication," *Journal of Personality and Social Psychology,* 23 (1972), 429–36.

In simpler terms: the larger the range of rejection, the more difficult the persuasion; the larger the range of acceptance or noncommitment, the less difficult; a large range of rejection predicts ego defensiveness.

Assimilation and contrast tendencies   Research on how humans make judgments about physical objects has given us insights into their social judgments as well.[67] One classic experiment is to put your hand into a pail of hot water for a minute or so, then put it into a pail of lukewarm water. You tend to judge the lukewarm water to be *colder* than it is. If you went from cold to warm water, you would tend to judge it *warmer* than it is. One pail of water serves as a referent point, or anchor, for your judgments that follow. When temperatures are in sharp contrast with the anchor, you tend to perceive it as farther from the anchor than it really is. When temperatures are close to that of the anchor, you tend to assimilate it—that is, perceive it as closer than it really is. Similar experiments in judging weights produce similar results.

This tendency for assimilation and contrast has been applied to attitude change. A receiver's initial attitude toward the persuasion serves as a referent point or anchor for making judgments about the message. In general, the more extreme the initial attitude (the anchor), the less attitude change one can expect. The less extreme the anchor, the more change one can expect.

After many creative researches, the authors of this theory of attitude change made the following predictions regarding our tendencies toward attitude assimilation and contrast:

> If a message or communication does not fall appreciably beyond the range of acceptances, the discrepancy will be minimized in placing the communication. Hence, the communication is likely to be *assimilated* into [the individual's] range of acceptances.
>
> If the message falls well beyond the range of acceptances, the individual will appraise it as more discrepant than it actually is. Its position will be displaced away from his acceptable range, and the extent of the *contrast effect* will be in proportion to the divergence of the communication from his acceptable range.
>
> The greater the commitment or dedication of an individual his stand on an issue, the greater the displacement of a discrepant message away from the bounds of his acceptance.[68]

A multiple response to a statement involving attitude is considered more accurate than a single response. Typical multiple-response instructions follow:

(✓ ✓)   most acceptable position
(✓)   acceptable positions
(✗✗)   most objectionable position

---

[67]See H. Helson, *Adaptation Level Theory* (New York: Harper & Row, Pub., 1964), chap. 2.

[68]Sherif, Sherif, and Nebergall, *Attitude and Attitude Change*, p. 226. For another viewpoint see Richard E. Petty and John T. Cacioppo, "Issue Involvement Can Increase or Decrease Persuasion by Enhancing Message-Relevant Cognitive Responses," *Journal of Personality and Social Psychology*, 37 (1979), 1915–26.

(X)   objectionable positions
(NC)   noncommitted positions[69]

Compare the single response shown in Figure 4–4 with the multiple response in Figure 4–5.

The neutral position indicated in Figure 4–4 might suggest that persuasion will be quite easy. But let's check the multiple responses we would obtain from this person if we were to use the latitude-of-attitude concept (Figure 4–5).

Our respondent is now seen to have a strong, ego-involved, neutral position and finds the extremes objectionable. Our persuasion doesn't appear quite so easy now.

How would you estimate your chances of persuasion on the basis of the information in Figure 4–6?

If you're in favor of the proposition, your persuasion of this receiver will be difficult since the latitude of rejection (that is, the latitude of objectionable positions) is so large. The more acceptable or noncommitted positions one observes, the wider the range of acceptable or noncommitted positions, and therefore the greater likelihood of attitude change. Examine Figure 4–7, for example.

Now consider Figures 4–8 and 4–9 which show how our assimilation and contrast tendencies work and what they tell us about the placement and strategy of our persuasion. In Figure 4–8 the receiver appraises the sender's position as further from his or hers than it really is. Suppose the sender tries a more moderate strategy or approach (Figure 4–9). The receiver now appraises the sender's position as closer to his or her own than it really is.

A slight alteration of strategy or perhaps a slight modification of one's own position often makes the difference between success and failure in persuasion.

This theory reminds us that truly ego-involved attitudes are more difficult to change. The type, order, and strength of the appeal—and even the credibility of the source—take on less importance for receivers having such attitudes. They listen primarily to people who agree with them. Parents

FIGURE 4–4

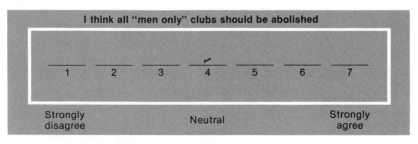

[69]Sherif, Sherif, and Nebergall, *Attitude and Attitude Change*, p. 152.

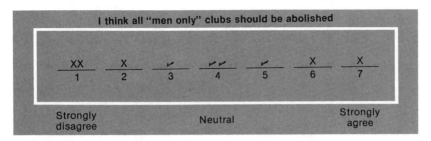

FIGURE 4–5

FIGURE 4–6

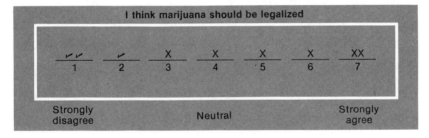

FIGURE 4–7

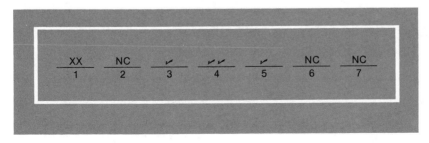

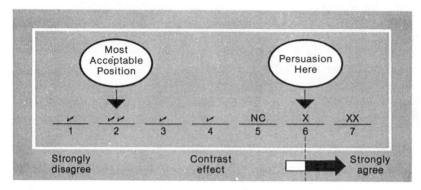

FIGURE 4-8

ordered to bus their four children to a distant, less-disciplined school may very well be more ego-involved than the person with no children who lives outside the busing district.

Self-Perception Theory

When put to critical analysis, Daryl Bem's theory of self-perception is perhaps more a behavioral theory than a cognitive one.[70] It makes predictions similar to those of consistency theory but offers different explanations of the results.

The basic proposition of self-perception theory is that "in identifying his own internal states, an individual partially relies on the same external cues that

FIGURE 4-9

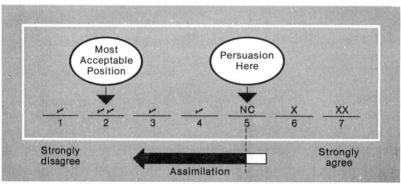

[70]This theory is advanced in the following studies by Bem: "An Experimental Analysis of Self-persuasion," *Journal of Experimental Social Psychology,* 1 (1965), 199–218; "Inducing Belief in False Confessions," *Journal of Personality and Social Psychology,* 3 (1961), 707–10; "Self-perception: An Alternative Interpretation of Cognitive Dissonance Phenomena," *Psychological Review,* 74 (1967), 183–200; and *Beliefs, Attitudes and Human Affairs* (Belmont, Calif.: Brooks/Cole, 1970).

others use when they infer his internal states."[71] In other words, we may think we are taking a direct reading of our cognitions, but we are really looking at our own behaviors and inferring our attitudes from them. We behave first and then decide our attitude.

We make attributions about ourselves the same way we infer the attitudes of others. If we see a person at an antinuclear power rally, we infer that the person has negative attitudes toward nuclear power. We base this inference on the person's behavior (attending the rally). We cannot get inside the person's head. Self-perception theory argues that we infer our own attitudes based on the behaviors in which we engage. The theory suggests that we systematically align and develop attitudes based on external cues or our own behaviors.

Recall our earlier discussion of dissonance theory. More attitude change resulted in the group of subjects who wrote the counterattitudinal essays for small amounts of money. This attitude change was attributed to the pangs of dissonance the subjects felt over engaging in the counterattitudinal task for little incentive.

Self-perception theory makes the same predictions as dissonance theory but simply explains the results differently. Bem would argue that the subjects in the dissonance-theory experiment did not feel pangs of dissonance and that internal tension was not the cause of their changed attitudes. Rather, they saw themselves behaving in a certain way (pro police) and then inferred the appropriate attitude from their behavior.

Self-perception theory has sustained serious criticism. Nevertheless, it should not be overlooked, for it points out the importance of external cues and attributes the causes of attitudes to our own as well as others' behaviors. Remember our discussion of the dimensions of attitudes in Chapter 1. Attitudes have not only cognitive and affective dimensions but also behavioral dimensions.

Attribution theory

Attribution theory deals with how and what we infer about the behaviors, attitudes, and intentions we observe or know, or think we know, in others and in ourselves.

I sat on a Jamaican beach in 1975 reading the novel *Jaws* by Peter Benchley. When friends bent on water fun tried to entice me into the ocean, I found my usual enthusiasm dulled by a strange reluctance. It wasn't the people, I was sure (after all, I liked them); it wasn't their manner or mode of persuasion (that had always been successful before); it had to be this scary book. I had conjured up visions of a great white shark stalking this beach.

---

[71]Bem, *Beliefs, Attitudes and Human Affairs,* p. 50. For a critical view of self-perception theory, see Jonathan L. Freedman, David O. Sears, and J. Merrill Carlsmith, *Social Psychology* (Englewood Cliffs, N.J.: Prentice-Hall, 1978), pp. 454–59.

My friends were perplexed by my reluctant behavior and I'm sure went through an array of attributions of cause. Ross doesn't like us any more; it was a bad time to interrupt him; he's had a recent bad experience with the water (they were close on that one). When they saw the book I was reading they roared with laughter. They made an attribution (a correct one) that the book had at least temporarily soured my love of the ocean.

The covariation principle   In the story above three or four things were related to my behavior; one was obviously the most responsible. Harold H. Kelley has called these variables covariants.[72] The swimming (and the book) are called the *entity;* my friends, the *person* influence; and the way and the time that they approached me, the *time/modality* influence.

Three years later the book *Jaws* was made into a movie. Safely back in the states, two of these same friends invited me to see it. Despite all the terror in the film, we enjoyed it tremendously and had a fun-filled evening and a great reunion.

Was our fun the result of the *entity* (a good movie)? Was it being with good friends—the *people* variable? Was it the beautiful and comfortable theater, or *modality?* The film could also have constituted *modality,* for the original story line was, after all, a print mode. Perhaps it was the *time.* I had been working hard, and this was a needed escape. All of these covariants also had something to do with our impression of the movie. As an entity *Jaws* will never be another *Gone With the Wind,* but it was a tempting attribution on that specific night.

The discounting effect   The first lesson of this story is that we tend to work backward from behavior to inferences about causes and often overlook the other critical influences that covary. Was the swimming reluctance caused *internally* by an abiding fear of the water, or was it mostly or exclusively caused by a scary story about a people-eating shark? In analyzing our own behavior we go through a similar attribution process. Were we laughing during the movie because it was so funny (external) or because of the happy mood of our reunion (internal)? This kind of analysis has been referred to as the *discounting* effect by Kelley: "The role of a given cause in producing a given effect is discounted if other plausible causes are also present."[73]

The second lesson is that we can do things that will make our impressions of others and our attributions to others more accurate. One means of doing this is by *taking another look.* Observe more of a person's behavior, preferably in different contexts. Is she under special external pressure? Is there free choice,

---

[72]Harold H. Kelley, "Attribution Theory in Social Psychology," in *Nebraska Symposium on Motivation,* ed. David Levine (Lincoln: University of Nebraska Press, 1967), pp. 192–240. For a recent collection of articles on attribution theory, see John H. Harvey, William Ickes, and Robert F. Kidd, eds., *New Directions in Attribution Research* (Hillsdale, N.J.: Lawrence Erlbaum Associates, 1978).

[73]Harold H. Kelley, "The Processes of Causal Attribution," *American Psychologist,* 28, no. 2 (1973), 108.

or does the job or the situation dictate all or part of the behavior? Does the hostage speak true treason, or is there a gun at his family's head? Another, often overlooked way of gathering more information is to ask the opinion of respected others who have observed the individual. This lesson also applies to ourselves. Check out the pressures and covariant influences that make you do the things you do. Solicited feedback from others can be a mind opener, but also sometimes an ego shaker.

Active persuasion Attribution theory can help us more objectively infer attitudes, intentions, and dispositions about receivers (as in audience analysis) or about the source of the persuasion if we are the receivers. Attribution theory attempts to help us improve subjective, probable-cause explanations of observed behavior (including our own). Our resulting evaluations of our explanations may lead us to revise or reinforce our attitudes or beliefs.

For a sender to facilitate this desired revision (or self-persuasion), the message and, where possible, the situation and context should be so arranged that the receiver infers his or her own underlying attitudes that support the sender's purpose. This harks back to consistency theory: having taken action (a counterattitudinal essay, an oath of office, a contribution to charity, and so forth), one then seeks consonance by revising his or her attitudes so that they justify the action.[74] The sender helps this search for consonance by very subtle or very little pressure to act, and by positive reinforcement of the personal and social benefits from such action. Where the persuasion takes place over time, repetition—in a variety of messages, situations, and contexts—should encourage these self-attributions. Political advertisements will often portray a candidate's best attributes in a variety of social settings; we are asked to repeat our pledges, oaths, and vows in settings ranging from the school and the church to the cemetery and the Super Bowl.

Whereas attribution theorists tend to view these facilitating efforts primarily as a passive process, communicologists see it also as an active process. Persuaders can appeal to receiver dispositions involving gain or loss, approval or disapproval, and hope for favorable cognitive evaluation. Rules are implied here.

SUMMING UP

A theory allows us to make sense of information, events, and observations. Theories are generalizations describing probable relationships between persuasive strategies and their effectiveness.

---

[74]See Russell H. Fazio, Mark P. Zanna, and Joel Cooper, "Dissonance and Self-Perception: An Integrative View of Each Theory's Proper Domain of Application," *Journal of Experimental Social Psychology*, 13 (1977), 464–79.

Rhetoric is the faculty of observing in any given case the available means of persuasion. The major classical rhetoricians were Aristotle, Plato, Isocrates, Cicero, and Quintilian. One classical speech organization pattern included: (1) exordium (introduction), (2) narration (facts), (3) confirmation (proofs), (4) refutation, and (5) peroration (conclusion). The basic assumptions of rhetorical theory are: (1) it is a useful art; (2) it can be taught; (3) it is based on the doctrine of the mean; and (4) it is the method of giving effectiveness to truth. The *canons* of rhetoric are: *invention (inventio), arrangement (disposito), style (elocutio), memory (memoria),* and *delivery (pronunciato).* James A. Winans, Charles Henry Woolbert, William Norwood Brigance, and Alan Houston Monroe were pioneering speech communication theorizers who made significant contributions to rhetorical theory. Others included A. E. Phillips, Winston Brembeck, William Howell, R. T. Oliver, and Franklin Knower.

Cognitive consistency refers to a kind of mental agreement between a person's notions about some object or event and some new information about those same objects or events. The assumption of cognitive consistency theories is that when the new information is contradictory or inconsistent with a person's notions and attitudes, it will lead to some psychological confusion and tension. This tension then motivates the person to alter or adjust his attitudes or behavior in the direction of reducing the inconsistency.

Balance theory is discussed in terms of the works of Heider, Newcomb, Abelson, and Rosenberg. According to balance theory, when two people interact with an event or object of mutual concern, the intrapersonal and interpersonal situation is cognitively either balanced or unbalanced. When it is balanced no persuasion is really possible. When unbalanced it produces tension and generates motivation or persuasion to restore or achieve balance. The individual respect and trust people have for each other in their interpersonal relations has much to do with the success of communication in reducing tension or strain. Rosenberg and Abelson built on the balance model in their affective-cognitive consistency theory. Attitude consists of two elements, feelings and beliefs. People seek balance between them. Persuasion is then possible by modifying either the affective or cognitive element.

Osgood and Tannenbaum's congruity principle explains how we strive to make our attitudes congruent or consistent when we have foreknowledge of the various strengths of attitudes about to come into association. We can then rhetorically predict the resultant scaler average of the attitudes.

The chief spokesman for cognitive dissonance theory is Leon Festinger. This theory argues that dissonance (inconsistency) is uncomfortable and motivates a person to achieve consonance. When dissonance is present a person will actively avoid situations and communications which would likely increase the dissonance. The theory postulates that behavior can cause persuasion. Festinger indicates that dissonance between two cognitions is typially caused by cultural mores, logical consistency, experience, and cases where one specific opinion is included by definition in a more general opinion.

There is wide support with literally hundreds of pieces of evidence to corroborate the idea that our cognitive systems seek a harmonious, agreeable, balanced, consistent set of relationships between our notions of the world and our latest perception of it. The various theories developing this idea might better be called inconsistency theories, since it is the inconsistency that causes the tension, motivation, and possible change in attitude or behavior.

Cognitive response theory suggests that people really persuade themselves through cognitive reevaluations. The basic sender strategy is to develop messages that (a) evoke favorable thoughts, and that (b) induce people to rehearse and remember these thoughts.

Social judgment theory provides us with the notion of range or latitude of attitude. In this theory, the larger the range of rejection, the more difficult the persuasion; the larger the range of acceptance or noncommitment, the less difficult; a large range of rejection predicts ego defensiveness. If the message can be encoded so that it does not fall appreciably beyond a person's range of acceptance, this theory predicts that it has a better chance of being *assimilated*. If it is so placed that it falls well beyond a person's range of acceptance, it will be *contrasted* away from the acceptable range and fail.

Self-perception theory argues that we infer our own attitudes based on the behaviors in which we engage. The theory suggests that we systematically align and develop attitudes based on external cues or our own behaviors. This theory makes the same predictions as dissonance theory, but explains the results differently.

Attribution theory deals with how and what we infer about the behaviors, attitudes, and intentions we observe or know, or think we know, about others and also about ourselves. The *covariation* principle involves three influences: the entity (or thing), the person, and the time/modality (when and how circumstances). The *discounting* principle involves a search for other, plausible causes for the effects observed. Suggestions are: take another look, consider the context, look for external pressures, and ask respected others. This theory helps us objectively infer attitudes and dispositions about senders as well as receivers of messages.

STUDY PROJECTS
AND TASKS

1. Make a brief study of the speeches of some political-action group in terms of cognitive consistency (congruity). Note particularly instances in which it becomes counterproductive (at least for some receivers).
2. Find and report three brief examples of persuasion that illustrate cognitive dissonance theory.
3. Write up a one-page case study in which behavior changed attitudes (for example: antipollution devices that caused problems with a new car softened your attitudes toward the automobile as a polluting agent).

4. Test self-perception theory by locating and describing attitudes that you developed after you had taken some action.

5. Prepare a two-to-four-minute persuasive message that attempts to accommodate a specific, hypothetical audience and is based on one or more of the persuasion theories discussed in this chapter.

6. Identify a group with serious anxiety problems (or a strong bias on an issue) who are almost impossible to persuade. Discuss.

7. Explain a situation where the *contrast effect* occurred. (Persuasion was perceived, at least initially, as more objectionable than it perhaps was.)

8. Explain a situation where *assimilation* took place. (Discrepancy was minimized and the persuasion appraised as more acceptable than it perhaps was.)

9. Collect three magazine or newspaper advertisements that make use of persuasion theories found in this chapter. Attach a one-page analysis and evaluation of the advertisements.

10. Prepare an oral report, essay, or study in which you attempt to prove or disprove any of the persuasion theories discussed in this chapter.

5

Audience Analysis

Audience Psychology
> The Nature of Audiences
> Types of Audiences
> Persuasibility

Mob Mentality

Audience Adaptation
> Descriptive Measures
> Rhetorical Sensitivity

Summing Up

Study Projects and Tasks

AUDIENCE PSYCHOLOGY

The Nature of Audiences

Persuaders are usually only as successful as their ability to adapt to their audience. Adapting involves knowing the obvious and not so obvious characteristics of receivers.

One sometimes needs to account for the superstimulation that arises when a number of people interact. A useful system of classifying such collective behavior is shown in Figure 5–1.[1]

Audiences are placed on the passive side of the diagram. A typical audience exhibits far less emotionality than a mob. The "group mind" is not as evident. Regressive acts are rare. Nevertheless, similar forces are present even in very casual audiences. More formal audiences, such as classes of students, church groups, and lecture gatherings, are motivated by more identifiable purposes. They may be seeking information or recreation; they may be seeking to be converted, as are the audiences attracted to religious and political rallies.

Audiences, like mobs, can vary considerably in size. We use the word *audience* to refer to relatively formal gatherings of roughly twenty or more persons.

For a *small group* to exhibit collective behavior, its members must have interaction—some reason for being together. A group of people waiting for a bus does *not* fit this description. Small-group members are often both senders and receivers of persuasion. Feedback is often swift, leadership changes, a group spirit frequently emerges. Small groups have been known to run wild (street gangs), audiences practically never (except in panics). Those attempting persuasion should realize that (1) small, agreeing groups develop a greater feeling of personal involvement and responsibility than do audiences, and (2) attitudes and behavior can be changed through group discussion.

Persuaders who are dealing with vast, unseen audiences, as in the mass media, should utilize a broader, more sociological analysis. Such an analysis should include primary contacts (such as family and friends), secondary contacts (religious and political affiliations, occupational ties, and so on), and definable social groups (publics) having common characteristics or interests. Nevertheless, much of what is said below will also apply to the mass-media audience. If the intermediary model applies—if opinion leaders pass information along interpersonally—then it may apply very closely indeed.

The audience has frequently been considered as a statistical source—that is, as a means of assembling a large amount of information about individuals

---

[1]See also Stanley Milgram and Hans Toch, "Collective Behavior: Crowds and Social Movements," in *The Handbook of Social Psychology*, 2d ed., eds. G. Lindzey and E. Aronson (Reading, Mass.: Addison-Wesley, 1969), vol. 4, pp. 507–610.

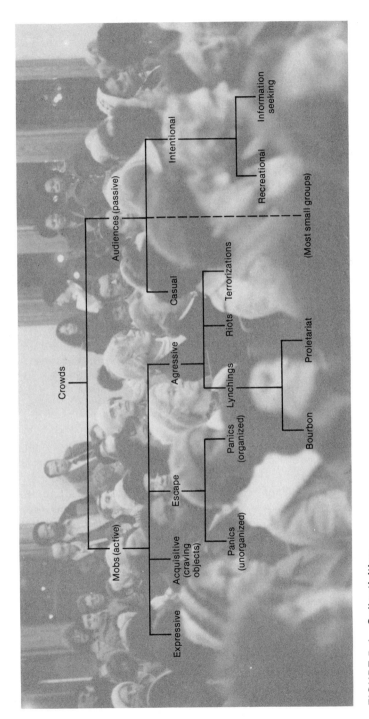

FIGURE 5–1 Collectivities

Adapted from Roger Brown, "Mass Phenomena," in *The Handbook of Social Psychology*, vol. 4, ed. G. Lindzey (Reading, Mass.: Addison-Wesley, 1954), p. 510.

(such as average age, income, nationality, and education) into manageable form. Audiences have also been classified into many general types, such as organized (or unorganized), unified, heterogeneous, apathetic, hostile, polarized, and bipolar. More will be said about types of audiences shortly. In general, the audience we are talking about is a fairly formal collection of individuals who assemble for a specific purpose. Patterns of interaction are reasonably predictable in such groups, given enough information about them.

Three of these patterns are *polarization, interstimulation,* and *feedback-response. Polarization* describes unusually homogeneous audience beliefs and attitudes. When two relatively homogeneous but opposing factions are present in an audience, the audience is referred to as *bipolar.* Debates often attract bipolar audiences. *Interstimulation* arises from some of the volatile behavior associated with mobs; it is similar to Floyd Allport's concept of social facilitation. It involves ritual, suggestion, and the reinforcement one receives from people behaving in similar ways at the same time. When all of those around us are angry, we are more apt to be angry; when all are happy, we are apt to be happy.[2] *Response to feedback* refers to a positive response to the efforts of the sender. If the speaker is strongly reinforced through positive feedback, he or she may become closely identified with some ideal. With strong interstimulation this identification may lead to exceptional, if only temporary, polarization among the speaker's listeners—an enviable situation as long as the persuader can control it and live with the results over a period of time. A highly stimulated audience may be only a few steps removed from a mob. Our ethical responsibilities, whether as sender or receiver, become critical.

Types of Audiences

Harry L. Hollingworth suggested that there are five types of audiences or receivers: (1) pedestrian, (2) discussion-passive, (3) selected, (4) concerted, and (5) organized. In referring to these audience types he used the term *orientation,* by which he meant "the establishment of a pattern of attention, when the group is considered, or a set and direction of interest, when we consider the individuals comprising the group."[3]

The *pedestrian audience* is a temporary audience, such as a group of pedestrians on a busy street corner. No common ties or lines of communication bind the members of the audience and the speaker. The speaker's first step, that of catching everyone's attention, is crucial. How far the process goes beyond that varies with the purpose of the speaker.

The *discussion group,* or *passive audience,* is one whose attention is already secured or guaranteed by rules of order. The persuader's initial problem is more likely to be the second step, that of holding attention or interest. Again,

[2]See Ladd Wheeler, "Toward a Theory of Behavioral Contagion," *Psychological Review,* 73 (1966), 179–92.

[3]Harry L. Hollingworth, *The Psychology of the Audience* (New York: American Book, 1935), p. 21.

how far the process goes depends upon the occasion or the success of the persuader.

The *selected audience* is one whose members are assembled for some common purpose but are not all sympathetic to one another or to the speaker's point of view. Impression, persuasion, and direction characterize the sender's undertaking here.

The *concerted audience* is one whose members assemble with a common, active purpose in mind, with sympathetic interest in a mutual enterprise, but with no clear division of labor or rigid organization of authority. Imparting a sense of conviction and delegating authority are the sender's chief responsibilities.

The *organized audience* is a group with a rigid division of labor and authority supported by specific common purposes and interests. The members know their tasks, having already been assigned them by the leader. Because the audience is already persuaded, the leader has only to issue clear instructions.

Before appearing in front of the audience, according to Hollingworth, a persuader ought to secure as full a knowledge as possible of the mode and degree of the audience's orientation. He or she must be prepared to shift tactics if the first reactions of the audience show that the initial judgment was wrong. Circumstances may, of course, alter an audience's orientation.

According to Hollingworth, the five fundamental tasks of a persuader are attention, interest, impression, conviction, and direction. By examining these we can gain a better picture of how to adapt to the five types of audiences. In Figure 5–2 the five tasks are listed under the types of audiences to which they

FIGURE 5–2 Hollingworth's Categorization of Audiences and Tasks
From H. L. Hollingworth, *The Psychology of the Audience* (New York: American Book Co., 1935), p. 21.

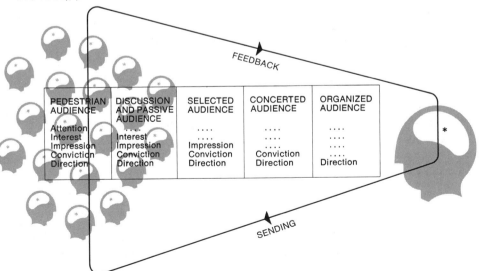

PEDESTRIAN AUDIENCE	DISCUSSION AND PASSIVE AUDIENCE	SELECTED AUDIENCE	CONCERTED AUDIENCE	ORGANIZED AUDIENCE
Attention	....	....	....	....
Interest	Interest	....	....	....
Impression	Impression	Impression	....	....
Conviction	Conviction	Conviction	Conviction	....
Direction	Direction	Direction	Direction	Direction

are most relevant. For instance, the primary tasks of a person speaking before a concerted audience are to instill conviction and provide direction.

This explanation assumes that the craving for an audience is a fundamental human need. One of the most significant characteristics of an individual is the type of audience that most readily motivates his or her thought and conduct. In *The Psychology of the Audience,* Hollingworth gives the word *audience* an extended meaning. To have an audience, in his view, is not only to be heard (this is the dominant meaning), but is also, more generally, to receive attention from other human beings.

Closely related to both interpersonal communication and speaker-audience interaction is Hollingworth's observation that there is often a striking conflict between our craving for an audience and our fear of it. We probably seek a certain amount of confrontation or encounter and at the same time resist it.

Audience configurations (Figure 5–3) — seating arrangement, degree of closeness, and so on — constitute an important aspect of collective behavior and audience analysis. In somewhat polarized formal audiences, the occasion and the ritual may become very important. The Japanese auto worker who as a ritual does five minutes of company-coordinated calisthenics, sings songs, and cheers his or her second-shift replacement is a different breed from most of the auto workers in Detroit.

We take the rituals of our social clubs, veterans' organizations, temples, and churches well in stride. However, persuaders are well advised to be cautious about upsetting the rituals of their audience. The old public-speaking adage prohibiting foul language is probably a useful one, especially where ritual is involved. The most foul-mouthed among us often becomes the purest of tongue in such situations. The audience's resentment against the blasphemer can be devastating. If a mob can become animalistic, audiences can in a flash become holier than thou![4]

The *physical setting* is part of the occasion and ritual. The pulpit in a church adds to the minister's message. The raised dais in the House of Representatives imparts extra authority to the Speaker's words. And the old Globe Theatre is no ordinary house. How we handle lighting, music, and pomp is also part of the physical setting and ritual, and it affects the message. The same message uttered in a church, a restaurant, and a fraternity house might be sacrilege in the first, rudeness in the second, and understatement in the third. People's expectations change in different settings and in different situations. The proximity of a speaker to an audience is also thought to be a factor in audience psychology. If you are on an elevated platform far removed from the first row of the audience, your style of delivery should differ from the style you would use if you were close to the group.

[4]Douglas G. Bock, Jeri Lynn Proffitt Butler, and E. Hope Bock, "The Impact of Sex of the Speaker, Sex of the Rater and Profanity Type of Language Trait Errors in Speech Evaluation: A Test of the Rating Error Paradigm," *Southern Speech Communication Journal,* 49 (Winter 1984), 177–86.

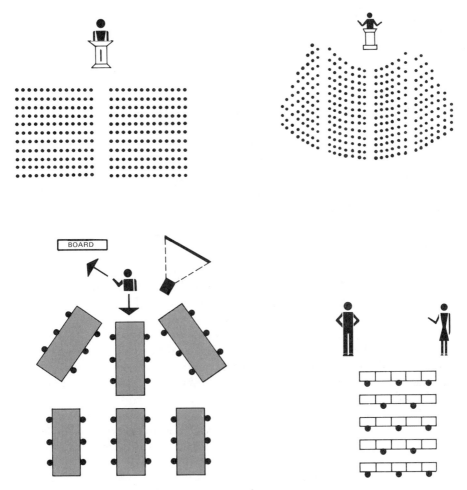

FIGURE 5–3 Audience Configurations

The arrangement of the audience also has an impact upon how the audience reacts to persuasion and influence, although evidence as to just how this works is mixed. Logical, factual persuasion is probably most effective when listeners are separated, and emotional appeals are probably most successful when listeners are close together.

Persuasibility

The attempt to understand how and why a person changes his or her mind is not new. Throughout the ages humanity has been striving to learn the secrets of why and how we change our beliefs and attitudes. What makes us susceptible to persuasion? How are we motivated to learn, to work, to fight? William McGuire suggests some important principles of persuasibility that allow a realistic analysis of receiver characteristics.[5] In the following discussion we have reorganized and simplified these principles.

Principles for analysis

THE MEDIATIONAL PRINCIPLE: THE SITUATION IS CRITICAL

Even when we know or think we know the receivers' predispositions or central personality traits, our analysis can be grossly inaccurate if we don't take into account the situation. If for some reason our receivers simply aren't paying attention or don't comprehend what's being said, the rest of our predictions may not be very meaningful. Not being able to hear adequately is, of course, another mediating factor. In short, people's predispositions do not hold as predictors across *all* situations.[6]

THE INTERACTION PRINCIPLE: THE SOURCE AND THE MESSAGE OFTEN OVERRIDE PREDICTIONS BASED ON PERSONALITY DISPOSITIONS

Who is doing the persuading often overrides all the other factors combined. How the receivers *perceive* the source is not only critical but often difficult to assess. (Refer to the discussion of status in Chapter 1 and credibility in Chapter 3.)

The *message* may also override predictions based on personality. A life-and-death message from a respected family physician may nullify Uncle Ben's anti–health care predispositions as predictors of his persuasibility.

THE CONFOUNDING PRINCIPLE: PREDICTIONS OF PERSUASIBILITY ARE CONFOUNDED BY THE INTERACTION BETWEEN A RECEIVER'S PERSONALITY TRAITS

If, as we will see later, low self-esteem is generally related to persuasibility as well as to depression and withdrawal—conditions that generally make people poor listeners—then what? Clearly an assessment of such confounding interaction is necessary before persuasibility can be predicted.

Immediate past experiences may also confuse your predictions. A person who usually has a positive, healthy self-esteem but who has just experienced a

---

[5]William J. McGuire, "The Nature of Attitudes and Attitude Change," in *Handbook of Social Psychology*, 2nd ed., eds. Lindzey and Aronson, Vol. 3, pp. 243–47.

[6]McGuire describes a *situational-weighting* principle that persuaders can use to analyze audiences across various situations.

stinging failure may very well be more susceptible than predicted. Also, a person may have more confidence about some matters than others; his or her self-esteem may change with the matter under discussion.

Some of these combined traits or characteristics may cause an averaging or even a canceling of persuasibility predictions.[7] A person who normally has low affiliation needs may find this need compromised or canceled in moments of great anxiety.

In addition to these three principles of McGuire's we would add a fourth:

WHAT HOLDS TRUE IN EXPERIMENTAL RESEARCH SETTINGS MAY NOT HOLD ACROSS ALL "REAL" SITUATIONS

McGuire's mediational principle alludes to this problem. We will attempt to use research that we feel does transcend the laboratory, either by design, replication in various contexts, or observation in a variety of situations.

Receiver characteristics   Keeping in mind all the guiding principles and warnings given above, we will now look at some receiver characteristics, assuming "other things are equal." Of course they never really are. However, the characteristics discussed below should provide some general benchmarks to help you start your audience analysis.

GENERAL TENDENCY

This has also been called *general trait,* but *tendency* may be the more appropriate word. In any event, the evidence suggests that some people are more open to persuasion than others. In one study some students were able to be swayed both pro and con on the same issue more readily than others. In another study some were found to alter their position on many topics more often than others.[8] A third study found that some children were more persuasible than others.[9] Evidence from earlier studies suggests that women may have more of this general tendency to be persuaded than men, but as we shall discuss under "gender," the general position of women today and their specific situations have altered this tendency.

---

[7]McGuire calls this the *compensation* principle.

[8]McGuire, "Nature of Attitudes and Attitude Change," pp. 241–43.

[9]Carl I. Hovland and Irving L. Janis, eds., *Personality and Persuasibility* (New Haven: Yale University Press, 1959), pp. 225–29.

INTELLIGENCE

In many respects an intelligent person is more difficult to persuade: he or she can be expected to have more highly developed critical abilities and a better basis for forming judgments. On the other hand, if the message is highly complex or subtle, a person needs intelligence simply to comprehend. This is probably why the research points to both a positive and a negative relationship between persuasibility and intelligence.[10]

Various intellectual abilities such as vocabulary, thinking, and concentration, which affect how a person attends to communication, suggest a positive relationship between persuasibility and intelligence. Without attention, persuasion is unlikely. When low intelligence is related to low self-esteem, there is perhaps a strong susceptibility to persuasion.

SELF-ESTEEM

Self-esteem is in large part the value you place on yourself. Arthur Cohen reports a study in which subjects previously determined to be of high and low esteem were analyzed in terms of persuasibility. The study found that persons of *low* self-esteem were generally more susceptible to persuasion. More specifically, such persons were more susceptible to persuasion by those with high self-esteem than by those with low self-esteem.[11]

In a study of self-esteem considered in terms of feelings of social inadequacy, low esteem was again found to be coupled with susceptibility (especially in men).[12]

Indeed, the events of Jonestown suggest that a large audience of people with low self-esteem were persuaded by a person they blindly held in high esteem.

Like people with intelligence, people with strong self-concepts may be better able to handle highly complex and challenging social-influence situations.[13] The less typical case of an unintelligent person with high self-esteem considerably complicates predictions. A highly antisocial, hostile personality with abnormally high self-esteem would of course be very difficult to

---

[10]See McGuire, "Nature of Attitudes and Attitude Change," pp. 243–49.

[11]Arthur R. Cohen, "Some Implications of Self-Esteem for Social Influence," in *Personality and Persuasibility*, eds. Hovland and Janis, pp. 102–20. See also Arthur R. Cohen, *Attitude Change and Social Influence* (New York: Basic Books, 1964), pp. 42–61; and Bonnie Spillman, "The Impact of Value and Self-Esteem Messages in Persuasion," *Central States Speech Journal*, 30, no. 1 (Spring 1979), 67–74.

[12]Irving L. Janis and Peter B. Field, "Sex Differences and Personality Factors Related to Persuasibility," in *Personality and Persuasibility*, eds. Hovland and Janis, pp. 55–68.

[13]McGuire, "Nature of Attitudes and Attitude Change," p. 250.

persuade.[14] It is unlikely that anyone could have persuaded James Jones to do much of anything in those last, terrible hours at Jonestown.

For all the variables of sex, circumstance, hostility, mental set, and changing self-image, some evidence clearly indicates that high persuasibility is related to low esteem.

AUTHORITARIANISM

About the authoritarian personality we have only limited generalizations to help would-be persuaders. The highly authoritarian personality is pre-occupied with power, makes absolute, either-or judgments about human values, relies on authority figures, is dogmatic rather than open-minded. When prejudice is involved, authoritarianism is, in part, a reaction against an out-group.

The source of authority in a persuasive communication is thought to be critical in a *prejudicial* way to the authoritarian receiver.[15] That is, authoritarians tend to be persuaded more by authorities cited in a persuasive message than by the information in the message.[16] Studies by Harvey and Beverly[17] and others[18] suggest that highly authoritarian people are more readily persuaded by a high-status source than are low-authoritarian people. The authoritarian personality apparently formulates beliefs primarily on the basis of authority rather than message content,[19] and may be both the most difficult and, in a restricted sense, the easiest personality to persuade. The status of the person who tries to persuade such personalities is important, as is the kind of evidence from authority that the person uses. For George Patton to be persuaded to apologize to the troops took an Eisenhower and a Marshall!

AGE

No hard evidence shows that age affects persuasibility, although we have many pronouncements that older people are more rigid (and therefore less

[14]Irving L. Janis and Donald Rife, "Persuasibility and Emotional Disorder," in *Personality and Persuasibility,* eds. Hovland and Janis, p. 130.

[15]F. A. Powell, "Open- and Closed-Mindedness and the Ability to Differentiate Source and Message," *Journal of Abnormal and Social Psychology,* 65 (1962), 61–64.

[16]John H. Rohrer and Muzafer Sherif, *Social Psychology at the Crossroads* (New York: Harper & Row, Pub., 1951), pp. 255–58.

[17]O. J. Harvey and G. D. Beverly, "Some Personality Correlates of Concept Change Through Role Playing," *Journal of Abnormal and Social Psychology,* 63 (1961), 125–30.

[18]I. H. Paul, "Impressions of Personality, Authoritarianism, and the Fait Accompli Effect," *Journal of Abnormal and Social Psychology,* 53 (1956), 338–44.

[19]See Milton Rokeach, *The Open and Closed Mind* (New York: Basic Books, 1960).

persuasible) than younger people. There is some evidence that children through age seven are influenced more heavily by adults than they are after age thirteen, but for all practical purposes we can make no generalizations about persuasibility and chronological age.[20] This is not to say that age is not a useful variable in audience analysis. The age range of an audience is certainly one of the elements of the speaker-audience situation. Age probably also has some relationship to certain personality traits. It is critical to remember not to consider variables in isolation when analyzing an audience. Audience characteristics tend to interact with one another.

GENDER

In several early studies gender was found to be related to persuasibility. Franklin Knower reported that (1) changes in attitude were more frequent among women than men; (2) men were more impressed by logical argument than women; (3) men were more effective with audiences than women; and (4) women were slightly more effective in face-to-face situations.[21] Thomas Scheidel found that women were significantly more persuasible than men and retained significantly less of the speech content..[22]

Irving Janis and Peter Field concluded that sex is a significant variable in persuasibility. They even warned that different generalizations regarding persuasibility may be necessary for the sexes.[23] These conclusions, however, probably reflect only the status of women at the time the research was conducted.

Evidence from more recent research is mixed. One study found female infants to be more compliant to maternal pressure.[24] Another study found Hindu women to be more persuasible than Hindu men.[25] When children aged three to eleven from six different cultures were studied in 1974, *no* overall sex differences were found.[26] But as recently as 1977, studies of classroom speech

---

[20]Gerald S. Lesser and Robert P. Abelson, "Personality Correlates of Persuasibility in Children," in *Personality and Persuasibility*, eds. Hovland and Janis, pp. 187–206.

[21]Franklin H. Knower, "Experimental Studies of Changes in Attitudes: I. A Study of the Effects of Oral Argument on Changes of Attitude," *Journal of Social Psychology*, 6 (1935), 315–47.

[22]Thomas M. Scheidel, "Sex and Persuasibility," *Speech Monographs*, 30, no. 4 (November 1963), 353–47.

[23]Irving L. Janis and Peter B. Field, "Sex Differences and Personality Factors Related to Persuasibility," in *Personality and Persuasibility*, eds. Hovland and Janis, p. 66.

[24]C. Minton, J. Kagan, and J. Levine, "Maternal Control and Obedience in the Two Year Old," *Child Development*, 42 (1971), 1873–94.

[25]V. Singh, "Sex and Age Differences in Persuasibility," *Journal of Social Psychology*, 82 (1970), 269–70.

[26]B. Whiting and C. Pope, "A Cross Cultural Analysis of Sex Differences in the Behavior of Children Aged Three to Eleven," *Journal of Social Psychology*, 91, no. 2 (December 1973), 171–88.

evaluators showed differences between the sexes.[27] However, the most impressive report on the question of gender and persuasibility cited more than seventy-five studies that *did not* as a whole support the earlier findings that females as a class are more persuasible than males.[28] However, there is evidence that receivers *expect* males to use more aggressive strategies than females and that deviations from these expectations may reduce persuasive effect.[29]

More recent research reflects the changing status of women and is generally freer of earlier tendencies to mistake levels of interest expectation or knowledge for genuine sex differences.[30] Once again the *context* makes a difference.

In modern America, male-female distinctions are often less meaningful than the attributions *people* (men or women) make about gender roles. An assessment of masculinity, femininity, and androgyny (the reflection of both male and female characteristics) may provide a better measure of sex-role adaptability.[31]

MOB MENTALITY

On December 3, 1979, eleven young Cincinnatians were stampeded to death in a tragic instance of mob insanity while waiting for a rock concert by The Who. Some comments by psychologists trying to explain:

[27]Douglas G. Bock, Larry Powell, James T. Kitchens, and James W. Flavin, "The Influence of Sex Differences in Speech Evaluation: Situational and Media Effects," *Communication Education*, 26, no. 2 (March 1977), 143–53. See also Douglas G. Bock and E. Hope Bock, "The Effects of the Sex of the Experimenter, Expectancy Inductions, and Sex of the Rater on Leniency, Halo, and Trait Errors in Speech Rating Behavior," *Communication Education*, 26, no. 4 (November 1977), 298–306; and L. R. Judd and C. B. Smith, "The Relationship of Age, Educational Classification, Sex, and Grade to Self-Concept and Ideal Self-Concept in a Basic Speech Course," *Communication Education*, 26, no. 4 (November 1977), 289–97.

[28]Eleanor E. Maccoby and Carol Jacklin, *Psychology and Sex Differences* (Stanford, Calif.: Stanford University Press, 1974).

[29]Michael Burgoon, James P. Dillard, and Noel E. Doran, "Friendly Or Unfriendly Persuasion: The Effects of Violations of Expectations by Males and Females," *Human Communication Research*, 10, no. 2 (Winter 1983), 283–94. See also Richard L. Street, Robert M. Brady, and Raymond Lee, "Evaluative Responses to Communicators: The Effects of Speech Rate, Sex, and Interaction Context," *Western Journal of Speech Communication*, 48, no. 1 (Winter 1984) 14–27.

[30]F. Sitrunk and J. McDavid, "Sex Variable in Conforming Behavior," *Journal of Personality and Social Psychology*, 17 (1971), 200–207. See also Dominic Infante and Robin Grimmett, "Attitudinal Effects of Utilizing a Critical Method of Analysis," *Central States Speech Journal*, 22 (1971), 213–17; and John E. Baird, Jr., "Sex Differences in Group Communication: A Review of Relevant Research," *Quarterly Journal of Speech*, 62, no. 2 (1976), 179–92; Alice H. Eagly, "Gender and Social Influence," *American Psychologist*, 38, no. 9 (September 1983), 971–80.

[31]Sandra L. Bem, "Sex Role Adaptability: One Consequence of Psychological Androgyny," *Journal of Personality and Social Psychology*, 31 (1975), 634–43. See also Charles L. Montgomery and Michael Burgoon, "The Effects of Androgyny and Message Expectations on Resistance to Persuasive Communication," *Communication Monographs*, 47 (1980), 56–57.

A blurring effect occurs.
The sense of self is lost.
The mob becomes your identity.
. . . regressive behavior, kid behavior, impulsive behavior.
Peer pressure to go along is very strong.
They lose a sense of physical self.
People actually forget they are crushing someone.
This could have happened at any large gathering.[32]

Our speech communication training typically involves more passive audiences that experience emotion through more deliberate interaction. However, we are meeting more active, expressive, and aggressive collections of people than ever before. In recent times we have witnessed demonstrations, panics, riots, and other types of collective behavior that challenge long-standing rhetorical advice. In these special situations people appear to be more susceptible to persuasion. To account for the superstimulation of a group of human beings, whatever its size, a new and more systematic classification of groups and perhaps an entirely new model of interpersonal influence is needed—a model involving contagion, regression, anonymity, suggestibility, violence, and other active dimensions not typically associated with more passive audiences. A useful system of classification was provided in Figure 5–1.

Panic illustrates how contagion, irrationality, and violence can spread through a crowd. The Chicago Iroquois Theatre fire of 1903, as described by the comedian Eddie Foy, who was on stage when it occurred, is another staggering real-life example.

"Fire!" . . . The crowd was beginning to surge toward the doors and already showing signs of a stampede. . . . They were falling into panic. . . . Especially in the gallery, they had gone mad.

The horror in the auditorium was beyond all description. . . . The fire escape ladders could not accommodate the crowd, and many fell or jumped to death on the pavement below. Some were not killed only because they landed on the cushion of bodies of those who had gone before. . . . Most of the dead were trampled or smothered. . . . In places on the stairways, . . . bodies were piled seven or eight feet deep. . . . The heel prints on the dead faces mutely testified to the cruel fact that human animals stricken by terror are as mad and ruthless as stampeding cattle. Many bodies . . . had the flesh trodden from their bones. . . .

From the start of the fire until all in the audience either escaped, died, or lay maimed in the halls and alleys, took just eight minutes. In that eight minutes more than five hundred perished. . . . Subsequent deaths among the injured brought the list up to 602.[33]

From the mob assaults of the French Revolution that were described so vividly by Gustave Le Bon to the protests, riots, and mass suicides of more

---

[32]*Detroit Free Press,* December 5, 1979, p. 1. Also see Peter Dublin, *Sociology: People in Groups* (Chicago: Science Research Associates, 1978).

[33]From the book *Clowning Through Life* by Eddie Foy and Alvin F. Harlow. Copyright 1928, by E. P. Dutton Inc. Renewal, © 1956 by Alvin F. Harlow. Reprinted by permission of the publisher, E. P. Dutton.

recent times, some very special mass persuasion has been recorded in history. It is not our purpose to evaluate these events as social movements. Our interest is rather in mob behavior, whatever the issues that motivate it. In 1913 E. A. Ross wrote a description of crowd behavior that is still useful today.

> The crowd [mob] may generate moral fervor, but it never sheds lights. If at times it has furthered progress, it is because the mob serves as a battering-ram to raze some mouldering, bat-infested institution and clean the ground for something better. This better will be the creation of gifted individuals or of deliberative bodies, never of anonymous crowds. It is easier for masses to agree on a Nay than on a Yea. Hence crowds destroy despotisms, but never build free States; abolish evils, but never found works of beneficence. Essentially atavistic and sterile, the crowd [mob] ranks as the lowest of the forms of human association.[34]

Le Bon suggests that when a crowd is focused into a mob, a *psychological law of mental unity* comes into play.[35] The participants become a sort of collective mind, and conscious personality is lost. Each person thinks and behaves quite differently from the way he or she would if acting alone. E. D. Martin described this phenomenon as *crowd mentality* and classified it with dreams, delusions, and automatic behavior. The collective mind seems to unleash our animal nature. According to Martin, the mob becomes "a device for indulging ourselves in a kind of temporary insanity by all going crazy together."[36] For Martin and Le Bon alike, the mob lurks under the skin of each of us. In this view mobs may be weapons of revenge. They are always uncompromising in their demands, and in no way do they respect individual dignity. Even their achievements are less a testament to their leadership than a consequence of their unbridled fury. In 1920 Martin wrote about mob behavior in words that have insight even today:

> The crowd, in common with paranoia, uniformly shows the quality of "megalo-mania." Every crowd *boosts* for itself, lauds itself, gives itself airs, speaks with oracular finality, regards itself as morally superior and will, so far as it has the power, lord it over everyone. . . .
> Every organized crowd is jealous of its dignity and honor and is bent upon keeping up appearances. Nothing is more fatal to it than a successful assault upon its prestige. Every crowd, even the casual street mob, clothes the egoistic desires of its members or participants in terms of the loftiest moral motive. No crowd can afford to be laughed at.[37]

---

[34]E. A. Ross, *Social Psychology* (New York: Macmillan, 1913), pp. 56–57. For social movement insights see Anthony Oberschall, *Social Conflict and Social Movements* (Englewood Cliffs, N.J.: Prentice-Hall, 1973).

[35]Gustave Le Bon, *The Crowd* (New York: Viking, 1960), p. 26.

[36]E. D. Martin, *The Behavior of Crowds* (New York and London: Harper & Brothers, 1920), p. 37.

[37]Ibid., pp. 74, 83. For other views see Helen Hughes, *Crowd and Mass Behavior* (Boston: Holbrook Press, Inc., 1972) and Jonathan Turner, *Sociology, Studying the Human System* (Santa Monica, Ca.: Goodyear Publishing Co., 1981).

For Le Bon, Martin, Ross, and others, the mob is a group in which people's normal reactions become secondary to unconscious desires and motivations. The major mechanisms leading to a state of collective mind or mob mentality appear to be *anonymity, contagion,* and *suggestibility.* One who is lost in the press of the mob loses much of his or her sense of responsibility. This anonymity gives rise to an inflated feeling of power. Contagion, well illustrated by the panic attending the Iroquois Theatre fire, is a kind of high-speed infectious mayhem. A heightened state of suggestibility leads to hasty, thoughtless, and rash action. Many of one's restraining emotions are lost—fear is often missing in battle, pity in a riot or a lynching.

A full-blown concept of collective mind includes, of course, the ethical and legal issues of sanity and of guilt or innocence. One can argue that stupidity and suggestibility exist in individuals as much as in mobs. Moreover, individuals vary in their degree of participation in mob action.[38] One can also argue, as Floyd Allport did, that mobs simply supply a form of *social facilitation.*[39] Individuals' desires are stimulated merely by the sight and sound of others

FIGURE 5–4

Photo credit: Irene Springer

[38]Ralph H. Turner and Lewis M. Killian, *Collective Behavior* (Englewood Cliffs, N.J.: Prentice-Hall, 1957, 1972).

[39]Floyd N. Allport, *Social Psychology* (Cambridge, Mass.: Riverside Press, 1924), p. 298.

behaving in similar ways. Roger Brown, a social psychologist, argues that "something new is created. To describe this new thing, this 'emergent,' as a 'group mind' does not seem to be seriously misleading. It may be a degree more illuminating to say that what emerges in the crowd is a payoff matrix that does not exist for the members when they do not compose a crowd."[40]

Collective behavior was surely manipulated at Jonestown, and apparently by a master at applying crowd suggestibility. A group mind is a frightening thing to students of persuasion. An understanding of collective behavior may help us keep cool heads when subjected to such mob pressures. An analysis of the mechanisms of crowd behavior may make us less susceptible to such influence.

Much remains to be uncovered about the behavior of crowds and mobs. They add a new dimension to persuasibility and audience analysis.

AUDIENCE ADAPTATION

Descriptive Measures

Locating springboards for what may or may not persuade a given group begins with an analysis of your receivers. Receivers are not the same in all situations. Your analysis must therefore include the occasion, situation, and any specific conditions that are pertinent.

The specific situation Recall the first principle of audience analysis discussed earlier: *The situation is critical.* As a speaker you will want to ask yourself the following questions:

1. What type of audience is involved? Can it be classified as pedestrian, passive, selected, concerted, or organized (the five categories suggested by Hollingworth)?
2. What is the total program? Am I all or part of it? Where do I fit in? Is ritual involved?
3. What is the audience arrangement? Is there fixed seating? Close seating? How large is the audience? Will I speak from a platform?
4. What is the physical setting? Is it inside or outside? In a church, a gym, or a theater?

If I see four thousand angry students looking at *me*—that's an audience. If they're looking in all directions—that's a mob!

Lee S. Drefus, Former Governor of Wisconsin, April 16, 1982

The audience-message relationship In our discussion of the principles of audience analysis we learned that the message and/or the source

[40]Roger Brown, *Social Psychology* (New York: Free Press, 1965), p. 760. Also see Ronald Federico and Janet Schwartz, *Sociology* (Reading, Ma.: Addison-Wesley, 1983), pp. 336–42.

often override all other measures with which we can make predictions about the audience. Jon Eisenson and his associates suggest several useful questions for *audience-message analysis.*

1. *What is the significance of the subject for the audience?* Is its interest in the subject only casual, or is it motivated by real needs and wants? How far has its thinking about the problem progressed?
2. *How much does the audience know about the subject?* Does it have essential factual information, or only opinions and sentiments? Are its sources of information sound, unbiased, and complete?
3. *What beliefs or prejudices does the audience have about the subject?* What are the probable sources or influences that led to these existing notions?
4. *What is the attitude of the audience toward the subject?* Is it possible to estimate the percentage who are in favor of, neutral to, or opposed to the subject?[41]

The source can override general audience dispositions as well. If the audience has an extremely high (or low) opinion of the speaker, this may affect how it receives the message. Remember to ask these obvious questions.

1. What does the audience know about me, the speaker? What impressions does it have of me?
2. Does it perceive me to be qualified, trustworthy, and sincere?
3. Do the people in the audience perceive my attitudes as being similar to their own?

Group memberships   Plato believed we reflect the society in which we live. Our family, school, temple and church are all thought to heavily influence our life and personality. This is not to suggest that people with similar backgrounds are carbon copies of one another. Even the strong influences of the culture in which we live determine only what we learn as members of a group, not what we learn as individuals. This explains in part why we alter our behavior and motivations in what seem to be the most inconsistent ways.

Living in a particular society requires us to adopt certain standards or patterns of behavior that are roughly agreed upon by the members of the group. Much random and impulsive individual behavior is held back out of respect for these group codes. The feelings of unity, purpose, and value that we experience as part of a group give us and the other group members a rough pattern of prediction, comfort, and understanding. The *conceptions* we have of our group often mold our personality more than the group itself does. Some groups have so dominated maladjusted individuals or those with low self-esteem that the personality of these persons becomes one of complete dependence and compliance.

Most of us belong to so many groups that predictions about the groups represented in even a uniform audience are often shaky at best. For example,

[41]Jon Eisenson, J. Jeffery Auer, and John V. Irwin, *The Psychology of Communication* (New York: Appleton-Century-Crofts, 1963), p. 279.

an audience at a political convention may be 100-percent Republican or 100-percent Democratic. Yet they may represent ever so many religious, ethnic, and occupational groups and hold widely divergent attitudes on key issues. However, the more we can learn about the groups those in the audience do or do not belong to, the more intelligently we can prepare our message.

Role and occupation   Role is another descriptive measure to which we should adapt our message. Sometimes the role we attribute to an audience is different from the role it attributes to itself, and sometimes several roles are involved.

Typing a person by his or her occupation is as dangerous as classifying a person according to role. Nevertheless, knowing a person's occupation is often useful. For instance, one can often predict the average income level of an audience by knowing the occupation of most of its members. Furthermore, we can predict that teachers will have college degrees, top management executives will have similar opinions about pieces of labor legislation, and so on.

People form roles on the basis of how they view themselves and how society and its subgroups expect them to behave. Surely people are motivated by appeals to their perceived role in life.

Special interests   Whatever their differences in primary-group membership, audiences are often highly polarized if their members have some special interest in common. A small community with a winning high school basketball team may ignore a guest speaker who is unaware of this special interest. Sometimes special interests are temporary, but speakers would be well advised to seek out and become familiar with any such interests that the audience expects them to know something about.

Education   A person's education is the sum of his or her learning. Do not confuse schooling with education, for a diploma is no guarantee of an education. Many college graduates remain uneducated. Nevertheless, formal schooling is usually a fast and systematic way of acquiring knowledge. Knowing a person's level of education may therefore help you plan your message. Your language and vocabulary should be adapted to your audience's educational level, previous schooling, and area of interest. An audience with a highly technical education will require a different approach than one with a religious or a liberal-arts background. Time invested in this kind of audience analysis is usually well spent.

Age   Despite the lack of generalizations available from the receiver characteristics discussed earlier, it is obvious that an audience of ten-year-olds will call for considerably different preparation than a group of forty-year-olds, even if the subject is Little League baseball. Even a few children in an otherwise all-adult audience can sometimes present a problem. If you choose (or are advised) to ignore them, you can be certain that the audience will not. Rather, it will establish norms of appropriateness and understanding based on the presence of the youngsters. A risqué story is less well received when even a single child is present.

Gender   As we have learned, sex differences in persuasibility are less significant than they once were. However, all women (and men) do not view the women's movement in quite the same way. One can presume a wider range of interests and sensitivities among women today. Some are intensely sensitive to the new role of women. Male and female sources had best be sensitive indeed about their language (watch out for chauvinism), illustrations, and humor. The modern audience is in no mood to be treated frivolously or labeled with stereotypes from the past.

Rhetorical Sensitivity

Rhetorical sensitivity involves effectively matching the message we are sending to the requirements of the receivers and the situation and context. It "is a particular attitude toward encoding spoken messages. It represents a way of thinking about what should be said and then a way of deciding how to say it."[42] According to Hart and Burks, it is "... that type of ... sensitivity which ... makes effective social interaction manifestly possible."[43]

Rhetorical sensitivity is a measure of a speaker's willingness to carefully consider the psychological environment before encoding messages. It is the ability to judge public and interpersonal encounters accurately and to sense when to be rhetorically sensitive and when to be rhetorically assertive.

In a study of hundreds of students in a speech-fundamentals course where audience analysis was heavily stressed, rhetorical sensitivity scores were found to be significantly higher at the end of the semester.[44] This was not true of students in other university courses.

Rhetorically sensitive people (RS) are usually considered to be inter-personally attractive. They judge encounters carefully before taking a stand on an issue; they distinguish between *content* and *relational* communication; and they know when to speak up and when to shut up. They deal with audience conflict forthrightly and yet with sensitivity.

People who are not rhetorically sensitive have been described as *noble*

[42]Roderick P. Hart, Robert E. Carlson, and William F. Eadie, "Attitudes Toward Communication and the Assessment of Rhetorical Sensitivity," *Communication Monographs,* 47, no. 1 (March 1980), 2.

[43]Roderick P. Hart and Don M. Burks, "Rhetorical Sensitivity and Social Interaction," *Speech Monographs,* 39, no. 2 (June 1972), 75.

[44]Ladene Schoen, "A Study of the Audience Sensitivity and Rhetorical Sensitivity of Students Enrolled in Speech 0200, Basic Speech, at Wayne State University and Implications for Pedagogy" (Ph.D. dissertation, Wayne State University, 1981).

FIGURE 5-5

Cliff Wirth, cartoonist, *The Detroit News*

selves (NS) or *rhetorical reflectors* (RR). The noble selves have been characterized as persons who see "any variation from their personal norms as hypo-
critical, as a denial of integrity, as a cardinal sin."[45] Rhetorical reflectors have
been described as persons who "have no self to call their own. For each person
and for each situation they present a new self."[46] They empathize with (or
at least appear to) and reflect each situation in which they find themselves.
Rhetorically sensitive speakers or receivers seek to moderate such extremes.
They are not braggarts, nor are they chameleons, fearfully reflecting and hiding
in each encounter. The range of sensitivity might be scaled as in Figure 5–6.

[45]Donald K. Darnell and Wayne Brockriede, *Persons Communicating* (Englewood Cliffs, N.J.:
Prentice-Hall, 1976), p. 176.
[46]Ibid., p. 178.

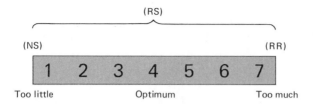

FIGURE 5–6
Sensitivity Toward Most Interactions
(NS=noble self;
RR=rhetorical reflector;
RS=rhetorically sensitive)

The research on rhetorical sensitivity suggests that the concept captures various special situations and contexts to which people are attracted. One study found that nurses with high RS scores tended to work in rehabilitation programs, outpatient clinics, and psychiatric wards; RRs worked as one might predict, with extended care and intensive care; nurses with higher NS scores tended to be supervisors.[47] In a study of military personnel, officers were found to be more rhetorically sensitive than sergeants; the sergeants tended to be noble selves, and the enlisted men were mostly rhetorical reflectors.[48]

Applying this concept, you, as a rhetorically sensitive speaker, should incorporate the following ideal personal characteristics in your audience analysis. The rhetorically sensitive speaker:

1. *Attempts to accept role-taking as part of the human condition.* To make this kind of adjustment you must decide what is an appropriate role to play at a given time. You cannot *not* play a role; the choice is among the roles available.
2. *Attempts to adjust verbal behavior.* You need not be all things to each and every complex audience, but you must try to adapt your language so that an audience is not so turned off that it misses your message or viewpoint.
3. *Is willing to undergo the strain of strategy adaptation.* Audiences differ in knowledge, mood, situation, and attitude. These differences call for organizational and rhetorical adaptations that often mean extra effort and extra patience.
4. *Discerns which information is acceptable for a given audience.* You must plan your speeches rather than speak off the cuff. You cannot say everything about anything, but you can easily say something stupid or offensive if you are not alert. Recall that a rhetorically sensitive person knows (or plans) when to shut up as well as when to speak up.
5. *Discerns which form and style are appropriate for communicating ideas.* There is more than one way to present information. You should calculate responses to different approaches or styles of speaking when you are analyzing the audience and preparing the message.[49]

It seems obvious that unless you are on a deserted island, you the speaker have a great need for audience analysis and rhetorical sensitivity. Remember

[47]Hart, Carlson, and Eadie, "Attitudes Toward Communication," p. 21.

[48]Dudley D. Cahn and Gary M. Shulman, "An Exploratory Study of the Relationship Between Rhetorical Sensitivity, Leadership Effectiveness and Rank in Military Organization," *Michigan Speech Association Journal*, 15 (1980), 1–11.

[49]These five characteristics are adapted from Hart and Burks, "Rhetorical Sensitivity and Social Interaction," pp. 79–91.

"WHAT SAY YOU GENTLEMEN, IF I OFFERED YOU THESE HILLBERRY THEATRE TICKETS AT HALF PRICE?"

FIGURE 5–7

Cliff Wirth, cartoonist, *The Detroit News*

also that some audiences are less rhetorically sensitive than others toward speakers.

SUMMING UP

Collective behavior includes such group varieties as *mobs, audiences,* and the *small group.* In the Brown taxonomy *crowds* becomes the generic term for collectivities. Mobs are described as *active* and audiences as *passive.* Mobs are subdivided into four categories: expressive, acquisitive, escape (including panics), and aggressive (including lynchings, riots, and terrorizations). Audiences are divided into casual and intentional (including recreational and information-seeking). In this chapter small groups are considered to be on the passive side of the Brown taxonomy.

In an audience the "group mind" is nowhere near as evident, the regressive acts are less gross, and there is typically far less emotionality and irrationality. The more formal audiences such as classes of students, church and temple groups, and lecture audiences, which are intentionally and purposefully organized, represent a collectivity with more ascertainable dynamics. Three reasonably predictable patterns of interaction are *polarization, interstimulation,* and *feedback response.*

H. L. Hollingworth suggests five basic kinds of audiences: (1) pedestrian, (2) discussion-passive, (3) selected, (4) concerted, and (5) organized. In this view a persuader has five fundamental tasks (attention, interest, impression, conviction, and direction), all of which are necessary for the nonpolarized *pedestrian* audience. Only the last (direction) is necessary for the highly polarized organized audience.

Audience configuration considerations include ritual, physical setting, arrangement, and seating.

Despite confounding variables some generalizations about receiver characteristics are possible: (1) general tendency (some people are more persuasible), (2) intelligence (no clear evidence), (3) self-esteem (people with low self-esteem are more susceptible to persuasion), (4) authoritarianism (not easily persuaded except by bigger authoritarians), (5) age (no clear evidence), (6) gender (reflects the status of women).

When a crowd reaches the focus and organization of a psychological mob, Le Bon suggests that there is a psychological law of mental unity or "collective mind" which makes a mob think and behave quite differently from their individual selves. The major mechanisms appear to be anonymity, contagion, and suggestibility. Mobs supply a stimulation and facilitation of individual desires, a kind of heightened response from the sight or sound of others making similar movements.

Audience descriptive measures include: the specific situation, audience-message relationships, group memberships, role, occupation, special interests, education, age, and gender.

Rhetorical sensitivity involves effectively matching the message we are sending to the requirements of the receivers and the situation and context. Rhetorically sensitive (RS) people judge encounters carefully; they distinguish between "content" and "relational" communication; and they know when to "speak up" or "shut up." Insensitive types have been described as "noble selves" (NS) or "rhetorical reflectors" (RR). Noble selves see any variation from their personal norms as a "sin"; rhetorical reflectors reflect each situation in which they find themselves. Rhetorically sensitive people seek to moderate such extremes and have the following characteristics: (1) accept role-taking as normal, (2) adjust their verbal behavior, (3) patiently adapt their strategies, (4) match information to the audience, (5) discern an appropriate rhetorical form and style.

STUDY PROJECTS AND TASKS

1. Observe audiences, live or through the media, until you find two clear-cut examples of (1) a mob and (2) an audience. Describe each in a page or less.

2. Prepare a two-minute speech designed to counterpersuade a hypothetical audience of twenty-five persons. Assume these people are (1) in a suggestible, active mood (for example, they are confronted with a fire, flood, or other threatening situation that does not really warrant panic), or (2) in a suggestible, aggressive state (for example, they are an angry group whose intended actions are clearly overreactions and not in anyone's best interest). Assuming that the speaker will receive some heckling might make this project more realistic.

3. Keeping in mind what we know about persuasibility, create a hypothetical character or audience that would be almost impossible to persuade (topic of your choice, or a common one for the class). Prepare a two-to-four-minute message in which you attempt to persuade this hypothetical audience.

4. Observe an active crowd until you can detect a sense of anonymity, contagion, or suggestibility. Write a highly specific account of the sensation, when it came on, and what seemed to cause it (possible examples: a protest, revival meeting, athletic event, fight, political meeting).

    Attend the meeting of a ritualized group and write a short report of the role of ritual and audience arrangement (possible examples: a church service, award ceremony, graduation, funeral service).

5. In one page describe a hypothetical audience—including such things as group membership, role, special conditions, and situation—that would be nearly impossible to persuade on a given topic (for example, a man one year from retirement who had just won the Irish Sweepstakes might be difficult to motivate to earn a living).

6. Describe a speaker or media personality who has exhibited the traits of a noble self or a rhetorical reflector.

7. Review the discussion of rhetorical sensitivity and assess yourself on the five ideal personal characteristics and the scale in Figure 5–6. Explain.

6

Organizing the Message

General Postulates and Principles
    Learning Postulates
    Rhetorical Principles
    Methods of Organizing
Strategies of Arrangement
    Normal Thinking Order
    Communication Tasks
    The Motivated Sequence
    The Effects of Order
    Both-sides Persuasion
Summing Up
Study Projects and Tasks

"Let me tell you why you're wrong," said a leader to an already antagonistic group. Even if the leader is right, this approach is poor persuasion. Logical organization is not always the most effective organization. Suppose the leader began like this: "I think I understand our differences; I appreciate and concede many of the arguments for your position; I should like to explain why I think we have come to differing positions." Would he or she get a better hearing with this approach?

Organization alone is no guarantee of persuasive success. As we discussed earlier, the whole context plays a part. One student with terrible organization had excellent persuasive effect. He had just spent a day in jail for failure to pay a speeding ticket and explained, in a disorganized way, that in our state failure to pay puts a driver on the wanted list.

This chapter, in an other-things-being-equal sense, will explain how we can best organize, order, and arrange the parts of a persuasive message. Message impact, as we have seen, depends in part on the credibility of the source. Message impact is also related to clarity, ease of retention, and interest.

We can learn much from the theories and research on effective ordering of the message parts. Moreover, organization alone can somewhat improve neutral or low credibility, particularly when we are attempting to persuade antagonistic receivers. These organizational strategies will also be discussed in this chapter.

Most of what is said in this chapter applies also to campaign persuasion. It certainly applies to the components of a campaign: the commercials, advertisements, and speeches. More specific treatment of campaign development, organization, and assessment appears in Chapter 8.

GENERAL POSTULATES AND PRINCIPLES

Learning Postulates

We learn *serially*. People tend as a rule to learn more readily when the things to be learned are in sequence. We teach youngsters addition and subtraction before multiplication and division. Although we could start with algebra, it is more efficient to use a sequencing based upon increasing difficulty. Many history courses follow a time sequence; others are organized around a sequence based on social issues.

How the parts can best be ordered will depend on the knowledge of your receivers, the complexity of your message, and your purpose. Receivers are learning serially when they can connect each portion of a sequence to the one that comes before it. One has not really learned to drive a car until accelerating, braking, and steering are so connected that the necessity of one automatically triggers the next.

We learn by relating the known to the unknown. One tends to understand and be affected by a message primarily as one brings previous experience and knowledge to bear on it. It follows that a sender should select and arrange the message content in a manner that best fits the knowledge and experience of the receivers. The general rule might be stated thus: Go from the known to the unknown. In trying to persuade someone of the merits of a new and relatively unknown political policy, one might select a known, similar policy for illustration. Analogies, comparisons, statistics, and testimony are further applications of this rule. Unnecessary confusion causes a frustration that affects persuasion as well as understanding. For example, bird watchers, assuming that everyone knows the size of an English sparrow, a robin, and a crow, typically relate the size of all unknown birds to one of these three. This simple relating of known to unknown has made the communicating and sharing of much information far less frustrating for serious bird watchers.

We learn through reinforcement. Theorists use S to stand for stimulus, R for response, and X for reinforcement. This X may be a reward for responding in the desired way or perhaps some form of repetition. One can also reinforce negatively! Our message may show receivers how to avoid embarrassment and punishment. This strategy involves appeals to *fear*—not phobic or abnormal fear, but a more reasoned, reflective kind. We tend to seek rewards and avoid punishments. Strong appeals to fear are generally more effective when they come from a highly credible source. If the president says we're close to war, we find the statement more frightening than if John Doe says it!

It is usually advantageous to use reinforcement close to the idea (or behavior) one is selling. The teacher who feeds back criticism with a smile, a frown, or a high grade is practicing a kind of reinforcement. So is the drill sergeant who uses a really loud voice. Reinforcement, then, may consist of repetition, a loud voice, a nonverbal cue, or some other form of emphasis.

In one experiment a fifteen-minute communication was delivered to various audiences in a relatively neutral mode of emphasis. Experimental speeches on the same subject were then given to similar audiences, but various kinds of emphasis were used. Twenty-one audiences participated. The primary means of emphasis, in the order of their effectiveness as measured by message retention, were as follows:

A. Significant differences
   1. Verbal emphasis ("Now get this," and so on, preceding a remark)
   2. Three distributed repetitions
   3. Immediate repetition early in the speech
   4. Speaking slowly (half normal rate)
   5. Immediate repetitions late in the speech

      6. Pauses
      7. Gestures (hand and index finger only)
  B. Moderate differences
      8. Four distributed repetitions
      9. Two distributed repetitions
    10. Soft voice (aspirate)
  C. Negative difference
    11. Forceful voice (almost bombastic) [1]

Significant differences in effectiveness were found between the neutral speeches and the experimental speeches given with the first seven kinds of emphasis. The kinds of optimal repetition used in the experimental speeches are thought to provide listeners with increased opportunities to cognitively process the information.[2] The experimental speeches utilizing the eighth, ninth, and tenth kinds of emphasis showed moderate or insignificant differences in effectiveness, and the experimental speech delivered in a loud voice resulted in a significant negative difference—that is, it was significantly less effective than the neutral speech.

This is strong evidence of the value of emphasis, whether it is supplied verbally, vocally, nonverbally, organizationally, or by some combination of the above. However, the results also carry some serious warnings for speakers. Note that although three repetitions had significant effect, four repetitions had only moderate effect and two appeared to be insignificant. Although the results in no way suggest that three is the magic number, they do imply that too much repetition is as bad as too little. All of us have grown weary of certain television and radio commercials that continually repeat the product name. We have also learned to appreciate the announcer or teacher who repeats and reviews things often enough, making them easier to understand. Voice volume also made a difference in this experiment. Reinforcement in the form of verbal, vocal, nonverbal, and organizational emphasis can be a strong asset. Be careful to adapt the amount and kind of reinforcement to your particular purpose, subject, situation, and receiver.

Rhetorical Principles

We learn through *unity, coherence,* and *emphasis.* These three great rhetorical principles have a profound bearing on how we should organize messages.

Unity In discussing tragedy, Aristotle said that a play must be so constructed that omission of any part damages the whole. Each part of the plot

---

[1]Raymond Ehrensberger, "An Experimental Study of the Relative Effectiveness of Certain Forms of Emphasis in Public Speaking," *Speech Monographs,* 12, no. 2 (1945), 94–111.

[2]See J. T. Cacioppo and R. E. Petty, "Effects of Message Repetition and Position on Cognitive Responses, Recall, and Persuasion," *Journal of Personality and Social Psychology,* 37 (1979), 97–109.

must contribute to the inevitability of the purpose or end of the play. By analogy, he said, it must have unity in the same manner as a living organism. We still use the term *organic unity* to express this concept. With regard to a more conventional message, organic unity means that the material should be unified to the point that it can be summarized in a single statement of purpose. In some messages this statement takes the form of a resolution or proposition that is forthrightly announced. In other cases it might suit the speaker's strategy to suppress the proposition. At all times the sender must understand the purpose if the message is to have unity. This specific purpose helps him or her evaluate the materials and ideas during preparation. The arrangement of the parts of a message should be unified in a way that welds receiver, source, and purpose.

Coherence Coherence is a function of the specific sequence of the parts of the message and one of the various methods of ordering and arranging ideas and details. To *cohere* is to be connected by a common principle or relationship, and a coherent message reflects a logically consistent subordination of ideas. The actual connecting of the various parts and ideas of a message is accomplished through words or phrases. An oral sender must be especially careful of connectives, often repeating and clearly labeling them. Unlike the writer, the oral persuader cannot go back and locate a lost thread of meaning. Therefore, coherence must always involve the audience. A sender may lose receivers when going from one point to another by falsely assuming that they will see the connection.

Emphasis Emphasis involves the location, space, form, and order given to the most important ideas. Should the most important idea be put first, last, or in a climactic order? Does the amount of space given the idea affect emphasis? (Ordinarily the main point is not buried under some very subordinate point.) If a number of important ideas compete for attention, which should be given the most emphasis? These questions can be best answered in terms of your subject, your knowledge, your audience, and the occasion. Location, space, form, and order do make a difference. The function of emphasis is to use these devices in harmony with the relative importance assigned to each part or idea in your message. Much more will be said of emphasis in the section on strategies of arrangement.

Methods of Organizing

We can organize *chronologically*, arranging materials according to the order in which a number of events took place. In discussing life on earth, we would probably organize the periods chronologically:

1. Archeozoic
2. Proterozoic

3. Paleozoic
4. Mesozoic
5. Cenozoic
6. present

Most historical subjects lend themselves readily to this method; so do processes that occur in a 1–2–3 order, such as film developing. Remember, however, that these subjects may be handled in other ways. History is often more interesting and meaningful if discussed topically. Persuasive messages may also be based on a psychological chronology, as first suggested by Aristotle. More will be said of this kind of chronology in the section on arrangement strategies.

We can organize *topically,* ordering the material according to general topics or classifications of knowledge. To continue the example of history, we might concentrate on the history of religion, war, government, education, or science. Organizing by topic may or may not violate chronological sequence and is a very useful way to start breaking down very broad subjects. We can, for example, look at the subject of racial integration in several ways—educationally, socially, militarily, economically.

We can organize *spatially.* This method is particularly useful for geographical or physical-order subjects. In a message about the United Nations, we might first describe each building, then discuss the offices in each building one floor at a time. In so doing we would be organizing the subject spatially. The same subject might also be treated topically if the audience were familiar with the general political structure of the United Nations. In discussing nationalism in Africa, we might simply divide the continent from north to south and east to west. It is obvious that chronological history might also be a useful method with this subject.

We can organize *logically.* This method involves generally accepted or obvious cause-and-effect relationships, whether they refer to the fall of the Japanese empire or the building of a house or a boat. When the order is natural or inherent in the subject or when the association of ideas is generally accepted, it may be convenient to organize our speech materials accordingly.

We can organize in terms of *difficulty.* For some subjects, particularly technical ones, it may be advantageous to proceed from the easiest aspect to the more difficult or complex ones. In discussing general principles of electricity, we might arrange our subject matter as follows:

1. the flashlight
2. switches
3. dry cells
4. light bulbs in a series
5. light bulbs in parallel
6. electromagnets
7. current and electrons

We can organize in terms of *need-plan*, arranging materials according to problems (needs) and solutions (plans). Usually people go along with the status quo unless a need for change has been demonstrated. An affirmative debate team concerned with a resolution on government health programs will typically divide its material into these two general categories. The first speaker will concentrate on the various needs in our present situation or in our present programs. The needs can be subdivided into such useful types as economic needs, health needs, and social needs. The second speaker will attempt to fit a solution (plan) to the specific needs. In analyzing various plans, the debater will discuss comparative advantages or show that the proposed plan offers the most advantages with the fewest disadvantages.

Having considered various ways of ordering the content of a message, we turn now to strategies for arranging the *parts* of persuasive messages.

STRATEGIES OF ARRANGEMENT

Normal Thinking Order

Aristotle used the Greek word *taxis* to denote division in his explanation of the most logical arrangement of the parts of a persuasive message. He felt that the following elements were most closely related to normal thinking habits: proem (introduction), statement, argument, and epilogue (conclusion).

Probably the most famous pragmatic thought sequence is the *reflective-thinking* pattern of John Dewey:

> (1) suggestions, in which the mind leaps forward to a possible solution; (2) an intellectualization of the difficulty or perplexity that has been felt into a problem to be solved, or question for which the answer must be sought; (3) the use of one suggestion after another as a leading idea, or hypothesis, to initiate and guide observation and other operations in collection of factual material; (4) the mental elaboration of the idea . . . ; and (5) testing of the hypothesis by overt or imaginative action.[3]

In applying this normal sequence notion to the organization of your persuasive message you should arrange your speech materials so that your audience will receive and decode them in the following typical thinking order:

1. attention and awareness of felt difficulty
2. a recognition of a problem or need
3. the sorting of objections and counterplans in search of the best solution
4. an elaboration and visualization of the proposed solution
5. an evaluation of the plan leading to acceptance or rejection of the solution

[3]John Dewey, *How We Think* (Boston: Heath, 1933), p. 107.

The *introduction* to every message is very important. It almost always involves the concept of attention. The following applications of normal thinking order are all designed to attract attention. The famous psychologist William James said, "What holds attention determines action. . . . The impelling idea is simply the one which possesses the attention. . . . What checks our impulses is the mere thinking of reasons to the contrary. . . ."[4]

Attention may be thought of as a readiness to respond. To think of attention alone as being capable of controlling behavior is a little frightening. This, of course, goes beyond James's meaning, but it does point out the importance of attention in persuasion. If one thinks of hypnosis as a state involving complete, undivided attention,[5] it does appear that "what holds attention determines action."

As we have seen, various forms of emphasis are useful. Recall that the audience in the Ehrensberger study was better able to recall and remember things that had been emphasized in certain ways. Emphasis can also be used to gain attention in the introduction of a message. If attention and interest help determine action and a readiness to respond, then they affect persuasion.

An audience's attention is selective, and other factors are constantly vying for it—sounds, sights, people, and conflicting ideas, to mention a few. Because of this, the persuader must concentrate on keeping the audience involved in the subject.

Arousing attention is only one requirement of an introduction. The beginning of your message should also strive to establish or reaffirm good will among you, the group you represent, and the receivers. If good will is hard to come by (when you are speaking before a hostile audience, for example), your introduction should establish a climate for a fair hearing.

In some situations a function of the message introduction is *orientation.* The communicator must sometimes supply background or definitions that will enable the audience to understand the message. A brief historical sketch often helps receivers gain perspective and orientation. Certain terms or language may be either vague or unknown; failure to define them may cause confusion.

Unless your persuasive strategy dictates otherwise, an introduction seeks to make your purpose clear. It is often a preview of what is to follow. This necessitates a certain amount of repetition, but remember that when the persuasion is oral, listeners, unlike readers, cannot go back to a previous page. Therefore, more repetition may be required.

In sum, the general functions of a message introduction are: (1) to secure attention, (2) to establish good will, or at least (3) to assure a fair hearing, (4) to orient the receiver, and (5) to make your purpose clear (unless your persuasive strategy involves withholding it).

---

[4]William James, *Psychology: Briefer Course* (New York: Henry Holt and Company, 1892), p. 448.

[5]Hypnosis is probably more similar to normal sleep.

The message *body* includes the bulk of your arguments, information, and evidence. However, persuasion starts even before the first word is spoken, as we learned in our discussion of source credibility. More will be said shortly about the psychological effects of the way a message is ordered.

Aristotle suggested that the major purpose of a message *conclusion* or epilogue was to help the memory. We should add that it helps rekindle attention. The conclusion is generally shorter than either the introduction or the body. It may and generally should include a short summary for clarity and reinforcement. If the sender's purpose is to elicit certain actions, the conclusion may include explicit directions.

In formal oral persuasion make it evident when you are finished; carefully consider your exit lines. Not knowing when a speaker is finished is frustrating to an audience and awkward for the speaker. This is the dangling or never-ending message caused by our own frustrations, improper preparation, or the ham actor in all of us. Much otherwise good persuasion is lost because we don't know when to stop. We won't or can't finish. Prepare your conclusion as carefully as the rest of your message. The ending serves as a good check on organic unity. And quit while you are ahead.

Communication Tasks

As we saw in the previous chapter, according to Harry Hollingworth's popular view of persuasion a communicator has five fundamental tasks to accomplish in winning an audience: maintaining attention, holding interest, creating an impression, instilling conviction, and providing direction.[6] These tasks should be specifically related to the disposition and makeup of the audience. In other words, situations differ and the persuader must determine the point at which he or she should begin the sequence.

Attention is maintained through all of the devices discussed under the previous heading. *Interest* must be held long enough to *impress* the details on a person's memory. These details must in turn carry enough persuasion to lead to *conviction*. The conviction then *directs* a person to take some specific action.

Hollingworth offers some practical rules for accomplishing these tasks. Do not attempt to gain attention through identical competition. For example, instead of using a louder sound in a noisy oral situation, try a sound that has a different quality or a striking rhythm. Even better, appeal to a completely different quality than the one operating: try a visual approach, perhaps simply raising your hand or displaying a visual aid. Since an unoccupied sensory channel is most receptive to attention devices, shift from one sensory field to another.

Maintaining *interest* is really a matter of keeping attention. The key to this task is *rapport*, a word that Hollingworth uses to include everything from an

---

[6]Harry L. Hollingworth, *The Psychology of the Audience* (New York: American Book, 1935), p. 12.

amusing story to language use and delivery. He counsels against using sentences longer than twenty-five words if the delivery is oral.

Hollingworth defines the *impression* task succinctly: "The audience appears to be more moved by what it hears, but more permanently impressed by what it sees."[7] He makes a strong case for visual aids, particularly for immature or inexperienced receivers. He suggests that visual aids are more effective when they precede rather than follow messages. He believes the most impressive point in a discourse is the opening statement.

Conviction is the heart of the process of persuasion. Acknowledging that audiences usually resent purely emotional appeals, Hollingworth argues that people are more alike emotionally and that emotional appeals are generally more effective than logical ones. However, emotional appeals should give the appearance of logical persuasion.

Direction means indicating the precise nature, place, time, and method of the proposed act. Hollingworth argues that the strength of direction varies directly with its spontaneity, vividness, positive form, prestige, and frequency. He recommends using a slogan or catchword to crystallize a whole program of persuasion.

These five—attention, interest, impression, conviction, direction—are thus the fundamental tasks of persuasion.

Hollingworth suggests that after a person commits an act or makes a choice, he or she then justifies it with intellectual or logical reasons. When social pressure or group sanctions influence the person's act or choice, there is a special effectiveness in the rationalization appeal in which an attitude or conclusion, first aroused emotionally, is given subsequent logical support by the speaker. Hollingworth makes a telling comment about gullibility: "Prevalent forms of specious argument to which the gullible easily yield are (a) confusing anecdote with proof; (b) mistaking analogy for evidence; (c) mistaking correlation with causal relation; (d) the argumentum ad hominem; (e) affirming the consequent; and (f) confusing obscurity for profundity."[8]

The Motivated Sequence

Alan Monroe, like Hollingworth and others, advocates a message-arrangement system—he calls it the motivated sequence—that he argues is based on a natural, normal thinking process. He reasons that

> the mental process of the listener as applied to the various general ends of speech is not different, but cumulative, [and] this normal process of human thinking is sufficiently uniform that . . . we can outline a form of speech structure that will conform to it rather closely on nearly all occasions. This form of speech structure we shall call *the motivated sequence: the sequence of ideas which, by following the normal process of thinking, motivates the audience to respond to the speaker's purpose.*[9]

[7]Ibid., p. 107.
[8]Ibid., p. 138.
[9]Alan H. Monroe, *Principles and Types of Speech* (Glenview, Ill.: Scott, Foresman, 1949), pp.

As we saw in the last chapter, the steps in this sequence are (1) attention, (2) need, (3) satisfaction, (4) visualization, and (5) action. First, one's attention must be caught. Second, one must be made to feel a definite need. Third, one must be shown how to satisfy this need. Fourth, one must be made to visualize the personal application of the proposal. And finally, there must be a definite suggestion as to how one should act. This sequence really embodies what is variously called a need-plan, problem-solution, or need-satisfaction emphasis.

Monroe suggests that in its full form a need step involves a fourfold development: (1) a *statement* of the specific problem; (2) an *illustration* of the need; (3) the *ramification* or reinforcement of the need through the enumeration of additional examples and evidence; and (4) a *pointing out* of the direct relationship of the need to the receivers.

The satisfaction step, when fully developed, consists of a fivefold procedure: (1) a clear *statement* of the belief or action you wish the receivers to adopt; (2) an *explanation* for further clarity; (3) a *theoretical demonstration* of how the solution specifically meets the need step; (4) the use of *practical experience*— that is, examples and evidence that prove the efficacy of your solution—and (5) the *meeting of objections*—that is, the forestalling of opposition to probable counterarguments.

Monroe divided persuasive speeches into three types, based on their general end—stimulating, convincing, and actuating (getting people to take action).

The argument for a general message-arrangement system based on some sort of normal thinking is a strong one. Several proposed systems are compared in Table 6–1. The following concepts are involved in all of them:

1. creation of attention and interest
2. arousal of a sense of deficiency, dissonance, need, and problem awareness
3. explanation of a solution or plan that satisfies the deficiencies
4. comparison of the advantages of one plan or solution over those of others
5. advisement regarding what action, belief, or direction the receivers should take

Remember that any message-arrangement system is a simplification of very complex communication problems. Nevertheless, the systems charted in Table 6–1 are very useful in showing the relationship of message, receiver, sender, and how one organizes the parts of the message. The complex question of ordering the arguments or issues of a message is the meat of the next section. But first let's look at a speech illustrating the use of one message-arrangement system.

308–9. See also Douglas Ehninger, Alan H. Monroe, and Bruce E. Gronbeck, *Principles and Types of Speech Communication* (Glenview, Ill.: Scott, Foresman, 1978), p. 142; and John A. McGee, *Persuasive Speaking* (New York: Scribner's, 1929), pp. 268–69.

TABLE 6-1 A Comparison of Some Message-Arrangement Systems

	CLASSICAL	ARISTOTLE	HOLLINGWORTH	McGEE	MONROE	ROSS
Introduction	Exordium	Proem	Attention	Attention	Attention	Attention
	Narration	Statement	Interest	Problem	Need	Need
Body	Confirmation	Argument	Impression	Solution	Satisfaction	Plan
	Refutation		Conviction	Visualization	Visualization	Reinforcement
Conclusion	Peroration	Epilogue	Direction	Action	Action	Direction

EASY ON THE BIG MAC

General End:	To persuade.
Specific Purpose:	To persuade the audience to make dietary changes to protect themselves against heart disease and stroke.

Introduction

Attention

I. Heart Attack... Stroke!
   A. That pain in my chest ... am I having a heart attack?
   B. Will I be paralyzed by a stroke?

II. Each year heart disease and stroke kill more people than any other disease.
   A. In the United States, more people die of these two diseases than the next seven diseases combined.
   B. They kill more people than cancer.

Body

I. There is a relationship between heart disease and the amount of cholesterol and saturated fats in one's diet.
   A. Countries with high-fat diets have high rates of heart disease.
   B. High rates of heart disease mean there is a high rate of arteriosclerosis.

II. Arteriosclerosis: what is it?
   A. This condition is a build-up of fatty deposits on the inner walls of the arteries and veins.
   B. The deposits narrow down the tubes through which the blood flows.

Need

      1. The blood flow is slowly squeezed off.

      2. This causes blood pressure to go up.

      3. Blood cells get trapped in pockets in the arteries and veins and stick together and form clots.

  C. This fatty deposit is made of saturated fats and cholesterol.

      1. Saturated fats are found in meat, particularly beef and pork.

      2. Cholesterol is a fatty substance that exists in all animal tissue.

  D. High blood levels of saturated fats make the red blood cells "sticky" and cause them to clump together and form clots.

III. Arteriosclerosis can cause the following diseases:

  A. High blood pressure: occurs when the arteries and veins are too narrow for the amount of blood that travels through.

      1. This can cause kidney failure and stroke.

      2. It can severely weaken the heart.

  B. Heart attack: occurs when clots block the arteries of the heart.

      1. The heart does not get enough oxygen and literally starves.

      2. This can lead to a severely deformed heart or death.

  C. Stroke: happens when the brain does not get enough oxygen.

      1. This lack of oxygen is caused by a clot blockage or hemorrhage.

      2. The effects of stroke range from death through a major paralysis to a minor paralysis of part of the body.

  D. Strain: the heart will have to work harder, so that it will have no reserve.

IV. Where does this fatty material come from?

  A. It comes from the food we eat (show Big Mac).

      1. Studies show a high correlation between the amount of fats eaten and heart disease.

      2. During WW II, Finland, Norway, and Sweden had a shortage of food rich in animal fats.

      3. They still had a plentiful diet, but their diet consisted of grains, potatoes, and fresh vegetables.

      4. The U.S. and Denmark, on the other hand, maintained their high-fat diets.

      5. A comparison of the two types of diets showed a strong relationship between arteriosclerosis and high fat intake.

V. Other studies have shown that angina attacks occur three to five hours after an intake of saturated fats.

Plan

VI. A change in diet can reduce the amount of cholesterol and saturated fats.
   A. A Big Mac has about one ounce of saturated fat in it.
   B. To eat the same amount of saturated fat, you could eat all of the food in this submarine sandwich (chart).
   C. Two pats of butter have more saturated fat than a whole cup of spaghetti, meatballs, sauce and cheese.

VII. There are two major changes to consider in your diet.
   A. Reduce the amount of saturated fats.
      1. Eat less beef, and more chicken, turkey, and fish.
      2. Eat fresh fruit and vegetables.
   B. Substitute polyunsaturated oils for saturated oils.
      1. They do not add fatty build-up to your arteries.
      2. They reduce the tendency of the blood cells to stick together and form clots.

Conclusion

Reinforcement

I. A change in your diet can keep arteries and veins open.
II. More blood and oxygen throughout your body will keep you feeling fit longer.
III. Why suffer from diseases that can be prevented?

Direction

IV. Reduce your saturated fats.
V. Use polyunsaturated oils.
VI. In other words, "Go easy on the Big Mac."

From a speech by Barbara-Ann Linthorst-Homan, a student at Wayne State University.

The Effects of Order

One usually effective order is the need-plan order shown in the speech outline above. Arouse the receiver's need first, then supply the information that satisfies that need. When the need is presented first, the receiver can quickly see how the solution is relevant to it.[10] Attention is also easier to maintain when the need is presented first.

This is a good example of what is meant by the effects of order. Some studies of order are concerned primarily with determining the arrangement of major arguments within a one-sided message. In the *climax order* the major arguments are presented last; in the *anticlimax order* they come first. Other studies are concerned with messages that are two-sided and in which it makes a difference which side is presented first. The assumption is that the issue presented first (the position of *primacy*) has the advantage and that the issue presented last (the position of *recency*) is at a disadvantage. Primacy-recency research has also investigated the effects of public commitment, contradictions and forewarning in the message, and the pro-con or con-pro order for neutral or favorably disposed receivers. In this section we will attempt to unravel some of the research on the climax-anticlimax and primacy-recency questions. We will discuss one-sided versus two-sided orders for unfavorably disposed receivers in the following section.

Climax-anticlimax   The question of where to put the best or strongest arguments is an old one. Answers from research are confusing and require interpretation if they are to make much sense.

On the question of where to put information in order to achieve the best retention and recall, the evidence is only slightly better. If one divides a message into a beginning, middle, and end, then we may remember better in that serial order, other things being equal. However, early learning studies by Arthur Jershild[11] and Carl Hovland[12] indicate that items placed in the middle of a presentation are by far the most difficult to recall and that items mentioned at the beginning are better remembered than those placed at the end. However, compared with the difficulty of remembering material in the middle, the differences in recall between material at the beginning and material at the end are not very meaningful.

On the other hand, a study in which the material was placed in an anticlimax (beginning) order, a pyramidal (middle) order, and a climax (end) order showed that the middle-position details were best remembered (although attitudes were not necessarily better affected).[13] Study of retention of items

---

[10]See Arthur R. Cohen, "Need for Cognition and Order of Communication as Determinants of Opinion Change," in *The Order of Presentation in Persuasion,* ed. Carl I. Hovland (New Haven: Yale University Press, 1957), pp. 79–97.

[11]Arthur T. Jersild, "Primacy, Recency, Frequency and Vividness," *Journal of Experimental Psychology,* 12 (1929), 58–70.

[12]Carl I. Hovland, "Experimental Studies in Role-learning Theory: II. Reminiscence With Varying Speeds of Syllable Presentation," *Journal of Experimental Psychology,* 22 (1938), 338–53.

[13]Halbert Gulley and David K. Berlo, "Effects of Intercellular and Intracellular Speech Structure on Attitude Change and Learning," *Speech Monographs,* 23 (1956), 288–97. See also Donald Thistlewaite, Joseph Kamenetzky, and Hans Schmidt, "Factors Influencing Attitude Change Through Refutative Communication," *Speech Monographs,* 23 (1956), 14–25.

presented in a radio newscast found greater recall of those items at the end of the newscast and poorest recall for those in the middle.[14]

To further complicate the picture on retention, an early study on modes of emphasis in public speaking yielded better remembering of items at the beginning of the message than items at the end.[15] However, a replication of this study yielded the opposite results.[16]

L. W. Doob found that when the message is written rather than oral, those passages (or controversial issues) presented first received higher retention.[17] Although spatial and size relationships may constitute a slightly different variable in written messages than they do in oral ones, the ordering principles are probably the same. A study by Adams is a case in point.[18] Adams constructed a large-sized and a small-sized magazine advertisement and then presented them in opposite orders. He found that readers presented with the advertisements in the large-small order recalled more than those given the small-large order.

It appears that some very strong variables are not being considered or controlled in these studies. The most critical and often the most subtle one is *initial attitude.* Attitude affects all communication reception, regardless of intent.

Those studies of climax-anticlimax order where the initial-attitude variable is not controlled or accounted for are vulnerable to the same problems as the retention studies. The literature is full of just such confounding results. Two classic studies in speech communication were conducted by Harold Sponberg[19] and Harvey Cromwell.[20] Sponberg's results indicate support for the anticlimax order and Cromwell's, support for climax order.

If we can assume that an audience has a neutral position (that initially it does not have a highly structured attitude toward the message), then related research yields meaningful results for such audiences. This is probably also true—at least where both-sides' (or affirmative-negative) dimensions are considered—when the audience is polarized either for or against a position. The results of research on highly polarized attitude groups are, in fact, very

[14]Percy H. Tannenbaum, "Effect of Serial Position on Recall of Radio News Stories," *Journalism Quarterly,* 31 (1954), 319–23.

[15]Arthur T. Jersild, "Modes of Emphasis in Public Speaking," *Journal of Applied Psychology,* 12 (1928), 611–20.

[16]Ehrensberger, "Emphasis in Public Speaking."

[17]L. W. Doob, "Effects of Initial Serial Position and Attitude Upon Recall Under Conditions of Low Motivation," *Journal of Abnormal and Social Psychology,* 48 (1953), 199–205.

[18]H. F. Adams, "Effect of Climax and Anti-climax Order of Presentation on Memory," *Journal of Applied Psychology,* 4 (1920), 330–38.

[19]Harold Sponberg, "A Study of the Relative Effectiveness of Climax and Anti-climax Order in an Argumentative Speech," *Speech Monographs,* 13 (1946), 33–44.

[20]Harvey Cromwell, "The Relative Effect on Audience Attitude of the First Versus the Second Argumentative Speech of a Series," *Speech Monographs,* 17 (1950), 105–22. See also Howard Gilkinson, Stanley F. Paulson, and Donald E. Sikkink, "Effects of Order and Authority in an Argumentative Speech," *Quarterly Journal of Speech,* 40 (1954), 183–92.

meaningful and will be discussed in the section on antagonistic receivers. The results of studies by Frederick Lund[21] and one by Franklin Knower[22] that appear to meet the initial-attitude condition (no highly structured attitudes), are probably valid, but only for that attitude condition. In this research half of the groups being studied read messages that presented a pro argument first and a con argument second. The other half read arguments presented in the reverse order. The argument presented first, whether pro or con, was found to be more persuasive in determining the group's attitude toward the proposition contained in the messages.

Gulley and Berlo made the assumption that there were no highly structured attitudes among their subjects. They commented perceptively on what probably happens psychologically when a subject is confronted with two arguments in succession.

> After reading the first argument a subject would be expected to form a definite attitude, probably in the direction advocated by the argument. When perceiving the second argument, the subject no longer has an unstructured attitude toward the proposition. For this reason, the demands made on the second message would be greater than on the first. While the initial stimulus needed only to persuade a subject to *form* an attitude, the second was required to *change* an existing one. The second task is much more difficult than the first; hence the greater effect of the first.[23]

It is difficult to counsel an anticlimax or climax order, even if all other things are equal. "Other things" in this context are seldom equal, foremost among them the elusive variable of initial attitude. When initial attitude is unstructured, subsequent attitude may be more affected by first-position arguments.[24] Perhaps this is also true of retention, but until we do more research in which the initial-attitude variable is better accounted for, the relationship between retention and anticlimax or climax order is still one of conjecture.

Primacy-recency   Unlike the question of climax or anticlimax order, which is concerned with where to put your best arguments, the primacy-recency question is concerned with the first (prime) position or last (most recent) position in a message, apart from the worth of the argument. Primacy-recency is usually concerned with opposing communications presented in alternate sequence. It can and should be considered in one-sided messages as well. As with climax and anticlimax orders, no general law of primacy has

[21]Frederick H. Lund, "The Psychology of Belief: IV. The Law of Primacy in Persuasion," *Journal of Abnormal and Social Psychology*, 20 (1925), 181–91.

[22]Franklin H. Knower, "Experimental Studies of Changes in Attitude: II. A Study of the Effect of Printed Argument on Changes in Attitude," *Journal of Abnormal and Social Psychology*, 30 (1936), 522–32.

[23]Gulley and Berlo, "Intercellular and Intracellular Speech Structure," p. 289.

[24]Arthur R. Cohen, *Attitude Change and Social Influence* (New York: Basic Books, 1964), p. 15.

emerged, but we have learned about some sets of conditions that affect primacy.[25] These are useful to keep in mind during message preparation.

Earlier we pointed out that information will be accepted more readily if need arousal is given first position. We seem to have a rule of primacy under this set of conditions. We also showed that when an audience initially has an unstructured attitude, first-position arguments are more persuasive.

If after hearing only one side (the primary side, because it's first) of a controversial issue a receiver publicly indicates his or her position, he or she is less persuaded by subsequent (recent) persuasion. Carl Hovland, Enid Campbell, and Timothy Brock[26] presented one side of a controversial issue (voting age) to a group of students without telling them that they would hear the other side later. They then asked half of the students to write their opinions for publication in a school pamphlet. The other half were asked to write their opinions anonymously. The other side of the argument was then presented to both groups, and the attitudes were measured again. A primacy effect was found. That is, public commitment hardened attitudes and made the committed students more resistant to the second side. If there is no *real* public commitment, the rule apparently does not hold. In a study by Hovland and Wallace Mandell, an anonymously written statement of opinion did not reduce the effectiveness of the second side.[27]

When inconsistency or contradiction appears within a communication, the part of the communication that is ordered first has more effect. This statement is based primarily on the research of Abraham Luchins,[28] who did a series of studies on first impressions. He found that material presented first was more influential in determining what the subjects felt were the main characteristics of the person being described in the communication.

In related experiments Luchins found that when the subjects were cued or *forewarned* about the dangers of first impressions without information, *recency* was more effective.[29] In a sense this reflects the verbal-cuing effect discussed previously in the modes-of-emphasis studies.

[25]C. W. Mayo and Walter H. Crockett, "Cognitive Complexity and Primacy-Recency Effects in Impression Formation," *Journal of Abnormal and Social Psychology*, 68 (1964), 335–38. See also W. Wilson and Chester Insko, "Recency Effects in Face-to-Face Interaction," *Journal of Personality and Social Psychology*, 9 (1968), 21–23.

[26]Carl I. Hovland, Enid H. Campbell, and Timothy Brock, "The Effects of 'Commitment' on Opinion Change Following Communication," in *The Order of Presentation in Persuasion*, ed. Hovland, pp. 23–32. See also Erwin P. Bettinghaus and John R. Basehart, "Specific Factors Affecting Attitude Change," *Journal of Communication*, 19, no. 3 (1969), 227–38.

[27]Carl Hovland and Wallace Mandell, "An Experimental Comparison of Conclusion Drawing by the Communicator and by the Audience," *Journal of Abnormal Social Psychology*, 47 (1952), 581–88.

[28]Abraham S. Luchins, "Primacy-Recency in Impression Formation," in *The Order of Presentation in Persuasion*, ed. Hovland, pp. 33–61.

[29]Abraham S. Luchins, "Experimental Attempts to Minimize the Impact of First Impressions," in *The Order of Presentation In Persuasion*, ed. Hovland, pp. 62–75. See also Charles A. Kiesler and Sara B. Kiesler, "Role of Forewarning in Persuasive Communications," *Journal of Abnormal and Social Psychology*, 68, no. 5 (1964), 547–49.

Previous persuasion (an order variable) has obviously considerable influence on the persuasiveness of later messages. However, there is good behavioral evidence that attitudes change more when highly desirable communications are presented to the receiver first and less desirable ones second. "The communicator who first presents undesirable content to the recipient excites responses leading to nonacceptance (withdrawing attention) because agreeing with these undesirable issues is unpleasant; by the time he gets to the rewarding part of his message he has lost the subject's attention."[30]

William McGuire demonstrated that the persuasiveness of a communication depends on its capacity "for evoking those other responses which must mediate between the presentation of the communication and the ultimate response of agreeing with its content."[31] He was among the first to suggest the problem of receivers rehearsing their arguments against the proposition along with the more standard problems of attention, comprehension, and acceptance. Surely the effect of earlier communications on later ones will be influenced by motivational states other than those studied here. Among such states McGuire suggests tolerance for ambiguity, the need for cognition, perceptual defense, the need to identify with a high-prestige source, and the need to conform to the norms of one's reference groups.

When an audience initially agrees with the position taken by a credible source (that is, when opposing arguments have a low probability of being spontaneously salient), then the pro-con order is superior to the con-pro order. This finding also supports the importance of primacy. It was confirmed in a study by Irving Janis and Rosalind Feierabend, among others.[32] In this study of persuasion promoting volunteering, one group received a pamphlet presenting arguments for civil defense first and arguments against civil defense second. Another group received a similar pamphlet that reversed the order. When questioned on their willingness to volunteer for civil defense, the group that received the pamphlet with the pro-con order was better persuaded. We should remember that this primacy rule is thought to hold only when some general agreement in attitude exists to begin with—that is, when the sender is not immediately confronted with antagonistic or hostile attitudes and when he or she has credibility.

---

[30]Cohen, *Attitude Change and Social Influence,* p. 12. See also William J. McGuire, "Order of Presentation in 'Conditioning' Persuasiveness," in *The Order of Presentation in Persuasion,* ed. Hovland, pp. 98–114.

[31]McGuire, "Order of Presentation," p. 112.

[32]Irving L. Janis and Rosalind L. Feierabend, "Effects of Alternative Ways of Ordering Pro and Con Arguments in Persuasive Communications," in *The Order of Presentation in Persuasion,* ed. Hovland, pp. 115–28. See also Norman Miller and Donald T. Campbell, "Recency and Primacy in Persuasion as a Function of the Timing of Speeches and Measurements," *Journal of Abnormal and Social Psychology,* 59 (1959), 1–9; and Norman H. Anderson and Alfred A. Barrios, "Primacy Effects in Personality Impression Formation," *Journal of Abnormal and Social Psychology,* 63 (1963), 346–50.

Both-Sides Persuasion

Effects on antagonistic receivers   The effects of both-sides persuasion versus one-sided persuasion are more easily generalized than the effects of order discussed so far. A classic study done for the War Department contains many insights into the psychology of persuasion, particularly when antagonistic receivers are involved.[33] The experiment involved the issue of a long war (World War II) and overoptimism. The subjects were 625 army personnel. The War Department felt that the weight of evidence indicated at least two more years of war in the Pacific. The specific question the experimenter wished to answer was this: When the weight of evidence supports the main thesis being presented, is it more effective to present only the arguments supporting the point being made or to introduce also the arguments opposed to the point being made?

The persuasion was transmitted by means of two prerecorded radio broadcasts. Both speeches were in the form of a commentator's analysis of the Pacific war. The commentator's conclusion was that the job of finishing the war would be tough and that it would take at least two years after V–E (Victory in Europe) Day. The first program (one side) presented only those arguments indicating the war would be a long one, arguments relating mainly to problems of distance and logistics. The second program (both sides) presented all the same arguments, but it also briefly considered arguments for a short war. Two of these arguments were our naval victories and superiority and our previous progress despite a two-front war.

A preliminary survey of estimates of the length of the war was used to determine initial opinions. To register a change in attitude, a man had to revise by at least six months or more his estimate of how long the war would continue. In addition, the scores of high-school graduates were compared with the scores of men who did not graduate from high school. Here are the researchers' conclusions.

1.   In the case of individuals who were initially opposed to the point of view being presented, presenting the arguments on both sides of the issue was

[33]Information and Education Division, U.S. War Department, "The Effects of Presenting 'One Side' Versus 'Both Sides' in Changing Opinions on a Controversial Subject," in *Readings in Social Psychology*, eds. Eleanor E. Maccoby, Theodore M. Newcomb, and Eugene L. Hartley (New York: Holt, Rinehart & Winston, 1947), pp. 566–77. See also Carl I. Hovland, Arthur A. Lumsdaine, and Fred D. Sheffield, *Experiments on Mass Communication* (Princeton, N.J.: Princeton University Press, 1949), pp. 201–27; Ralph L. Rosnow, "One-Sided Versus Two-Sided Communication Under Indirect Awareness of Persuasive Intent," *Public Opinion Quarterly,* 32 (Spring 1968), 95–101; Glen Hass and Darwyn Linder, "Counterargument Availability and the Effects of Message Structure on Persuasion," *Journal of Personality and Social Psychology,* 23 (August 1972), 219–33; and J. W. Kohler, "Effects on Audience Opinion of One-sided and Two-sided Speeches Supporting and Opposing a Proposition," in *The Process of Social Influence,* eds. Thomas Beisecker and Donn Parson (Englewood Cliffs, N.J.: Prentice-Hall, 1972), pp. 351–69.

more effective than giving only the arguments supporting the point being made.

2. For men who were already convinced of the point of view being presented, however, including arguments on both sides was less effective for the group as a whole than presenting only the arguments favoring the general position being advocated.

3. Better-educated men were affected more favorably by the presentation of both sides; poorly educated men were affected more by the communication that used only supporting arguments.

4. The presentation of both sides was least effective for the group of poorly educated men who were already convinced of the point of view being advocated.

5. An important incidental finding was that the omission of a relevant argument was more noticeable and detracted more from effectiveness in the both-sides presentation than in the one-side presentation.[34]

The most important of these findings for our purposes is the first one. Although the second finding is less important since it does not involve antagonistic receivers, it is interesting to note.

When the same both-sides strategy was tried in a mass-communication advertising study, essentially the same results were found. Edmond Faison exposed people to three one-minute commercials about an automobile, a gas range, and a floor wax. Half were exposed to one-sided commercials presenting only the positive features of the product (conventional commercials). The other half were exposed to a comparable two-sided commercial that presented both positive and negative features of the product in relation to their competitors. Here are the general conclusions:

1. Two-sides advertising communication seems to be an effective means of influencing economic attitudes. Two-sided arguments for all three products were more effective in influencing attitudes than comparable one-sided mass communications messages.

2. Effectiveness of two-sided advertising was related to intelligence. Upper-level subjects were more influenced by two-sided arguments, lower-level subjects by the one-sided presentations.

3. For audience members who were initially opposed to the point of view presented in the commercials (those who used competitive products), the two-sided arguments were superior. For those with a prior positive attitude (those who used the recommended), the one-sided commercial tended to be superior.

4. The relative amount of influence of both types of media advertising seems to be related to the product. The commercials concerning the least expensive product (floor wax) produced a much greater change in attitude than did those for the most expensive product (automobile).

5. Four to six weeks after the commercials were presented, neither the one-sided nor the two-sided arguments had shown diminishing attitude effects. For those exposed to the two-sided commercials there was a continuing increase in the favorableness of attitude toward the products. Thus, the two-

[34]Maccoby, Newcomb, Hartley, eds. *Readings in Social Psychology,* p. 577.

sided commercials were significantly more effective than the one-sided commercials in influencing attitudes over time.

6. The more knowledge a person has about a given subject the less influential the commercial, whether one-sided or two-sided.[35]

Both-sides persuasion works best when initial attitudes are hostile. It may help maintain positive attitudes by supplying an inoculation effect against counterpersuasion. In some experiments where the initial-attitude variable was not carefully controlled, results were not as dramatic as in the studies cited above.[36]

Both-sides persuasion almost always involves some kind of concession. The advertisements in Figures 6–1 and 6–2 are good examples: Seagram concedes the disrupting effects of too much alcohol, and the Tobacco Institute makes concessions to nonsmokers. The separation of nonsmokers from *anti*smokers is interesting persuasion—a concession that you can't win them all.

Effects on counterpersuasion   If we know that a convinced group will be exposed to counterpersuasion at a later date, then what kind of communication decision should we make? Fortunately, a study similar to the previously mentioned study done for the War Department has thrown light on this issue. The amount of resistance produced by a one-sided versus a two-sided propaganda presentation was compared. Once again, the experimental design involved prerecorded radio programs. A one-sided speech (program A) and a two-sided speech (program B) were drafted; as before, these were intended to combat overoptimism. The main difference between this study and the one previously described is that here, half of the subjects (half who heard program A and half who heard program B) were exposed to counterpropaganda one week after the speeches.

The researchers found that the groups who were previously persuaded with both-sides argumentation were more resistant to counterpropaganda than those persuaded with one-sided argumentation. Only 2 percent of the latter groups maintained the desired attitude when subjected to counterpropaganda, whereas 61 percent of the former groups resisted the counterpropaganda and maintained the desired opinion. The researchers concluded that "a two-sided presentation is *more* effective in the long run than a one-sided one (a) when, regardless of initial opinion, the audience is *exposed* to subsequent counterpropaganda, or (b) when, regardless of subsequent

[35]Edmond Winston Jordan Faison, "Effectiveness of One-Sided and Two-Sided Mass Communications in Advertising," *Public Opinion Quarterly,* 25 (1961), 468–69.

[36]See, for example, Robert D. Dycus, "Relative Efficacy of a One-Sided vs. Two-Sided Communication in a Simulated Government Evaluation of Proposals," *Psychological Reports,* 38 (1976), 787–90.

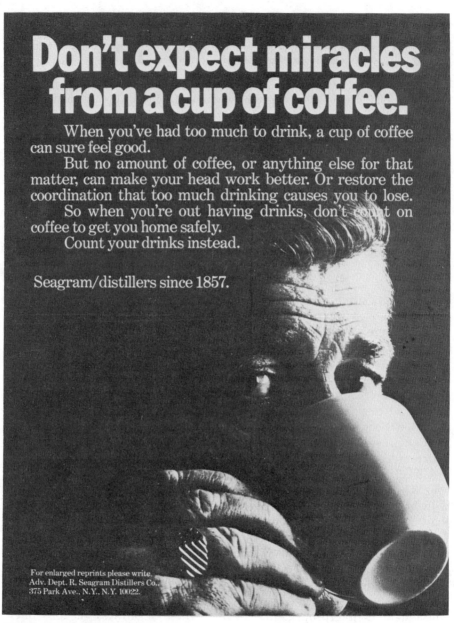

FIGURE 6–1　Moderation Series

From Seagram Distillers Co., New York, 1979.

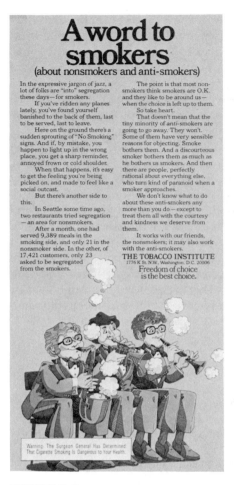

FIGURE 6–2

The Tobacco Institute.

exposure to counterpropaganda, the audience initially disagrees with the commentator's position."[37]

It is readily apparent that this study supports the War Department study. It shows that we must consider the use of both-sides persuasion because of the possibility that an audience may be exposed to counterargument later on.

Many speech studies have measured the effects of both-sides persuasion. Among such studies, many indicate that other factors are so important as to make generalization dangerous. For example, the role of a speaker's prestige

[37]Arthur A. Lumsdaine and Irving L. Janis, "Resistance to Counter-Propaganda Produced by a One-Sided Versus a Two-Sided Propaganda Presentation," *Public Opinion Quarterly,* 17 (1953), 311–18.

may seriously offset any advantage that he or she is predicted to have.[38] When receivers are required to publicly commit themselves to a position, sidedness becomes secondary.[39] There is also evidence that in full-blown, emotional, political oratory, a straightforward argumentative approach may be more effective than a both-sides presentation.[40]

Both-sides persuasion nevertheless has the appeal of objective, rational evaluation. It is a subtle and honest call for fair play. Opposing arguments are not omitted, and therefore opposed receivers are not antagonized. Listening should be more favorable because the listener will not be involved in rehearsing counterarguments during your positive (pro-side) persuasion. Both-sides persuasion not only helps insulate receivers against counter-arguments but also forces senders to be more audience-oriented. Both-sides persuaders must be more sensitive to their audience's attitudes and to all the arguments and issues pertaining to their subject. One student, after much research on both sides of his subject, reported that he was now convinced of the validity of the "other" side of the subject. Both-sides persuasion is more effective than one-sided persuasion, according to Russell Jones and Jack Brehm, because of *psychological reactance.*[41] That is, people react strongly against harsh, one-sided persuasion and are less defensive about both-sides persuasion.

Here are some specific characteristics of both-sides persuasion:

1. *Objectivity:* fair, honest, bias based on evidence
2. *Suspended judgment:* avoids superpositive statements, creates doubt, makes frequent use of the hypothesis form
3. *Nonspecific opponents:* does not identify receiver as the opposition, suggests receiver is undecided, creates a common ground
4. *Critical willingness:* arouses receiver's reevaluation, motivates receiver to reconsider the "other" side
5. *Qualified language:* does not overstate the position and the evidence, is careful of overgeneralized statements
6. *Sensitivity to audience:* adapts the presentation to feedback signs, considers alternative actions before making the speech or sending the message
7. *Ethical approach:* above all, honest, presents significant opposing arguments in an objective manner; recognizes that honesty is the best practical policy

[38]Stanley F. Paulson, "The Effects of the Prestige of the Speaker and Acknowledgment of Opposing Arguments on Audience Retention and Shift of Opinion," *Speech Monographs,* 21 (November 1954), 267–71.

[39]Erwin P. Bettinghaus and John R. Basehart, "Some Specific Factors Affecting Attitude Change," *Journal of Communication,* 19 (1969), 227–38.

[40]Thomas Ludlum, "Effects of Certain Techniques of Credibility Upon Audience Attitudes," *Speech Monographs,* 25 (November 1958), 278–84.

[41]Russell A. Jones and Jack W. Brehm, "Persuasiveness of One-and-Two-Sided Communications as a Function of Awareness: There Are Two Sides," *Journal of Experimental Social Psychology,* 6 (1970), 47–56.

He who knows only his side of the story doesn't know that—

J. S. Mill

Here is an outline of a speech that utilizes both-sides persuasion.

THE BATTLE OF THE DRINKING AGE

General End:	To persuade (both-sides approach).
Specific Purpose:	To persuade the audience to vote yes on Proposal B (changing the legal drinking age from twenty-one to nineteen).

Introduction

I. Today is election day. Many of you who are going to the polls today have already decided how you're going to vote on each of the proposals. Before you vote, however, I would like you to consider the pros and cons of proposal B—the proposal to reduce the legal drinking age from 21 to 19 years of age.

II. In 1972 the drinking age in our state was lowered from 21 to 18. In April of 1978 the Michigan Legislature passed a law raising the drinking age from 18 to 19. That same year voters passed a proposal that raised the drinking age back up to 21. The battle of the drinking age continues this year with a proposal to lower it back down to 19.

Body

I. Drinking has bad connotations.
   A. The citizens of the United States as a whole

are heavy drinkers.
1. The alcoholism rate is higher than in most other countries.
2. Drinking is referred to as a social disease.
B. Drinking is a drug.
1. It is a depressant.
2. It can be habit-forming (as in alcoholism).
C. Many people believe that drinking is more important to the younger generation today than when they were that age.

Concessions to Con Side

II. Drunk-driving accidents.
A. Most drunk-driving accidents involve people under the age of 25.
B. Dr. Richard L. Douglass and Alexander C. Wagenaar, of the University of Michigan Highway Safety Research Institute, have developed evidence that changing the legal drinking age from 21 to 19 would result in an additional 1,000 or more alcohol-related traffic accidents a year, many of them involving injuries and death.
C. This same Douglass-Wagenaar study covered all of 1979. They surveyed police accident reports and concluded that among 18-to-20-year-olds the raised drinking age of 21 resulted in 1,650 fewer alcohol-related accidents—a 17.7% decline.

III. Keep drinking out of high schools.
A. It is believed that 21-year-olds purchase liquor for their 19- and 20-year-old friends.
B. If the drinking age were lowered to 19, this would make liquor more accessible to 17- and 18-year-olds.

IV. Overcrowded bars. Many people above the age of 21 would like to keep 19- and 20-year-olds out of the bars they frequent so that the bars are not so crowded.

Transition Con to Pro

However important and convincing these arguments may be, there is another side to this proposal that must be considered. Let's now evaluate the arguments for lowering the drinking age to 19.

I. Equity
A. If the age of majority is 18, it ought to be 18 for all things.
1. In 1971 18-year-olds were given the right to vote, and in the following year the Michigan Legislature voted to give them full rights—which included lowering the drinking age.

2. Although equity calls for a drinking age of 18, supporters of Proposal B have compromised on the age of 19 in order to keep drinking out of the high schools.

B. 19- and 20-year-olds are adults.
   1. They are able to vote, buy property, and pay taxes.
   2. Many are married and holding full-time jobs.
   3. They receive the same punishment for crimes as any other adult.
   4. They have been sent to war and have died for their country.

II. How can you give a right or a privilege to someone on the basis of age discrimination?
   A. If going by age, why not raise it to 25?
      The secretary of state's report of 1978 said that "18-to-20-year-olds with legal access to liquor are not behaving significantly different from those people 21 to 24 years old."
   B. Why not set drinking limits according to sex, race, religion, or social status?
      Martin Lee, the secretary of state's main traffic-safety researcher, had this to say, and I quote: "Keeping the drinking age at 21 discriminates against young people. If your sole aim is to cut traffic deaths, it would be more logical to prohibit all men from drinking, since they have 10 times more alcohol-related accidents than women."

Pro-side Arguments

III. Disagreements on drunk-driving statistics.
   A. Kenneth Eaton, the state substance-abuse director, disagrees with the Douglass-Wagenaar studies.
      1. He accuses them of oversimplification and sloppy methodology.
      2. Quote: "I'm taking their report to other experts to look at their methodology. I simply disagree with them. If I thought for a moment there would be damage to young people [by lowering the drinking age], I would not take this position."
   B. Secretary of State Richard Austin and Governor Milliken also favor lowering the drinking age.

IV. A lower drinking age is realistic.
   A. Whether it is legal or not, young people will continue to drink. The Governor's Special Commission on the Age of Majority put out a report in February of 1971. The report read, "The fact is that the 18-, 19- and 20-year-old has already entered an adult social

and employment world and he will drink if he wants to whether it is legal or not."
1.   Rather have drinking in bars instead of cars.
2.   Driving to Canada to drink is more dangerous than going to the corner bar with friends.

B.   Laws are made to be broken. If no one broke the law, there would be no use for the law.
1.   By making drinking illegal, are we not in effect raising the desire to drink?
2.   If drinking is legal, might it not be taken for granted and perhaps in some cases be done less frequently, as in European countries?

C.   Educational programs for the wayward.
1.   Secretary of State Richard Austin and Kenneth Eaton, state substance-abuse director, favor educational programs for dealing with young drinking drivers.
    a.   Eaton's office has involved 5,000 young people in alcohol counseling programs.
    b.   Eaton believes these programs would be jeopardized if he is seen as a prohibitionist.
2.   Reasoning is always more effective than the use of force.
    "We believe, on balance, that reducing the drinking age back down to 19 years of age will ultimately offer a greater potential to reduce the drinking problems of young people."
                              Quote from Kenneth Eaton

Conclusion

As you go to the polls this afternoon I would like you to keep in mind what I have said to you today. The drinking age of 21 has not worked. It certainly has not stopped me or anyone that I know from drinking. I would like to state that I do not condone drinking. Drunk driving is a serious problem in our society and it is a problem for *all adults* no matter what age. Prohibiting a certain number of adults from drinking, aside from clearly being a case of discrimination, is not a solution to the problem. Vote *yes* on Proposal B.

From a speech by Catherine Foley, a Wayne State University student.

SUMMING UP

Message organization and arrangement is related to how we learn. We learn serially; we learn by relating the known to the unknown; we learn through reinforcement. Both temporal contiguity and reinforcement have great practical usefulness for the communication and persuasion theorist. We must be careful to adapt the amount and kind of reinforcement to our particular purpose, subject, situation, and receiver. We also learn through unity, coherence, and emphasis. These three great rhetorical principles have a profound bearing upon how we should organize messages.

Organizing includes the following classic methods: chronological, topical, spatial, logical, difficulty, and need-plan.

The natural sequence in terms of psychological order is thought to be most closely related to the thinking habits of man, as in the system of John Dewey. The following natural sequence concepts are probably involved in all successful persuasion and motivation efforts:

1. Creation of attention and a feeling of felt difficulty.
2. Arousal of problem awareness and need.
3. Explanation of the solution in terms of the problem, need, previous experience, knowledge, and personality of the audience.
4. Visualization of the solution and anticipation of all important objections.
5. Evaluation and reinforcement of the solution leading to action.

The "fundamental tasks" of Hollingworth (attention, interest, impression, conviction, direction), and the "motivated sequence" of Monroe (attention, need, satisfaction, visualization, action), illustrate attempts to adapt organizational schemes to the normal thinking process.

The order question of climax-anticlimax, or where to put your best or strongest arguments, is an old one. Answers from research are confusing and need interpretation. It is difficult to generally counsel an anticlimax or climax order for message preparation even in an other-things-being-equal sense. Other things in this context are seldom equal. The elusive variable of initial attitude is of overriding concern. With unstructured initial attitudes it may be that subsequent attitude is more affected by first position arguments. Perhaps this is also true of retention, but until we do more research where the initial attitude variable is better accounted for, it is still conjecture. Primacy-recency is concerned with the first (prime) position or last (most recent) organizational message position apart from the worth or strength of the argument. No general law of *primacy* has convincingly emerged, but we have knowledge about some of the sets of conditions which affect primacy. If you divide your message into need arousal and information, you will have your information more readily accepted if you put the need arousal in the first or prime position. When the conditions of unstructured attitudes are met, it was also shown that first position arguments are probably more persuasive. If after hearing only one side (the primary side because it's first) of a controversial issue, a receiver makes a response publicly indicating a position, he or she is less persuaded by subsequent (recent) persuasion. When the condition of inconsistency or contradiction appears within a communication, that part ordered first (primary) has more effect, at least where personality impressions are concerned. Your previous persuasion and human transaction impact has considerable influence upon the persuasiveness of later messages. When an audience initially agrees with the position taken by a credible source, the pro-con order is superior to the con-pro order. This primacy rule is thought to hold only when there is some general agreement attitudinally, that is, when one is not confronted with antagonistic or hostile attitudes, and when the source has credibility. Other variables in terms of primacy include such things as tolerance for ambiguity, need for cognition, perceptual defense, need for identifying with a high prestige source, and need to conform to the norms of one's reference groups.

The arrangement effects, in terms of organization for antagonistic receivers, particularly when initial attitudes are known, are quite generalizable. A most important research finding is that both-sides persuasion was significantly better than one-sided persuasion when the audience was opposed to the point of view being presented. The one-sided arguments were more effective when the audience was already convinced of the point being presented. Groups previously persuaded with both-sides argument, regardless of initial attitude, were more resistant to counterpropaganda than those persuaded with one-sided argumentation. Both-sides persuasion has the appeal of objective rational evaluation. It is a subtle and honest appeal to fair play. An opposed listener is not subject to being antagonized by omission of arguments on his or her side of the issue. Listening should be more favorably oriented because the receiver will not be involved in rehearsing counterarguments. Both-sides persuasion not only helps insulate the receivers against counterargument, but also forces the source to be more audience oriented.

STUDY PROJECTS AND TASKS

1. Prepare a detailed outline for a five-to-seven-minute persuasive speech based on a motivated sequence. The five major divisions of the outline could be labeled:

I.	Attention		I.	Attention
II.	Need		II.	Need
III.	Satisfaction	or	III.	Plan
IV.	Visualization		IV.	Reinforcement
V.	Action		V.	Direction

    Indicate the primary motives, appeals, and other devices you are relying on in your outline (safety, esteem, self-preservation, and so on).

2. Clip three newspaper or magazine advertisements and evaluate them in terms of the sequences in project 1. Create an ad of your own.

3. Report and illustrate a radio or television commercial or other appeal (whether for antagonistic groups or not) that makes use of both-sides persuasion. Create one of your own. See the examples in the chapter. Discuss.

4. Prepare an eight-to-ten-minute persuasive speech on a topic toward which your class audience is relatively hostile. (For example, pick the unpopular side of a social issue.) Meet the significant opposition arguments first and make concessions where you must before turning to the other side of the question. Utilize the specific characteristics of both-sides persuasion listed on page 152. See project 5 for further assistance.

5. Use the following criteria in building your own both-sides persuasive speech. Use them also in judging and critiquing others.
    a. Did the speaker impress the audience with his or her objectivity, open-mindedness, and bias based only on evidence? Could any of the following methods be identified?
        (1) Presented the significant opposing arguments.
        (2) Did not try to hide his or her own stand on the issue.
        (3) Did not grant opposing arguments reluctantly.
    b. Did the speaker develop a oneness with the audience and prevent the audience from identifying itself as the opposition? Could any of the following methods be identified?
        (1) Avoided "I"; used "we" and "you and I."
        (2) Was nonspecific about the opposition; identified people other than the audience as opponents.
        (3) Suggested audience was an undecided group; created a common ground.
    c. Did the speaker develop suspended judgment in the audience and arouse a critical willingness to consider both sides? Could any of the following methods be identified?
        (1) Avoided superpositive statements, created doubt, made frequent use of hypothesis form.
        (2) Created doubt rather than certainty, did not overstate the position and evidence, was careful of overgeneralized statements.
        (3) Was above all ethical; presented significant opposing arguments in an objective, honest manner.

6. The following topics were found to be controversial to 25 percent or more of the college students asked. They might be used as topics for projects 4 and 5.
    a. U.S. Olympic athletes should be subsidized by the federal government.
    b. Sex education should be required in all public schools.
    c. College students should hold a part-time job while in school.
    d. Premarital sexual relations should be discouraged.
    e. Women should be drafted into the armed forces.
    f. The federal government should enact a law to require the sterilization of the feeble-minded and the insane.
    g. College social fraternities and sororities should be banned.
    h. Most college students drink too much.
    i. The population explosion should be curbed by a federal law limiting families to two children.
    j. Movies should be taxed according to their movie-code rating.
    k. Gambling should be legalized in our state.
    l. Affirmative action is demeaning to capable minorities.

     m. The honors system for taking exams should be adopted at this school.

     n. Marijuana should be legalized.

     o. Cigarettes should be taxed more heavily.

     p. Conviction for drunk driving should be automatically penalized by loss of license.

     q. Men are unfairly treated in divorce proceedings.

     r. Further manned exploration of space is worth the expense.

     s. The choice of abortion should rest solely with the pregnant female.

     t. Men are better suited for high political office than women.

     u. Aid to Dependent Children should be eliminated.

7. Analyze a campaign, editorial, or advertisement and locate the natural-order steps shown in project 1.

8. In a campaign, editorial, or advertisement, locate appeals to any of the following human needs: physiological, safety, love, esteem, self-actualization. Take into account the specific audience.

9. In what ways do projects 7 and 8 use the theories of cognitive consistency?

7

Reasoned Supports of Persuasion

Emotive and Rational Supports
Forms of Logical Support
        Authority
        Examples
        Statistics
Forms of Reasoning
        From Cause
        From Generalization
        From Analogy
        From Sign
Elements of Argument
        Pattern of Analysis
        Definitions of Elements
Fallacies
        Overgeneralization (*secundum quid*)
        False Cause (*non sequitur*)
        Begging the Question (*petitio principii*)
        Ignoring or Ducking the Issue (*ignoratio elenchi*)
Sender-Receiver Considerations
Summing Up
Study Projects and Tasks

EMOTIVE AND
RATIONAL SUPPORTS

In this chapter we are concerned primarily with rational reasoning and argument—that is, with the logical rather than the psychological and emotive supports of persuasion. The ancient Greeks used the words *logos* and *pathos* to make this distinction. *Pathos* refers to the emotive elements. We may also use the word *cognition* for *logos* and *activation* for the rest.[1] We take a more holistic view of reasoning today, recognizing that it is not always possible to know where rationality begins and emotion ends. Logic is almost always mixed with some emotion or affect. By the same token, emotional persuasion usually contains some logic. According to the modern view of reasoning, both types of support must be known and considered from the point of view of the audience, not just that of the speaker. In this sense both emotive and logical supports can be *rational* if the emotive supports lead to some logical deliberation.[2]

We learned in Chapter 1 about belief systems that shape our attitudes and our thinking. These vertical and horizontal structures affect what we view as logical or rational. The supports and the reasoning we will discuss in this chapter are surely conditioned by how prominent or primitive a belief system is involved. Most of our religious and philosophical beliefs are central and relatively unstructured. Less basic beliefs, as we learned earlier, are quite a different matter. We have learned, for example, to be more cautious about our perceptions of authority and credibility. If the Surgeon General says that smoking causes cancer, and if the Surgeon General is an expert, then we logically conclude that smoking causes cancer, correct? Well, not quite: we are aware that the surgeon general is not perfect and might possibly be in error.

We may reach the same conclusion as another person, but for quite different reasons. We may engage different belief systems. The Surgeon General may conclude on the basis of detailed, health-centered syllogistic reasoning that smoking causes death; another person may reach the same conclusion because he views smoking as a sin and his central belief system tells him that the wages of sin are death.[3]

Humans are clearly different from animals in that they have the capacity to reason at high levels of abstraction. They are as a result vulnerable to unethical or confused appeals that sound logical. Those who intentionally muddle their arguments or befuddle their receivers are perhaps the most

[1]Gary L. Cronkhite, "Logic, Emotion, and the Paradigm of Persuasion," *Quarterly Journal of Speech,* 50, no. 1 (February 1964), 13–18.

[2]G. E. Yoos, "Licit and Illicit in Rhetorical Appeals," *Western Journal of Speech Communication,* 42, no. 4 (Fall 1978), 222–30.

[3]For an interesting discussion of belief systems, see Daryl J. Bem, *Beliefs, Attitudes and Human Affairs* (Belmont, Calif.: Brooks/Cole, 1970), pp. 4–13.

unethical persuaders of all. Our discussion of fallacies should help receivers detect such messages. We should be aware of unethical or confused arguments and the overlapping nature of emotive and rational appeals as we study the *primarily* logical supports of persuasion. Other things being equal, good, clear reasoning and argument should enhance the quality and stature of your persuasion.

FORMS OF
LOGICAL SUPPORT

Aristotle was one of the first to make the distinction between extrinsic and intrinsic proof. *Extrinsic* proof is based on facts in the world about us or statements based upon such facts—that is, observable phenomena. If you were to go to Baldwin School and count 525 students, that number would be a fact that you had observed. It would still be considered a fact if a document written by the principal said there were 525 students in Baldwin School. *Intrinsic* proof depends on reasoned effort—that is, on the application of rhetoric and logic.

Essentially, the sources of logical support are objects or things that are observable or reports about things that are observable. The most useful forms of logical support for our purposes are (1) statements by authorities, (2) examples, and (3) statistics.

Authority

This form of logical support typically takes the form of testimony from a person better qualified than the speaker to give a considered opinion about something. However, the value of an authority depends on how much of an expert the person is. Perhaps the testimony simply supports the observations of the speaker rather than proving his or her point. Authority was discussed briefly in Chapter 3, where it was translated into intent, trustworthiness, and competence.

The idea or statement being supported determines in part who the experts are. If you are trying to prove that the man who crashed into your car ran a red light, the expert is the lone person who was standing on the corner and saw the whole thing. If you are relying on this kind of nonprofessional testimony you often need more than one witness. If you are trying to prove that you have observed a bird considered extinct, such as the passenger pigeon, you will need the testimony of a qualified ornithologist. This expert will insist on firsthand observation of a captured bird in this exceptional case.

Authorities are qualified to give expert testimony by virtue of their closeness to a firsthand observation or experience and by virtue of their training in observing the phenomenon in question. The authority should be an expert *on the topic under discussion.* You would not ask a doctor of medicine to diagnose a problem in an airplane engine.

Problems may arise from your audience's knowledge and opinion of the authority quoted. The bias the audience assigns your expert may be very troublesome. When the audience simply does not know who John Doe is, then you must explain why his testimony is authoritative (for example, "John Doe is professor of economics at Cornell University and a member of the U.S. Tax Commission").

Examples

An example is a specific illustration, incident, or instance that supports a point you are trying to make. A hypothetical example may be of substantial aid to clearness and is often very persuasive, but it is not demonstrated logical support. We are concerned here with real, factual examples.

To prove that a person can operate normally in a state of weightlessness, we can cite one example of an astronaut who has done so successfully. However, in some situations *one* factual example, though proving its own case, may be so unique or exceptional that it does not truly support a generalization. If you were arguing that Volkswagens were assembled poorly and carelessly and you supported this statement with only *one* example of a car that was indeed assembled poorly, then your proof would be suspect. How many specific examples does one need? The answer involves inductive reasoning, which we'll discuss shortly.

Statistics

A joker once said, "First come lies, then big lies, then statistics." (Or was it "Figures don't lie, but liars figure!") There are fraudulent uses of statistics, but the truth is that we live by statistics. We accept data on births, deaths, and accidents as facts. However, the complexity of statistics as a method bewilders many people. You do not have to be a statistician to realize that a *mean* (an average) is not always the most representative measure. Let's take eleven hypothetical educators and their yearly incomes:

	SALARY		SALARY
Educator A (Administrator)	$45,000	Educator G	$20,000
Educator B (Administrator)	40,000	Educator H	18,000
Educator C	30,000	Educator I	17,200
Educator D	25,500	Educator J	16,000
Educator E	22,500	Educator K	15,000
Educator F	20,000		

The mean income of these eleven educators is $24,472. The problem is obvious: two educators (the administrators) make the figure unrepresentative, particularly if you are more concerned with teachers than with administrators. Counting halfway down the list of salaries, we find $20,000. This is the *median*, in this case a much more meaningful and representative figure. If we do not include the two administrators, the average income of the teachers is $20,466 and the median is $20,000. You could then figure the amount by which each income differs from the average; the average of these differences is the *average deviation*. If you were to translate these deviations from the average onto a so-called normal distribution, you could then determine the *standard deviation* (also known as *sigma*).

It should now be evident that statistics can very quickly become complicated, capable of many applications, and (if we are not careful) meaningless. The lessons are (1) to select the most appropriate statistics for your point or proposition and (2) to make sure your audience will understand them. Statistics (figures) do not lie, but liars *do* have the opportunity to "figure"!

FORMS OF REASONING

From Cause

If we were to see a man accidentally shoot a live man and then see the victim fall dead with a bullet in his heart, we could say the *effect* was death and the *cause* was the bullet or the man with the gun. Even this simple, observed, cause-to-effect relationship is full of problems. If the shooting were deliberate, would it in any way change the relationship? Let us suppose you found a dead man (the effect of something) with a bullet in his heart. Can we conclude absolutely that the bullet is the cause? This is reasoning from effect to cause—*a posteriori* reasoning. The bullet is certainly a possible cause, but as any Simon and Simon fan knows, the man might have been killed by arsenic

FIGURE 7–1
Which To Use?

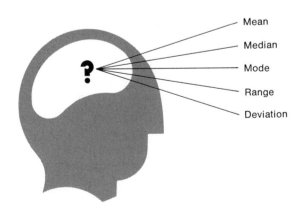

poisoning, then shot after his death as a means of hiding the real cause. We should expect causes to be complex and interrelated.

One more example: Suppose a man dashes into your classroom, shoots a gun at your professor, and dashes out. Your professor falls to the floor and everyone runs out screaming. You observed the cause and concluded that the effect was murder or attempted murder. (Perhaps it was a role-play instead.)

Your car battery is weak, you observe that it's ten degrees below zero, and you conclude that your car isn't going to start. This is before-the-fact, or *a priori*, reasoning. The conclusion is based upon circumstances you observed before the disputed fact. You are reasoning from *cause to effect.*

If when you get up tomorrow morning you say "It's ten below zero; my car won't start; I'll be late for school," you are reasoning from *effect to effect.* Both your faltering battery and your tardiness (as well as the thermometer reading) are the effects of a common cause—low temperature. In arguing from effect to effect, you must first sort out the effect-to-cause and cause-to-effect elements and then apply the general requirements for arguments based on causal relations. These requirements are as follows:

Effect to cause
1. Is the attributed cause able to generate the particular effect?
2. Is the claimed cause the only possible cause of the effect?
3. Has coincidence been mistaken for cause?[4]
4. The alleged cause must not have been prevented from operating.

Cause to effect
1. Is the alleged cause relevant to the effect described?
2. Is this the sole or distinguishing causal factor?
3. Is there reasonable probability that no undesirable effect may result from this particular cause?
4. Is there a counteracting cause?
5. Is the cause capable of producing the effect?
6. Is the cause necessary and sufficient?
7. How does a new cause affect the system?[5]

From Generalization

Reasoning from generalization involves inducting from fair and sufficient samples or examples. *Induction* is the process of reasoning by which we arrive at a conclusion or generalization through observing specific cases or instances. "Properly conceived [it] may be thought of as the synthetic process used in moving from particulars to probable conclusions."[6] If you were to

[4]The first three items of this list are taken from Craig R. Smith and David M. Hunsaker, *The Bases of Argument* (Indianapolis: Bobbs-Merrill, 1972), pp. 88–89.

[5]This list is taken from Austin J. Freeley, *Argumentation and Debate,* 5th ed. (Belmont, Calif.: Wadsworth, 1981), pp. 121–26.

[6]George W. Ziegelmueller and Charles A. Dause, *Argumentation: Inquiry and Advocacy* (Englewood Cliffs, N.J.: Prentice-Hall, 1975), p. 88.

observe 500,000 spiders and if each one had eight legs, it would be reasonable to conclude that spiders have eight legs. The induction is perfect for the 500,000 cases, since there were no exceptions. To be intolerably scientific, however, our induction is merely a prediction (although a highly probable one) when applied to all the spiders in the world. Assuming we are happy with the generalization "All spiders have eight legs," we can then conclude *deductively* that this particular eight-legged thing in our garden is a spider. In sum, induction starts with particular cases and proceeds to a generalization, whereas in deduction we start with a generally accepted observation or principle and apply it to a particular case. Here are some tests for good generalizing:

1. Is the example relevant?
2. Are there a reasonable number of examples?
3. Do the examples cover a critical period of time?
4. Are the examples typical?
5. Are the negative examples noncritical?[7]

From Analogy

Analogies can make things clear, vivid, and interesting. Some analogies are figurative or emotive, others more literal. All offer support, but the literal are thought to be the more logical.

Abraham Lincoln made good use of a *figurative* analogy for political persuasion. During the Civil War there were those who loudly criticized his method of conducting the war. At that time, a tightrope walker named Blondin became famous for walking and riding a two-wheel bicycle on a rope strung across Niagara Falls. In explaining the dangerous position of the nation, Lincoln directed the following analogy at his critics:

> Gentlemen, I want you to suppose a case for a moment. Suppose that all the property you were worth was in gold, and you had put it in the hands of Blondin, the famous rope-walker, to carry across the Niagara Falls on a tightrope. Would you shake the rope while he was passing over it, or keep shouting to him, "Blondin, stoop a little more! Go a little faster!" No, I am sure you would not. You would hold your breath as well as your tongue, and keep your hands off until he was safely over. Now the government is in the same situation. It is carrying an immense weight across a stormy ocean. Untold treasures are in its hands. It is doing the best it can. Don't badger it! Just keep still, and it will get you safely over.[8]

A *literal* analogy is open to less argument but is nevertheless always imperfect proof. Its effectiveness depends on how close the comparison really is. In arguing for gun control Senator Edward Kennedy tried a *literal* analogy:

[7]From Freeley, *Argumentation and Debate,* pp. 116–18.
[8]Quoted in *Town Meeting,* 11 (October 11, 1945), 24.

Opponents of firearms laws insist that gun licenses and record-keeping requirements are burdensome and inconvenient. Yet they don't object to licensing automobile drivers, hunters, or those who enjoy fishing. If the only price of gun licensing or record-keeping requirements is the inconvenience to gun users, then the public will have received a special bargain. Certainly sportsmen will gladly tolerate minor inconvenience in order to protect the lives of their families, friends, and neighbors.[9]

George Ziegelmueller and Charles Dause analyzed this analogy as follows: "Senator Kennedy asserts that gun licensing is like automobile, hunting, and fishing licensing in an essential characteristic (inconvenience), and he suggests that it will be like the other forms of licensing with regard to the characteristic (tolerance) known in the other forms but not known in the instance of guns."[10]

From Sign

We reason from circumstances or clues that act as signs. Some are better at this than others. Sherlock Holmes was an expert at reasoning from subtle signs. Consider his assessment of Dr. Watson:

"But do you mean to say," I said, "that without leaving your room you can unravel some knot which other men can make nothing of, although they have seen every detail for themselves?"

"Quite so. I have a kind of intuition that way. Now and again a case turns up which is a little more complex. Then I have to bustle about and see things with my own eyes. You see I have a lot of special knowledge which I apply to the problem, and which facilitates matters wonderfully. Those rules of deduction laid down in that article which aroused your scorn are invaluable to me in practical work. Observation with me is second nature. You appeared to be surprised when I told you, on your first meeting, that you had come from Afghanistan."

"You were told, no doubt."

"Nothing of the sort. I *knew* you came from Afghanistan. From long habit the train of thoughts ran so swiftly through my mind that I arrived at the conclusion without being conscious of intermediate steps. There were such steps, however. The train of reasoning ran, 'Here is a gentleman of a medical type, but with the air of a military man. Clearly an army doctor, then. He has just come from the tropics, for his face is dark, and that is not the natural tint of his skin, for his wrists are fair. He has undergone hardship and sickness, as his haggard face says clearly. His left arm has been injured. He holds it in a stiff and unnatural manner. Where in the tropics could an English army doctor have seen much hardship and got his arm wounded? Clearly in Afghanistan.' The whole train of thought did not occupy a

[9]Quoted in "Tighter Gun Controls—Both Sides of the Dispute," *U.S. News and World Report*, July 10, 1972, p. 69.

[10]Ziegelmueller and Dause, *Argumentation*, p. 98.

second. I then remarked that you came from Afghanistan, and you were astonished."

"It is simple enough as you explain it," I said, smiling.[11]

Some tests that Holmes always applied are useful for all of us:

Are the signs reliable?
Are they in sufficient number?
Do any contradict one another?

ELEMENTS OF ARGUMENT

If reasoning is how we go about generating and testing ideas that support a position we are taking or a claim we are making, then argument is the scheme by which we link and demonstrate the logic of our claims.

Pattern of Analysis

Suppose you had argued that the great football running back Billy Sims of the Detroit Lions would return to play for the Lions in 1984. That was your CLAIM. First, some background:

Headline: July 1, 1983. "Sims Signs with Houston Gamblers"
Headline: December 16, 1983. "Sims Signs Second Contract with Detroit Lions"
Rumor: Sims has signed a third contract.
Coach Clark: "Billy wants to stay; we want him to stay."

For all the controversy, you still reasoned that there was good argument that Billy would play for Detroit next season. That was your (1) *CLAIM.* You argued on the (2) *GROUNDS* that the facts were that Billy had a valid, signed contract with the Lions, and that the earlier Gamblers' contract was invalid since Sims' agent (Jerry Argovitz) misrepresented the facts of the contract. You further argued (or reasoned) that the link between your claim and grounds was (3) *WARRANTED,* since formal contracts are not legally binding if there is deception, fraud, or conflict of interest, and you could cite for (4) *BACKING* legal statutes and the facts that the USFL constitution prohibits a holder (Argovitz) of any interest in a member club from acting "as the contracting agent or representative for any player," and that Billy said he wanted to play for the Lions. Since there was no certainty in this kind of a situation, you (5) *QUALIFIED* by saying, "so probably," or "presumably" he would play for Detroit, *unless* some rare counterarguments, circumstances (Argovitz sold his

[11]A. Conan Doyle, *A Study in Scarlet* (New York: Harper & Brothers, 1892), p. 14.

agency in September, 1983), or (6) *REBUTTALS* interceded. There were several reservations about your claim to consider. Billy might elect to break his Detroit contract. The courts might delay a decision for a year or more. The courts might decide that Sims had adequate choice and clues to protect himself, or that Sims had *two* legal contracts.

These elements of argument can be diagrammed in the following useful pattern as shown in Figure 7–2.

FIGURE 7–2

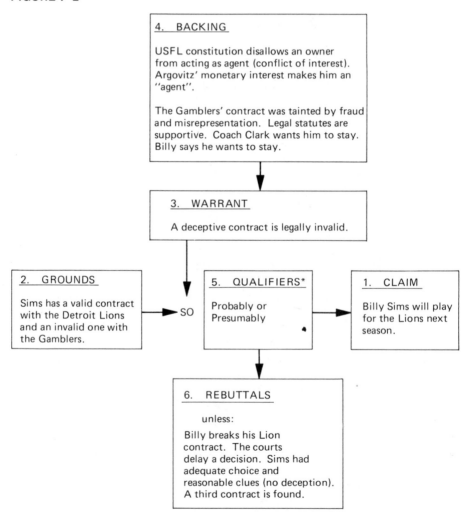

*These are also referred to as "model qualifiers."

Definitions of Elements

Claims   This is your stand on an issue, the position you are taking, your purpose for arguing. "I claim, despite the contract controversy, that Billy Sims will play for the Detroit Lions next season." (1984)

Grounds   This is the evidence, facts, data, and information that are the reasons for your claim in the first place—a reasoned beginning. "Sims has a legal, ethically negotiated contract with the Detroit Lions for next season and a deceptively negotiated one with and by the Gamblers."

Warrants   These form the link between *grounds* and *claims*. What justifies the connection? Some warrants are natural (gravity, for example); some are axioms (means, opportunity, or motivation, in the language of criminology); many are ethical principles or legal statutes. In the Sims case ethical principles and legal statutes are probably both backing and warrants. Both Sims and the Lions hired separate lawyers. One strong proclaim warrant is that a contract is not legally binding if deception was involved in its signing.

Backing   This is the general body of information that supports and clarifies a warrant. In this case it ranges from ethics and legal statutes to testimony from Coach Clark, Billy Sims, agents, and others.

Qualifiers   This is your parachute or escape hatch. Since so little is certain in practical reasoning, you must evaluate the strength of your conviction. "This is probably (possibly, presumably, etc.) true—*unless* the unforeseen, the improbable, the bizarre happens."

Rebuttals   Here is where you specifically assess how or under what circumstances a claim might prove false or untenable. New information in the Billy Sims' drama might prove enough rebuttal for you to drop your claim. Suppose Billy has signed a third contract!

Bumper Sticker: "Honk if Billy has signed a contract with you."

Given this confusion, it would be tempting to reason from *sign* (or perhaps *cause*) and attribute recklessly: Billy is sick; Billy was deceived; Billy is manipulating both teams. Clearly we never really know, and we can't win them all. Indeed, even in this case simple cause-and-effect reasoning appears to be quite naive. Nevertheless, some arguments have more rational merit than others. Some have more legal merit; some, like this one, have more *ethical* merit.[12] Stephen Toulmin, Richard Rieke, and Allan Janik put it well:

[12]On February 10, 1984, U.S. District Judge Robert E. DeMascio rescinded the Gamblers' contract with Billy Sims. It was judged invalid because "the defendant, Jerry Argovitz, breached his fiduciary duty when negotiating the Gamblers' contract and because the contract was otherwise tainted by fraud and misrepresentation." Memorandum Opinion, Civil No. 83CV5649DT.

Evidently an eloquent speaker or writer can dress up his arguments in all kinds of ways so as to conceal their defects and make them attractive to his audience. To the extent that he understands the tastes and prejudices of the audience, he will be able to slant his arguments to take advantage of those inclinations. But in most cases, it is possible to separate the features that give our arguments genuine "rational merit" from those other rhetorical devices that have the effect of making them more attractive and persuasive than they deserve to be. So let us begin here by setting aside all considerations of charm and eloquence and by concentrating on those rational merits alone.

—It must be clear just what *kind* of issues the argument is intended to raise (aesthetic rather than scientific, say, or legal rather than psychiatric) and what its underlying *purpose* is.

—The *grounds* on which it rests must be relevant to the *claim* made in the argument and must be sufficient to support it.

—The *warrant* relied on to guarantee this support must be applicable to the case under discussion and must be based on solid *backing*.

—The *modality*, or strength, of the resulting claim must be made explicit, and the possible *rebuttals*, or exceptions, must be well understood.[13]

FALLACIES

Fallacies are by definition deceptive and unsound rational reasoning, yet they are often very persuasive. They are not always designed to deceive or confuse; they can be quite accidental. To further complicate matters, an argument that is fallacious in one context may be sound in another. Persuaders and receivers should work diligently to untangle fallacious reasoning and be gracious in attributing intent. As a practical rule of reasoning, beware of unwarranted assumptions and ambiguous language.

Aristotle devised a classification of fallacies that has been the springboard for all systems to this day. (See Figure 7–3.)

Aristotle himself admitted that there were problems in his system, so we may presume to rearrange it. We shall examine four major types of fallacies, together with their subtypes. The four are *secundum quid*, or overgeneralization—"They're all dumb"; *non sequitur*, or false cause—"The dance caused the rain"; *petitio principii*, or begging the question—"Everybody knows they're crooks."; and *ignoratio elenchi*, or ignoring or ducking the issue—"What discrimination?" A *sophism* is a deliberate use of a fallacy for some expected argumentative gain. The intentional use of these devices is called *sophistical reasoning*.

[13]Stephen Toulmin, Richard Rieke, and Allan Janik, *An Introduction to Reasoning* (New York: Macmillan, 1979), p. 106. See also Richard D. Rieke and Malcolm O. Sillars, *Argumentation and the Decision Making Process* (Glenview, Ill.: Scott, Foresman, 1984), esp. chap. 4. For a detailed discussion of the elements of argument, see the Toulmin, Rieke, and Janik text. See also J. Vernon Jensen, *Argumentation: Reasoning in Communication* (New York: D. Van Nostrand, 1981).

"They're all dumb."

"The dance caused the rain."

"Everybody knows they're crooks."

"What discrimination?"

FIGURE 7-3

Overgeneralization (*secundum quid*)

Snap judgments based on insufficient evidence or experience belong in the category of overgeneralization. This fallacy results in going from the general case to a specific case, or vice versa. The process is similar to that of deduction and induction.

Overgeneralization causes the most trouble when we encounter exceptions to generally accepted rules. We would all agree that it is wrong to kill a person. However, the specific case of killing in self-defense is for most of us an exception to this rule. To take another example, there could be several exceptions to the rule "Alcohol is harmful."

Sampling A group of star high-school football players were being oriented to a certain Big Ten campus when they observed a dozen chic females coming out of a campus building. To a man their generalization was "Wow! What coeds this place has!" The coach did not bother to tell them that these women were all professional fashion models who had just come from a faculty program. Consider the size and representativeness of your sample before generalizing. A rash of teenage delinquencies may cause some to conclude that all teenagers are juvenile delinquents, but this would be an unfair generalization.

The most treacherous part of this fallacy is that it does start with facts. There *were* twelve stylish females on a given campus; teenage delinquency *has* been recorded. It is our lack of objective analysis of our sample that gets us into trouble.

Extrapolation   Stuart Chase refers to this fallacy as the "thin entering wedge." It is also known as the "camel's nose in the tent." It is a form of sampling trouble (as are all overgeneralizations), except that this one is keyed to prediction and probability. Chase put it well: "You chart two or three points, draw a curve through them, and then extend it indefinitely!"[14] Space scientists extrapolate or else they do not predict at all. So do economists and meterologists. Scientists typically know the dangers of extrapolation; to offset these dangers, they generally phrase their predictions in terms of statistical chance or confidence. Scientists draw predictive curves only when they have located enough points to make a qualified prediction. We are well advised to do the same.

False Cause (*non sequitur*)

This is the fallacy of assigning a wrong or false cause to a certain happening or effect. It also involves refutation by means of irrelevant arguments. Superstitions belong here. If you blow on the dice and win, was it the blowing that brought you luck? We still sell rabbits' feet, and most hotels still have no floor labeled 13.

Post hoc ergo propter hoc   This translates "after this, therefore because of this." Superstitions fit here too, but in our saner moments we are not really unaware of their fallacy. It's the more subtle misuse of time sequence that hurts us. If new city administrators come into power after a particularly rough winter and are faced with badly damaged roads, you may find it easy to hold them responsible as you survey a ruined $100 tire: "We didn't have roads like this until after their election." After this, therefore because of this. The great Roman Empire fell after the introduction of Christianity—care to try that one?

Tu quoque   This fallacy translates "thou also" and consists of making a similar, but essentially irrelevant, attack upon one's accuser. A discussion between a Brazilian student and several Americans about Communist infiltration in Latin America became quite heated. Suddenly, the Brazilian said "Communists? How about segregation in your country?" The retort was equally brilliant: "How about Nazis in Argentina?" A classic instance of this

---

[14]Stuart Chase, *Guides to Straight Thinking* (New York: Harper & Row, Pub., 1956), p. 6. This book is an excellent supplement to your reading on fallacies.

fallacy occurred in a Marine Corps basic-training mess line. The mess steward put a salad on top of a private's mashed potatoes. When told what an ignoramus he was, the steward retorted in a most effective (if illogical) way: "Yeah? What about those poor guys in Lebanon?" Or how about "Tell it to Ronnie!"

Consequent This fallacy simply involves the corruption of the reasoning used in conditional syllogisms. The problem lies with possible, partial, or even probable truths. If he lies, he will be expelled from school; he was expelled; therefore, he lied. (In actuality, he may have been expelled for poor grades.)

When we use a conditional syllogism and argue from the truth of the consequent (he was expelled) to the truth of the antecedent (he lied), or when we argue from the falsity of the antecedent to the falsity of the consequent, we are committing the fallacy of the consequent.

Either-or Surely there are things in this world that are either one way or another. You are either living or dead; the lake is frozen or it is not. However, when a statement or problem with more than two possible solutions is put in an either-or context, we have a fallacy. "The fight is either Jan's or Jim's fault." It may be neither's fault, or it may be the fault of both. There are shades of gray in most things. All too often we hear either-or arguments that only slow real solutions: science versus religion, capitalism versus socialism, suburban versus city living, and so forth.

Loaded question This device usually involves asking two questions as if they were one. It typically puts you in an awkward position no matter how you answer. In a speech it may take the form of a great many questions, the combination of answers leading to fallacious reasoning. The answers typically sought are yes or no. The classic loaded question is "Have you stopped beating your dog?" Yes or no? If you answer no, you are an admitted beater. If you answer yes, you are an admitted former beater. Either way, the loaded question stacks the deck against you.

Begging the Question
(petitio principii)

This fallacy assumes the truth or falsity of a statement or claim that lacks substantial evidence.

Arguing in a circle (circulus in probando) This is the classic form of using two or more unproved propositions to prove each other. Professional boxing should be outlawed for it is inhumane; we know it is inhumane because it is a practice that should be outlawed. Take "Speech and Communication Theory" at Northwestern University because it is the best course in the country. Why is it the best in the country? Because it is taught at Northwestern University.

Direct assumption   In this form of the fallacy, language is carefully selected to help conceal bald assumptions. Many statements may be used, or perhaps just a word or two is subtly inserted. In a discussion of big-time college football an opposition speaker started with the words, "It is my purpose to show that buying professional players is not in the best interest of college football." This statement begged the whole proposition by assuming at the outset that colleges buy professional players. Unless the statement is supported, it remains an assertion.

Ignoring or Ducking the Issue
(*ignoratio elenchi*)

This fallacy can be a subtle, persuasive (if not detected), and often vicious process. It almost always involves using apparently relevant but objectively irrelevant arguments to cloud or duck the real issue or argument. This fallacy has several types, and each is worthy of a word of warning to the receiver and the unsophisticated sender.

Personal attack (ad hominem)   When a speaker attacks the personal character of an opponent rather than the issue at hand, that person is using *ad hominem* argument. When intended as deception, this kind of argument becomes a question of ethics as well as one of decency, as we saw in Chapter 1.

Partisan appeal (ad populum)   This is an appeal to the people in terms of their prejudices and passions. The symbols of motherhood, the flag, race, and sin are typical partisan themes. Vicious and often unsupported attacks have been made against liberal-minded Americans in the name of un-Americanism. The charge of Romanism was leveled by some in the John Kennedy presidential campaign of 1960. We hope that bald-faced *ad populum* appeals will become less successful as the general population becomes better educated and more sophisticated.

False appeals to authority (ad verecundiam)   This type of fallacy involves an appeal to authority and dignity. When the authority is legitimately connected to the subject, as Aristotle is to logic, we have no problem. However, if in our reverence of Aristotle we use him to oppose modern probability theory, we are guilty of *ad verecundiam*. Reggie Jackson and Billy Sims are well-paid experts in their highly specialized fields. They are probably not authorities on contracts, laser theory, or even shaving cream or candy bars. If you are impressed because Dr. Whosis says that alcohol causes cancer, find out if Whosis is an M.D. or an English professor!

Appeals to ignorance (ad ignorantiam)   Here the speaker hides his or her weak arguments by overwhelming an audience with impressive materials that they know little about. A twelve-cylinder vocabulary can screen many a feeble argument. An improper use of statistics (or even a proper one) in the presence of people ignorant of the theory or the numbers involved is a good example of *ad ignorantiam.* This is not to say that vocabulary and statistics are the problem. It is the intent with which the speaker adapts them to the audience.

SENDER–RECEIVER CONSIDERATIONS

The practical and ethical role of the sender seems clear: support statements with facts and evidence; avoid deliberate or accidental fallacious reasoning. However, a frustrated sender or one deeply involved with an issue may unintentionally say illogical things. Then too, receivers may decode messages in ways not intended by the source. We need tolerance on both sides of this kind of behavior.

In some difficult situations, receivers may simply be in no mood for logical reasoning or argument. The driver who has just waited four hours for gasoline and then paid two dollars a gallon for it is probably not psychologically ready for a carefully reasoned argument on energy conservation or even mass transportation. At another time perhaps. In all persuasion, timing is important, especially when one is primarily using reasoned supports.

Sometimes a person's argument is logical but his or her reasoning is in error. The British scientists who reasoned that the General Motors design for a diesel locomotive was theoretically impossible were shocked when Boss Kettering showed them one in action. When they asked how they could have been so wrong, Kettering replied that they weren't illogical, "they just started out wrong."

The sender should also consider how much reasoned support is needed. This will depend in part on how much receivers already know about the issue or how much credibility they perceive the sender to have. If receivers are not aware of or misjudge a source's high credibility, they may judge the message to be short on support. Remember, credibility carries some of its own proof if the issue at hand is related to the sender's expertise. An astronaut would not need as much evidence on the subject of weightlessness as a nonastronaut. But he or she might need considerable support if the topic were modern art. When the goal is justified and is not illogical and the means have sufficient reason, a more emotional appeal *is* sometimes ethical. Receivers must sort out relationships between seemingly unrelated claims and grounds before branding the reasoning fallacious. They must exercise tolerance according to the sender's intent, but only to a point. The most notable intent does not justify unrepresentative facts or faulty reasoning. A receiver's obligation is to recognize blatant fallacies, know how to challenge them, and then challenge.

SUMMING UP

Other things being equal, good, clear reasoning and argument should promote your persuasion. Extrinsic proof deals with facts in the world about us or statements based upon facts—self evident, observable phenomena. Intrinsic proof depends upon reasoned effort on our part—upon the application of rhetoric and logic. The most useful sources of logical support are authorities, examples, and statistics.

Four basic forms of reasoning are: (1) from cause, (2) from generalization, (3) from analogy, and (4) from sign. The Toulmin pattern of argument includes the following elements of argument: claims, grounds, warrants, backing, qualifiers, and rebuttals. One is advised to first determine the underlying purpose of the argument and then evaluate as follows: (1) the *grounds* must be sufficient to support the *claim;* (2) the *warrant* must be applicable and based on solid *backing;* (3) exceptions and possible *rebuttals* must be considered.

There are four major types of fallacies: (1) overgeneralization, (2) false cause, (3) begging the question, and (4) ignoring or ducking the issue. Specific cases of the last type attack the personal character of an opponent rather than the issue, appeal to popular prejudices and passions, appeal to authority and dignity for inappropriate subjects, and appeal to audience ignorance.

STUDY PROJECTS
AND TASKS

1. Search a newspaper or newsmagazine and locate three good examples of the use of persuasive evidence. Try to find one of each of the following:
   a. statement by authorities
   b. example or illustration
   c. statistics
2. Check your thinking habits on the following items and discuss:
   a. An archeologist found a coin marked 45 B.C. How old was it?
   b. If you divided 30 by ½ plus 10, how much would you have?
   c. Which side of a horse has more hair?
   d. How far can a dog walk into the woods?
   e. If you went to bed at eight and set the alarm to ring at nine in the morning, how many hours of sleep would you get?
   f. Does England have a Fourth of July?
3. Find or create an example of each of the four forms of reasoning: from cause, from generalization, from analogy, from sign.

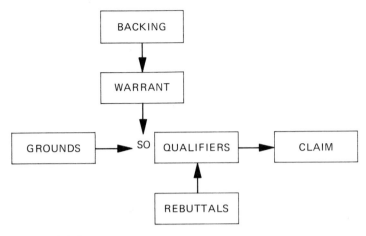

FIGURE 7-4

4. Set up a proposition or claim (for example, Billy Sims will play for the Houston Gamblers) and diagram your argument using the elements of argument discussed in this chapter.

5. Search the newspapers and locate two examples of fallacious reasoning. Define and explain the fallacies in terms of the discussion of fallacies in this chapter.

6. Prepare a two-to-three-minute oral exercise in which you attempt to use as many fallacies as possible. See if you can fool your classmates, but be prepared to explain your sophistry should you prove too successful at deceiving them.

7. Prepare a detailed two-to-three-page outline for a two-to-three-minute persuasive one-point speech in which you use primarily the logical supports of persuasion (authority, examples, statistics, forms of reasoning, and elements of argument).

8. Critically evaluate the logical support for your classmates' speeches. Watch especially for fallacious reasoning. Write out your critiques and be prepared to cross-examine each speaker.

8
Campaign Persuasion

Social Movements
Campaigns
        General Stages
        Dramatistic Description and Analysis
        Psychological Description and Analysis
Mass-Communication Aspects of Campaigns
        Innovation-decision Process
        Opinion Leaders
        Adopter Categories
        Social-system Structure
Codes and Regulations of Conduct
        Professional Standards for Public-relations Campaigns
        Code of Ethics for Political-Campaign Advertising
        Principles of Journalism
        Code of the National Association of Broadcasters
Summing Up
Study Projects and Tasks

In this chapter we discuss persuasion over time—persuasion that comes about through a series of events and persuasive efforts. When the persuasion consists of systematic efforts of relatively short duration, we call it a *campaign*. When the persuasion is prompted by spontaneous events followed by long-term planned and unplanned motivation, we call it a *movement*.[1]

SOCIAL MOVEMENTS

Examples of social movements are the antiwar protests of the 1960s, the black search for equality and identity, and the women's and ecology movements of today. Campaigns are usually a large part of a movement once directions and limited goals emerge. Forced busing and affirmative-action campaigns have been part of the black movement (as well as other movements). The Equal Rights Amendment (ERA) is a campaign associated with the women's movement.

If our interest in movements lies primarily in their tactics and strategies, we should consider these questions offered by Charles Stewart, which we have shortened and rearranged for our purposes.

HOW DO SOCIAL MOVEMENTS:
1. Propose or defend their strategies and tactics?
2. Alter proposals or defenses of strategies and tactics when communicating with different target audiences?
3. [Adjust] as they encounter changing rhetorical situations and unexpected events?
4. [Adjust] when they encounter varying degrees of opposition from inside and outside of the movement?
5. [Adjust or respond] when the opposition aims its criticism at specific strategies or tactics?
6. [Adjust] as they progress from stage to stage, and eventually approach termination, because of age, oppression, failure or institutionalization?[2]

Charles Reed, combining a sociological model of movements with Kenneth Boulding's concept of image, hypothesizes that a "movement can progress from one stage to the next as it is able to modify the existing images of the receivers." He suggested that five major image alterations must occur during a successful movement:

---

[1]For an excellent discussion of different ways of studying movements, see the entire issue of *Central States Speech Journal*, 31, no. 4 (Winter 1980). See also Bernard L. Brock, ed., "Special Report: Social Movements," *Central States Speech Journal*, 34, no. 1 (Spring 1983), 67–82.

[2]Charles J. Stewart, "A Functional Perspective on the Study of Social Movements," *Central States Speech Journal*, 34, no. 1 (Spring 1983), 77–80.

MOVEMENT STAGES
1. in the stage of social unrest, a change by the masses from frustration and discontent to hope for a better future
2. in the stage of collective excitement, a change by the establishment from indifference toward the movement to fear of its gains
3. in the stage of formal organization, a change by the movement from respect for the institution to hatred of its policies and leaders
4. also in the stage of formal organization, a change by the institutional moderates from a mediating position between the rival factions to identification with the movement
5. in the stage of institutionalization, a change by the movement, the establishment, and the masses from hostility toward one another to the necessity of peace and reunion[3]

These five stages have also been described as a life cycle which goes through: (1) genesis, (2) social unrest, (3) enthusiastic mobilization, (4) maintenance, and (5) termination.[4]

For some theorists, a movement goes through three broad rhetorical stages: (1) mobilization, (2) exercise of external influence, and (3) resistance to counterinfluence. Within these stages the movement has the following specific tasks:

MOVEMENT TASKS
1. justifying the movement's mission to its constituents and to third parties
2. infusing the mission with a sense of urgency
3. acquiring material and nonmaterial resources
4. organizing activists into a disciplined and cohesive unit
5. gratifying constituents' personal needs
6. selling to or imposing upon the movement's targets its program for action
7. discrediting oppositions
8. countering efforts at social control[5]

Leland Griffin, who is concerned with the broader aspects of movements, suggests the following focus for analysis:

[3]From Charles R. Reed, "Image Alteration in a Mass Movement: A Rhetorical Analysis of the Role of the Log College in the Great Awakening," *Dissertation Abstracts International*, 33 (February 1973), 4571–A.

[4]Charles Stewart, Craig Smith, and Robert E. Denton, Jr., *Persuasion and Social Movements* (Prospect Heights, Il.: Waveland Press, 1984), p. 37.

[5]From Herbert W. Simons, Elizabeth Mechling, and Howard N. Schrier, "Functions of Communication in Mobilizing for Collective Action From the Bottom Up: The Rhetoric of Social Movements," in *Handbook of Rhetorical and Communication Theory*, eds. Carroll C. Arnold and John W. Bowers (Boston: Allyn & Bacon, 1983).

Let us say that an historical movement has occurred when, at some time in the past: 1. men have become *dissatisfied* with some aspect of their environment; 2. they desire change—social, economic, political, religious, intellectual, or otherwise—and desiring change, they make efforts to alter their environment; 3. eventually, their efforts result in some degree of success or failure; the desired change is, or is not, effected; and we may say that the historical movement has come to its termination.[6]

Griffin specifically suggests that a movement contains three phases of development: *inception, rhetorical crisis,* and *consummation.*[7] *Inception* usually involves some striking event that captures the attention of a share of the public. The *rhetorical-crisis* period involves pro-con exchanges between spokespersons who succeed in bringing the issue to a head. The *consummation* period finds some resolution of the crisis: ERA is passed; the war is at an end.

In a study of the Black Action Movement, Bruce Gronbeck postulated the following rhetorical functions. (The three phases proposed by Griffin are shown at the left.)

RHETORICAL FUNCTIONS	
INCEPTION PHASE	1. Defining: Somebody or some group takes the first step. A problem is defined and a solution is urged.
	2. Legitimizing: Legitimizers can lend positive authority, a regional or national presence to a budding movement.
RHETORICAL CRISIS PHASE	3. In-gathering: The movement builds a power base, a group of adherents ready to talk, march, and fight for the cause.
	4. Pressuring: The movement also mounts a campaign urging reform or revolution.
CONSUMMATION PHASE	5. Compromising: After direct confrontation, usually some sort of compromise must be worked out.
	6. Satisfying: Leaders must be able to return to the masses of their movement, proclaiming victory, even if only partial gains have been made.[8]

Movements provide a background or context for better understanding campaigns that relate to them. An advertising campaign may or may not relate to any special social movement. Some political campaigns (such as elections) may pretty much stand alone; others may reflect larger political movements.

[6]Quoted in Bernard L. Brock and Robert L. Scott, *Methods of Rhetorical Criticism: A Twentieth Century Perspective* (Detroit: Wayne State University Press, 1980), p. 397.

[7]See Leland M. Griffin, "A Dramatistic Theory of the Rhetoric of Movements," in *Kenneth Burke,* ed. W. H. Rueckert (Minneapolis: University of Minnesota Press, 1969), pp. 456–78.

[8]From Bruce Gronbeck, "The Rhetoric of Social-Institutional Change: Black Action at Michigan," in *Explorations in Rhetorical Criticism,* eds. Gerald P. Mohrman, Charles Stewart, and Donovan Ochs (University Park, Pa.: Pennsylvania State University Press, 1973), pp. 96–113.

CAMPAIGNS

Campaigns generally involve three primary persuasive orientations: (1) efforts to improve the *image* of an organization or person; (2) the
selling of a *product* (or service); and (3) efforts to form or change attitudes on an
issue. All three start with a felt difficulty, need, or sense of urgency. Lloyd Bitzer
calls this a rhetorical *exigence:* "a defect, an obstacle, something waiting to be
done, a thing which is other than it should be."[9] Foul weather, a flat tire, death,
and earthquakes are obvious exigencies, but these cannot be modified by
persuasion and hence are not rhetorical. The initial problem must be
modifiable by persuasion and discourse.

The campaign situation must also be rhetorical. The receivers of the
persuasion must have some capacity for being influenced and must be at least
modest mediators of change.

The campaign situation also involves *constraints* on the actions needed to
resolve the problem. Attitudes, images, interests, traditions, and credibility are
among these constraints.

Several institutions, such as *advertising, political groups, social groups, and
public-relations organizations* make use of these three campaign orientations.
Their use is part of the general strategy to be considered in a campaign. Some
are more a part of one orientation than another. Advertising, for example, is
clearly a large part of any campaign to sell a product.

General Stages

Effective campaigns demand planning, effort, promotion, and
follow-up. Five basic tasks are generally considered in the planning of a
campaign:

1. *Identifying the effects and goals desired:* What kind of an image? How much market
   expansion? What kind of service? How much attitude change? What major and
   minor issues? What is the urgency? What is the rhetorical exigence?
2. *Selecting and/or analyzing the audience(s):* What is the target audience? What is its
   susceptibility to influence? How might its members mediate or affect change?
   How do we know who they are? What is their latitude of attitude?
3. *Planning the persuasive strategy:* What is our basic message? How should it be
   handled—one-sided or two-sided? hard or soft? logical or emotional? What
   persuasion theories should we apply? Timing—what should we be doing, and
   when? What are the legal and ethical constraints?
4. *Detailing the transmission of messages:* Who will be responsible for what? What
   media will we use, and when? What coordination is necessary? Do we meet the
   ethical codes of the media and agencies involved?
5. *Evaluating success:* What measures of image change and attitude or opinion
   change are available? What behaviors suggest success or failure: votes, sales,

[9]Quoted in Douglas Ehninger, *Contemporary Rhetoric* (Glenview, Ill.: Scott, Foresman, 1972),
p. 43.

complaints, publicity, profits? What measurements should we initiate: attitude surveys, opinion polls? Did we fairly meet the legal and ethical codes governing strategy and methods? Where are we in terms of future campaigns?

THE NELSON ROCKEFELLER PRESIDENTIAL CAMPAIGN OF 1960

His organization was specialized so that a division did reconnaissance work among Republican party and financial leaders; a speech-writing unit gathered information, generated ideas and prepared speeches on national and world issues; an "image" staff of Madison Avenue talents was assigned the problem of personal public relations; a scheduling unit did the "advance" work and arranged Rockefeller's trips and appearances; press relations were entrusted to the Governor's press secretary in Albany; and a citizens' division carried on the function of dealing with potential public supporters.[10]

If your campaign candidate is female, the data in Figure 8–1 might be of special interest in either the planning or the follow-up stages.

The campaign model in Figure 8–2 condenses the five tasks listed above into the three stages of *planning, promotion,* and *follow-up.* It suggests appropriate questions for campaign analysis.

The five-stage model of campaign tasks in Figure 8–3 has also been proposed. This model is quite clear except perhaps for the word *legitimation.* For the campaign to achieve legitimation is for it to achieve a level of *credibility*—that is, to be taken seriously by the receivers it seeks.

Some scholars who have examined the campaigns of emerging nations suggest five similar steps: *identification, legitimacy, participation, penetration,* and *distribution.*[11] The *identification* step consists of providing a recognizable "handle," or name, whether for a new nation or a new product. *Legitimacy* is the same as legitimation. The campaign establishes a legitimate credibility, demonstrating that it can support its identity. In the *participation* step more people become directly involved. *Penetration* is the extension of the campaign

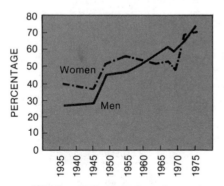

FIGURE 8–1

Historical Trends in Percentages of American Men and Women Who Are Willing To Vote for a Woman Presidential Candidate

From Stuart Oskamp, *Attitudes and Opinions* (Englewood Cliffs, N.J.: Prentice-Hall, 1977), p. 350.

---

[10]Wallace C. Fotheringham, *Perspectives on Persuasion* (Boston: Allyn & Bacon, 1966), p. 234.

[11]Leonard Binder et al., *Crisis and Sequence in Political Development* (Princeton, N.J.: Princeton University Press, 1971). See also Charles U. Larson, *Persuasion: Reception and Responsibility,* 3rd. ed. (Belmont, Calif.: Wadsworth, 1983), pp. 168–74.

1. *The Planning Stage*
   a. What were the effects and goals desired?
   b. What was the target audience? Why?
   c. What were the major roadblocks or constraints?
   d. What was the basic persuasion strategy?
2. *The Promotion Stage*
   a. What resources were mobilized?
   b. What media were used? Why?
   c. How was the persuasion strategy applied?
   d. At what point did the campaign achieve credibility?
3. *The Follow-Up Stage*
   a. What results indicated success or failure?
   b. Did the campaign meet ethical standards?
   c. What should have been done differently?

FIGURE 8–2   Three-stage Campaign Model

FIGURE 8–3   Campaign Stages and their Components

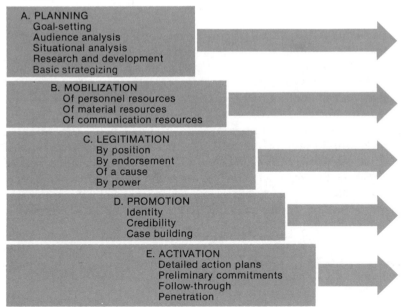

START

A. PLANNING
Goal-setting
Audience analysis
Situational analysis
Research and development
Basic strategizing

B. MOBILIZATION
Of personnel resources
Of material resources
Of communication resources

C. LEGITIMATION
By position
By endorsement
Of a cause
By power

D. PROMOTION
Identity
Credibility
Case building

E. ACTIVATION
Detailed action plans
Preliminary commitments
Follow-through
Penetration

to newer markets. (Ford may penetrate the Chevrolet part of the automobile market.) The *distribution* step makes available the goals and rewards of a campaign, whether they be products or social reforms. The campaign must show accountability and make good on its promises.

Dramatistic Description and Analysis

Kenneth Burke views movements and campaigns as a kind of drama with a recurring plot. He borrows five terms from drama—*act, scene, agent, agency,* and *purpose*—to help us understand what happens as a campaign unfolds. Burke considers these terms to be interdependent. That is, they function as a system making up the campaign.[12] Thus, they are important not only in isolation but as they relate to one another. The degrees of interrelationship of the terms can provide the student of campaigns or movements with a flexible and accurate method of describing the drama of an unfolding campaign.

BURKE'S PENTAD
1. ACT: What was done?
2. SCENE: When or where was it done?
3. AGENT: Who did it?
4. AGENCY: How was it done?
5. PURPOSE: Why was it done?

In this system the structure and bureaucracy of society provide all of us with a role that we sometimes accept and sometimes reject. When we reject or are out of step with this social *order* it is as if the order is *polluted.* This pollution leads to a sense of *guilt.* We strive tirelessly to cancel this guilt and thereby *purify* ourselves and attain the general goal of *redemption* (salvation or rescue). These five—pollution, guilt, purification, and redemption—are thought to be good benchmarks for describing a campaign or movement. According to Bernard Brock and Robert Scott, they also offer the critic a theoretical framework and vocabulary with which he or she can judge the effectiveness of persuasion.[13] Surely the Watergate affair is amenable to this kind of analysis. The nation found itself in conflict with the hierarchy (the establishment). Guilt was everywhere. The lengthy hearings and trials were examples of purification and ultimately redemption.

---

[12]Kenneth Burke, *The Grammar of Motives and the Rhetoric of Motives* (Cleveland: World, 1962), p. 544. Burke refers to the five terms as the *pentad.*

[13]Brock and Scott, *Methods of Rhetorical Critism,* pp. 349–51.

Psychological Description and Analysis

Psychological description and analysis of campaigns are based on the consistency, social-judgment or assimilation-contrast, both-sides, cognitive-response, and other theories of psychological persuasion discussed in previous chapters. Though more psychological than rhetorical in origin, such evaluation and description constitute a large part of what is called contemporary rhetoric.

The use of *consistency* theory in a campaign, whether consciously or unconsciously, can usually be discovered through the persuader's strong efforts to make people uncomfortable about an issue. Remember that this theory assumes people prefer a consistent set of relationships between what they know of the world and their latest perception of it. It assumes people will actively avoid situations and information that will increase the dissonance or inconsistency they feel. The campaign strategist may find, for example, that the suburban citizens he or she is addressing do not know about urban blight, yet they feel they are responsible people. To make them feel inconsistent, dissonant, or uncomfortable, the strategist may spend a lot of his or her campaign efforts (and wisely so) bringing these attitudes into association. The audience's efforts to reduce the inconsistency will, the strategist hopes, alter their attitudes about the problem of urban blight. Theoretically, they will be more amenable to the specific program the campaigners have in mind to resolve urban blight. If some of the citizens were avoiding this uncomfortable issue, the campaigners might use more confrontation—perhaps pictures or other evidence of the spread of urban blight to nearby areas. The campaigners would attempt to involve people in the issue. If the analysis indicates that there is already considerable dissonance, then the campaigners will seek to show that their program meets the problem with less discomfort than others. Some people will change their attitudes because of the campaign, some will reject or modify the argument of the campaign, and some will avoid the issue and the campaign. These are all ways of reducing discomfort or inconsistency. The campaign strategist makes good use of this knowledge.

When *assimilation-contrast* or *social-judgment* theory is a large part of a campaign, it will be detected by how hard or vigorously the campaigners push (or don't push) a point. Remember that according to this theory, people have latitudes or ranges of acceptance, rejection, and noncommitment. The theory clearly suggests that if your persuasion is overly strong and falls way beyond a person's (or public's) range of acceptance, you will encounter reverse persuasion. The campaign strategy is to go to the very edge of the public's range of acceptance (or into the noncommitment area). This, the theory tells us, will cause the receivers to assimilate the message and perceive it to be closer to their attitudes than it really is.

The campaign should be characterized by a greater-than-usual amount of sensitive audience analysis. Placing the persuasion is dependent on knowing the ranges of attitude you are apt to be dealing with. An affirmative-action campaign that bluntly asked that incompetents be hired would probably fall so far outside the range of acceptance of most people that it would create reverse persuasion and be hurt rather than helped.

Some early women's-rights campaigns were less than successful with housewives who had generally been sympathetic with the movement. Harsh persuasion was placed far outside their latitude of acceptance, and they rejected the persuasion.

Of course, you can't persuade all segments of your audience, but you should be aware of these segments and recognize what you give up or lose when you decide on a particular persuasive strategy. Assimilation-contrast theory can help campaigners know why they are (or were) apt to be more successful with some segments of their audience than with others.

When *both-sides* persuasion is used extensively in a campaign, we should be able to detect it by its concessions. Remember that both-sides theory predicts that (1) some people are more readily persuaded by arguments that include some acknowledgment or concession to the other side, and (2) all people are more resistant to counterpersuasion if they are first forewarned (or inoculated).

You should find the material in Chapter 6 on both-sides persuasion valuable in assessing campaign strategy. Antagonism is part of most campaigns, but when it is unusually intense, wise campaigners will rely on both-sides theory. Two-sided persuasion also works well with sophisticated audiences, but it may backfire with unsophisticated groups who are already somewhat convinced of the position the campaigner is advocating. However, if the latter group is apt to meet a clever campaigner of the opposite persuasion, the first campaigner may have to make some tough strategy decisions. Sales campaigns by the liquor industry have made good use of both-sides theory (see Figure 8–4).

In our discussion in Chapter 1 of the functions that attitudes serve, we learned that attitudes help protect people's egos. Campaign strategists often direct their appeals at these needs for ego defense. In doing so they walk a psychological (as well as ethical) tightrope, for too much of such an appeal may cause the receivers to despair and ignore them. On the other hand, enough is needed to cause the necessary dissonance or inconsistency. Campaigns can break down when the strategists misread temporary ego defense as a long-term attitude. A Nazi campaigner may hear frustrated people say, "I've had enough of minorities. What about the majority?" His opportunistic appeals may effect some momentary success, but once the projection (and frustration) ceases he may find that such a campaign backfires. Nevertheless, it is clear that some campaigners try to take advantage of our conflicts and frustrations.

Dramatistic and psychological notions can probably be better used in describing and evaluating rather than planning a campaign. In the 1960s, some postriot campaigns to supply food to inner-city rioters and victims were

enormously successful in the suburbs. Surely some of this was "purification," or compensatory behavior for feelings of guilt.

People's egos can make or break campaign persuasion. An unintended insult to an ethnic group can undo an entire political campaign. One joke about minorities by Earl Butz cost him his job as secretary of agriculture. In analyzing campaigns for ego-defense tactics, look for such incidents and consider their impact and how the campaigners (and their opposition) reacted.

MASS–COMMUNICATION ASPECTS OF CAMPAIGNS

Campaigns occur over time. Persuasion fails to gain campaign status unless large groups of people are reached. This section explains how audience behavior is taken into account by campaign strategists.

Whether the persuaders are interested in changing an image, selling a product, or changing attitudes on an issue, they are trying to get a mass audience to adopt an innovation. An *innovation* can be an idea, attitude, or product. What makes it an innovation is that it is *new* or different from what the audience has experienced.

In campaigns the sender normally cannot *directly* influence every individual of the social system he or she is trying to reach. The persuader must depend on individuals to spread the word to other individuals. These people influence still other people until a large number have adopted the innovation being promoted.

Mass-communicated messages aimed at the mass audience will have little persuasive effect if the members of that audience fail to talk to one another about the message. An understanding of the *innovation-decision process, opinion leaders, adopter categories,* and *social-system structure* will greatly aid the campaign manager and the campaign analyst.

Innovation–decision Process

Research has shown that members of a mass audience go through four basic steps in adopting an idea: knowledge, persuasion, decision, and confirmation.[14] In the *knowledge* step the audience is simply made aware of the innovation. The campaign strategists, when they have access to the mass media, can make people aware through advertising, campaigning, slogans, and so forth. The actual persuasion and decision steps are contingent upon the interpersonal influence of significant others or opinion leaders within the social system. Once the decision to adopt the innovation or idea has been

---

[14]Everett M. Rogers and F. Floyd Shoemaker, *Communication of Innovations: A Cross Cultural Approach,* 2nd ed. (New York: Free Press, 1971), p. 25.

made, the change agent can reinforce or *confirm* the decision through the mass media.

Opinion Leaders

Opinion leaders have the most direct and powerful persuasive affect on people in the social system. Campaign strategists are well advised to tailor their messages so that they will influence opinion leaders within the social system. Everett M. Rogers and F. Floyd Shoemaker suggest that opinion leaders have the following characteristics.

1. They tend to be able to informally influence other's behavior and attitudes and tend to be held in high esteem by others.
2. They tend to be more aware and responsive to communication originating outside the social system.
3. They tend to be more cosmopolitan or eclectic in their ideas and attitudes than their followers.
4. They tend to be more predisposed toward change (innovativeness).[15]

Finding and influencing opinion leaders significantly affects the success of a campaign.

Adopter Categories

As we have suggested, campaigns are not one-shot persuasive affairs. They develop over time. The entire social system is not instantly persuaded. Certain people within the social system tend to be more innovative than others. Research has defined five basic categories of people who adopt an innovation. They are defined below in the order that they can be expected to be persuaded.

1. *Innovators:* These are the first to adopt. They tend to be only fringe members of the social system and can afford the potential negative consequences of adopting the new idea or innovation.
2. *Early Adopters:* They tend to be well-integrated, higher-status members of the social system. Most opinion leaders are located in this category.
3. *Early Majority:* They tend to be average members of the social system. They tend to make use of mass-media communication channels more than other social system members.
4. *Late Majority:* They tend to be somewhat below average in social status. They tend to come under more direct influence of peers through interpersonal communication.
5. *Laggards:* These are the last members of the social system to be persuaded. They tend to be highly traditional in their socialization.[16]

[15]Ibid., p. 35.
[16]Ibid., p. 27.

Social–system Structure

Social systems themselves place constraints on the acceptability and rate of diffusion of new ideas within them. The campaign strategist must tailor the messages so that they function as effectively as possible within the social structure.

Social systems' norms vary on a continuum ranging from modern to traditional. It should be stressed that most social systems fall somewhere between the two. According to Rogers and Shoemaker, modern social systems (as opposed to traditional social systems) have the following characteristics:

1. Positive feelings toward change
2. Positive attitudes toward science and education
3. A more complex division of labor
4. A more rational attitude toward social relations as opposed to familial
5. More cosmopolitan perspectives: tend to interact more with others outside the social system[17]

Obviously, a campaign for a new product would most likely be met with less resistance in a modern social system than in a more traditional system. In a traditional social system the change agent's primary efforts should be directed at influencing opinion leaders.

CODES AND REGULATIONS OF CONDUCT

Your planning and analyzing of campaigns should involve ethics. In a legally constituted democracy the law also becomes a campaign obligation. American laws and professional rules or codes of ethics address primarily the means and methods of persuasion, not so much its content. Free speech permits you to speak on either side of the abortion issue. Our advertising laws and codes are most specific about the means. The American Civil Liberties Union may not particularly approve of the Nazi party or the Ku Klux Klan, but they will vigorously defend their right to be heard. However, should these groups pursue their goals through illegal and unethical *means* they will be legally tried with equal vigor. Ethical persuasion demands honesty; pressure free of violence; perceived choice; tolerance for legitimate strategy; fair hearing; and a willingness to comply with persuasion from legitimate authority. Campaigners have a responsibility for the strategies they employ and for their social consequences. In most codes, techniques and strategies are unethical when they are dishonest, unfair to the facts, or so subtle as to be deceptive.

[17]Ibid., pp. 32–33.

In addition to these general guidelines for evaluating campaign persuasion, many useful, specific codes and rules are available. These come from public-relations, advertising, and publicity organizations, among many others. These are fair and reasonable criteria for us to apply to campaigns. Some selected examples follow. Check the footnotes for the location of the complete code.

Professional Standards for Public-relations Campaigns

1. A member shall not engage in any practice which tends to corrupt the integrity of channels of public communication.
2. A member shall not intentionally disseminate false or misleading information and is obligated to use ordinary care to avoid dissemination of false or misleading information.
3. A member shall be prepared to identify to the public the source of any communication for which he is responsible, including the name of the client or employer on whose behalf the communication is made.
4. A member shall not make use of any individual or organization purporting to serve or represent some announced cause, or purporting to be independent or unbiased, but actually serving an undisclosed special or private interest of a member or his client or his employer.[18]

Advertising Code of American Business

1. **Truth** Advertising shall tell the truth, and shall reveal significant facts, the concealment of which would misled the public.
2. **Responsibility** Advertising agencies and advertisers shall be willing to provide substantiation of claims made.
3. **Taste and Decency** Advertising shall be free of statements, illustrations, or implications which are offensive to good taste or public decency.
4. **Disparagement** Advertisement shall offer merchandise or service on its merits, and refrain from attacking competitors unfairly or disparaging their products, services, or methods of doing business.
5. **Bait Advertising** Advertising shall offer only merchandise or services which are readily available for purchase at the advertised price.
6. **Guarantees and Warranties** Advertising of guarantees and warranties shall be explicit. Advertising of any guarantee or warranty shall clearly and conspicuously disclose its nature and extent, the manner in which the guarantor or warrantor will perform, and the identity of the guarantor or warrantor.
7. **Price Claims** Advertising shall avoid price or savings claims which are false or misleading, or which do not offer provable bargains or savings.

---

[18]Public Relations Society of America, "Declaration of Principles: Code of Professional Standards for the Practice of Public Relations With Interpretations." See your library or Doug Newsom and Alan Scott, *This Is PR: The Realities of Public Relations* (Belmont, Calif.: Wadsworth, 1976), pp. 265–93.

8. **Unprovable Claims** Advertising shall avoid the use of exaggerated or unprovable claims.

9. **Testimonials** Advertising containing testimonials shall be limited to those of competent witnesses who are reflecting a real and honest choice.[19]

Code of Ethics for Political–Campaign Advertising

1. ☐ The advertising agency should not represent any candidate who has not signed or who does not observe the Code of Fair Campaign Practices of the Fair Campaign Practices Committee endorsed by the American Association of Advertising Agencies.

2. ☐ The agency should not knowingly misrepresent the views of stated record of any candidates nor quote them out of proper context.

3. ☐ The agency should not prepare any material which unfairly or prejudicially exploits the race, creed or national origin of any candidate.

4. ☐ The agency should take care to avoid unsubstantiated charges and accusations, especially those deliberately made too late in the campaign for opposing candidates to answer.

5. ☐ The agency should stand as an independent judge of fair campaign practices, rather than automatically yield to the wishes of the candidate or his authorized representatives.

6. ☐ The agency should not indulge in any practices which might be deceptive or misleading in word, photograph, film, or sound.[20]

Principles of Journalism

1. Responsibility
2. Freedom of the press
3. Independence
4. Truth and accuracy
5. Impartiality
6. Fair play[21]

Sigma Delta Chi, the Society of Professional Journalists, was more specific. Their updated code (1973) details what is meant by responsibility, freedom of the press, ethics, accuracy and objectivity, and fair play.

---

[19]Created, developed, and distributed by the American Advertising Federation and the Association of Better Business Bureaus International.

[20]Adopted by the Board of Directors of the American Association of Advertising Agencies, February 22, 1968.

[21]Code of ethics adopted by the American Society of Newspaper Editors, October 23, 1975.

Code of the National
Association of Broadcasters

Sections IV, VII, VIII, and IX of the National Association of Broadcasters' code pertain to all campaign strategists and critics. They enable us to better understand the constraints on campaign persuasion.[22]

Section IV consists of *special program standards*. It explains the rules for dealing with violence, narcotics, discrimination, obscenity, family life, fictional dramatizations, and even subliminal communication.

Section VII is concerned with *political telecasts*. It can also help receivers better understand campaign persuasion. It states that political telecasts should be clearly identified as such. They should not be presented by a television broadcaster in a manner that would lead listeners or viewers to believe that the program is of any other character.

Although there is very little federal regulation of the message content of the broadcast media, you should be aware of two critical components of broadcast law that apply to political campaigns: the *fairness doctrine* and the *equal-time provision*. Both laws are "policed" by the Federal Communications Commission. If broadcasters fail to meet the letter of these laws, they run the risk of losing their license.

The fairness doctrine applies primarily to controversial issues. Broadcasters are required by law to give fair treatment to all sides of controversial issues of public interest. This does not mean that all sides of an issue must be given equal air time—it only suggests equitable treatment.

The equal-time provision applies only to the exposure of political candidates during campaigns. Broadcasters are required by law to offer all political candidates equal amounts and *quality* of air time. Offering one candidate a one-minute television spot at nine o'clock in the evening and another candidate a one-minute spot at one o'clock in the morning would be a violation of the equal-time provision because the quality of air time would be different.

Section VIII pertains to *religious programs*. If you are concerned with the advantages and constraints resulting from the use of media in religious campaigns, then you will find section F of the radio code even more specific in this area.

Section IX covers *general advertising standards*. These apply specifically to telecommunication but are necessary reading for anyone interested in advertising campaigns. The standards cover such topics as integrity of the advertisers, objectionable products and services, exaggerated claims or promises, and good taste.

Standards of broadcast ethics reflect the law of the land and generally the

[22]Under U.S. District Court Judge Harold Greene's order of November 23, 1982, the National Association of Broadcasters is enjoined from "distributing" any code concerning television commercial time standards.

codes of the responsible agencies shown above. They also reflect the codes of the legal, educational, and medical associations.

SUMMING UP

Campaigns are persuasive efforts over time through a series of events and strategies. When the persuasion is prompted by spontaneous events followed by long-term planned and unplanned motivation, we call it a movement. Movements go through phases. One scheme suggests: (1) inception phase (defining and legitimizing the cause or problem), (2) rhetorical crisis phase (in-gathering of adherents and pressuring), (3) consummation phase (compromising and proclaiming gains).

There are three primary campaign orientations: (1) efforts to improve the *image* of an organization or person, (2) the selling of a *product* or service, and (3) efforts to form or change attitudes on an *issue*. A campaign must be rhetorical, the receivers must have some capability for being influenced, and be mediators of change. Effective campaigns demand planning, effort, promotion, and follow-up. Five basic functions are involved: (1) identifying effects and goals, (2) selecting and analyzing the audience, (3) planning the strategy, (4) detailing the messages, and their transmission, and (5) evaluating success. Some suggest a dramatistic model for describing campaigns. Kenneth Burke's pentad involves: (1) *act* (What was done?), (2) *scene* (When or where was it done?), (3) *agent* (Who did it?), (4) *agency* (How was it done?), and (5) *purpose* (Why was it done?).

Campaign analyses derived from psychological descriptions are based on the consistency, social judgment, assimilation-contrast, both-sides, cognitive response, and other persuasion theories. They can be used for evaluation as well as description.

Mass communication audiences go through four steps in the *adoption* of an idea: knowledge, persuasion, decision, and confirmation. Campaign strategists should tailor their messages to influence *opinion leaders* who are thought to be more disposed toward adopting change. Adopter categories are: *innovators* (the first to adopt), *early adopters* (high status members of society), *early majority* (average members), *late majority* (below average in social status), and *laggards* (highly traditional in socialization).

Social systems place constraints on the acceptability of new ideas. Modern social systems offer less resistance than more traditional ones. In the latter the persuasion should be directed at opinion leaders.

Campaigners have an ethical responsibility for the strategies employed and for the social consequences that result. Campaigners are also responsible to the laws of the land, and the codes and regulations of related professions. Some of these are: Public Relations Society of America, Advertising Code of

American Business, American Association of Advertising Agencies, The Society of Professional Journalists, and the National Association of Broadcasters.

STUDY PROJECTS AND TASKS

1. Make a brief study of
   a. a political action campaign
   b. a product- or service-advertising campaign
   c. an image campaign
   d. an issue-oriented campaign.

As a basis for your analysis use the descriptive sequences or systems discussed in Chapter 8. Also see Chapters 4 and 6. In an introduction state the specific purpose of the campaign and identify the analytic scheme you will use. Clearly label the main steps or phases in your outline. Include a brief evaluation of success. See the models in Appendix B. Your analysis should not exceed four typed, double-spaced sheets. You should be prepared to present a seven-to-ten-minute oral report in class.

SOME CAMPAIGN TOPICS

Note that some are current, some historical; some are local, others national; some are personal, some are conducted by professional agencies. They all teach lessons about campaign persuasion. Some are part of movements; others are not.

Jimmy Carter's presidential campaign
Boy Scouts of America (ongoing)
A church recruitment campaign
The Jonestown campaign
The Edsel campaign (Ford Motor Company)
Automobile rebates
Census promotion
The FBI's new-look campaign
University recruitment campaign
Bell long-distance campaign ("Reach Out")
Draft registration
Nixon's 1968 presidential campaign (why he won)
People's Park, Berkeley, California, 1968
X cars (General Motors)
Semta Park and Ride (bus)
The BBC in the Middle East
Health Occupations Students of America (HOSA)
"Go 4 It" (television-station campaign)
Farrah Fawcett—sex goddess
Chunky Soups (Campbell)

Presidency of student residence hall
New Detroit campaign
Repeal of Prohibition
WLLZ radio (share of market)
McDonalds' crew motivation
Racial tension (Denby High School)
Muscular dystrophy
New Chrysler Corporation image
Nixon's 1960 presidential campaign (why he lost)
Mayor Young's 1974 campaign
Afro-American Mission's summer program
1975–77 Cougar campaign (Ford Motor Company)
Delta Zeta rush
Disadvantaged students (Project 350)
Transcendental-meditation campaign
Hitler campaign, 1927–33
Antislavery campaign (Lincoln)
Preventive dentistry
Safe-toys campaign
Anti–drunk-driving campaign
Tylenol recovery
Say yes to Michigan

SOME SEQUENCES (see also Chapter 8)

Burke's Pentad	*Binder et al.*	*Griffin*
Act (what was done)	Identity	Inception
Scene (when or where)	Legitimacy	Rhetorical Crisis
Agent (who)	Participation	Consummation
Agency (how)	Penetration	
Purpose (why)	Distribution	
Simons	*Bitzer*	*Brock and Scott*
Planning	Exigence	Order
Mobilization	Audience	Pollution
Legitimation	Constraints	Guilt
Promotion		Purification
Activation		Redemption

TYPICAL CAMPAIGN ANALYSIS
(See also model, p. 187)
1. Identify the goals desired.
2. Identify the target audience.
   a. general description
   b. attitudes
3. Identify the persuasive strategy.
   a. rhetorical

> b. psychological
> c. ethical considerations
> 4. Implement the strategy.
>   a. organizational plan
>   b. use of media
>   c. ethical codes and standards
> 5. Evaluate success.
>   a. behaviors
>   b. attitudes
>   c. compliance with ethical code

2. Do a one-page historical analysis of an older campaign (such as the Watergate cover-up) in which you illustrate the fivefold sequence of order, pollution, guilt, purification, and redemption.

3. Describe the consumer movement and explain its development to date. What are some specific campaigns within the movement? Be prepared for a general class discussion.

4. Join a campus or community campaign. Keep a communication log of the persuasion principles and strategies that you observe.

5. Describe and illustrate a short-term advertising campaign. Explain how various persuasion theories and strategies were utilized.

6. Prepare a three-to-four-minute persuasive speech for a current campaign. Take one to two minutes to orient the class to the current situation.

7. View thirty minutes of television campaign materials and evaluate their ethics according to the standards (political, advertising, public-relations, and so forth) outlined in the last section of this chapter. Prepare to report orally for one to three minutes.

8. Analyze several print offerings (newspapers, magazines, and so forth) on a particular campaign and evaluate them according to the codes presented in the last section of this chapter.

Appendix A
Model Speech
Outlines

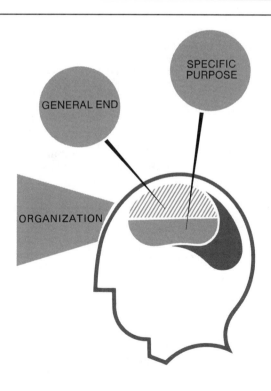

BOTH-SIDES ORGANIZATION

MANY HAPPY RETURNS

General End: To persuade (both-sides organization).

Specific Purpose: To persuade the class to put the environment first and to resist the campaign to repeal the deposit law.

Introduction

Attention

I. Are these a familiar sight to you?
    (Exhibits: several bottles and cans)
    A. As you know, last December third the deposit law went into effect.
        1. It requires a deposit on all beer and soft-drink containers.
        2. Deposits are then repaid when consumers return the containers for reuse or recycling.
    B. Since most of you probably drink soft drinks or beer, this law affects you directly.

Body (Con Side)

I. And you as consumers know this law does affect your pocketbook.
    A. The Can Manufacturing Institute's recent survey of shelf prices indicates that beer and soft drinks cost about one dollar a case more in Michigan than in states that don't have deposit laws.

Concessions to Con Side

    B. The Stroh Brewing Company and Coca-Cola of Detroit concede: "Unfortunately the cost of doing business has to be passed on."

II. Industry spokesmen show that the price increases are due to the extra handling that the law creates.
    A. When the consumer returns the bottles and cans, the retailer has to store them until the bottler picks them up.
    B. Many retailers and bottlers are complaining about storage problems and sanitation problems that increase costs.
        1. They need more warehouse space to store empties.
        2. They need bottle washers.
        3. They need additional delivery trucks to transport the empties.
        4. They also need to hire more drivers.

III. There are other complaints about the law.
    A. It eliminates some jobs in glassmaking (bottles are reused).
    B. The law probably wastes energy by forcing trucks to make additional trips with empty containers.

Body (Pro Side)

Transition

I. But if you really think about it, what are we supposed to do?
    A. Repeal the law, like the Associated Food Dealers want to do?
    B. Then go back to all the cans, bottles, and broken glass on our streets, highways, and landscaping?
    C. I think not; listen to the reasons for supporting our deposit law.

Evidence

II. Volunteers have recently staged a cleanup throughout the state.
    A. Of 9,000 items picked up, only 9 were returnables.
    B. Look at the differences in our roadsides and our neighborhoods (before-and-after pictures).
    C. Our litter fines obviously were not doing the job.

III. Five other states now have deposit laws.
  A. A survey in Oregon (whose law went into effect in 1972) says that 95% of the people still favor the law.
  B. Oregon's deposit return rate is 94 percent.
  C. In Vermont (which also has a deposit law) a study shows:
    1. A 76-percent decline in beverage litter.
    2. A 35-percent reduction in total litter volume.
    3. A 31-percent decline in state costs for litter pickup.
    4. The law has created about 400 new jobs in sorting, storing, and truck driving.
    5. Vermont figures that the container manufacturers save 708 million BTUs in energy annually as a result of recycling and reuse. (That's enough energy to heat the homes of 15,000 people.)

Meeting Objections

IV. The increase in the prices of beer and soft drinks may also be caused by other factors.
  A. The Michigan United Conservation Clubs recently asked the attorney general to investigate the increases in prices. They found:
    1. Many bottlers changed their product designs.
    2. Bottlers switched to metric volumes. (Display one half-liter Coke bottle.)
    3. Bottlers installed new equipment.
  B. These are new and mostly one-time costs.
  C. Once these costs are assimilated, bottle and can prices should drop.
    1. The average bottle is used over and over (about fifteen times).
    2. The aluminum cans are recycled over and over and over, which reduces the cost of aluminum and saves our natural resources.
    3. A Faygo spokesman said that the deposit law will result in some reduced prices after the new equipment is paid for.

Conclusion

Visualization

I. The deposit law is a way to deal with the problem of litter from beverage containers.
  A. Isn't it nice to see the Michigan streets cleaner again?
  B. Wouldn't it be even nicer to see the whole country cleaner?

  C. Because people have to pay a deposit on a container, it's more than likely they will return it rather than throw it around.

  D. As we have seen, the deposit law is not solely responsible for our current price increases.

  E. It may be inconvenient returning the containers, but isn't it worth the trouble?

Action   II. This law is a major step in cleaning up this country. Support the deposit law—resist the repeal campaign.

  A. If someone asks you to sign a petition to repeal the law, *don't do it.*

  B. If, by some chance, it comes on the ballot in 1983, vote to keep our deposit law.

  C. There is talk of a nationwide deposit law to clean up the whole country. I urge your support.

  III. The benefits greatly outweigh the inconvenience.

  A. Help keep Michigan and the nation clean.

  B. "Many happy returns."

From a student speech by Richard Mietlinen.

MOTIVATED-
SEQUENCE ORGANIZATION

A RAMPANT KILLER

General End: To persuade.

Specific Purpose: To persuade the audience that they should have their chests X-rayed.

Attention

Possible Procedures   I. There is a subtle killer loose in the room.
Startling Statement   A. It killed 40,000 people last year.
Illustration   B. It likes young people.
Rhetorical Question   II. No one is immune to tuberculosis.
Reference to the Subject   A. You may be infected now!
           B. How long has it been since you had a chest X ray?

Problem (Need)

Development	I. Despite wonder drugs, TB is our number six killer disease in America.
Statement	
Illustration	A. Last year 40,000 Americans died from it.
Ramification	B. Nearly 2,000 died in Michigan alone.
Pointing	II. No one is immune to TB.

Development
Statement
Illustration
Ramification
Pointing

I. Despite wonder drugs, TB is our number six killer disease in America.
  A. Last year 40,000 Americans died from it.
  B. Nearly 2,000 died in Michigan alone.
II. No one is immune to TB.
  A. You can get it by contagion.
  B. The most susceptible ages are from fifteen to thirty-five.
III. It maims and handicaps as well as kills.
  A. Many of those who recover cannot lead normal lives.
    1. They cannot travel in warm, damp climates.
    2. They cannot exert themselves.
      a. Cannot run to class.
      b. Cannot dance.
      c. Cannot play athletic games.
  B. TB may spread to other parts of the body.
    1. One may lose a limb.
    2. If often attacks the spine.
    3. One can lose a vital organ such as an eye or a kidney.

Solution (Satisfaction)

Development
Statement
Explanation
Demonstration
Illustration
Objections

I. A yearly X-ray checkup is the surest way to avoid a serious case of TB.
  A. It can be stopped most effectively if caught in time.
    1. For the most part it is a slow-developing disease.
    2. Its growth depends on the resistance of the victim.
    3. Even if TB is detected in its early stages, a cure would take at least six months.
  B. An X-ray checkup is the most positive means for detecting the disease.
    1. A patch test merely indicates the presence of TB germs, but the disease may not actually be present.
    2. A lesion is the positive sign when it shows on the X ray.

II. We can benefit from an X ray easily and quickly.
   A. It is free.
      1. The money from the sale of Christmas Seals pays for the X rays and other tests you get.
      2. The state is particularly interested in preserving the health of its young, college-age people.
   B. It is convenient to get.
      1. The mobile unit comes to the campus during the first week of the semester.
         a. It is open weekdays from 8 A.M. to 4 P.M.
         b. It parks near the Health Center.
      2. There is also a permanent clinic in town.
         a. It is open five days a week for adults from 8:30 A.M. to 4:30 P.M.
         b. A special appointment may be arranged after 4:30 P.M.
         c. It is located on the corner of Cass Street and Putnam Avenue.
         d. The phone number there is 831-0100.
   C. It is painless and quick.
      1. If you've ever had an X ray, you know it doesn't hurt.
      2. You need only remove your outer garments, such as coats and jackets.
      3. You can be in and out in five minutes.
   D. The results are mailed to you.

Visualization

Project the Future
Methods
  Summary
  Challenge
  Inducement
  Specificity

I. A few minutes now can beat this killer.
   A. Avoid pain and suffering.
   B. Avoid years in a tuberculosis sanitarium.
   C. Avoid physical handicaps.
II. Enjoy a normal life physically and psychologically.

Action

I. Get a chest X ray this week.

II. It is simple and convenient.
   A. The mobile unit is on campus at the library.
   B. It will take just five minutes of your time.
   C. It is absolutely free.

III. The X-ray examination program is an effective way to fight this disease.

1. INTRODUCTION
2. BODY
3. CONCLUSION

ROCK MUSIC

General End: To persuade.

Specific Purpose: To persuade the audience that rock music has significant social impact.

Introduction

Attention

I. Rock music blares out on our radios and TVs.
   A. Radio-tape demonstration.
   B. TV-tape (audio) demonstration.

II. Thousands pay to see and hear rock stars.
   A. Festivals have been big.
   B. Club bookings are big.
   C. Records are popular.

Body

I. The history and evolution of rock.
   A. Originally the music was improvised from the blues.

      1. Chuck Berry.
      2. Little Richard.
  B. Big stars won rock fans.
      1. Elvis Presley.
      2. The Beatles.

Interest
  C. New electronics advanced rock.
      1. The San Francisco sound.
      2. Electric instruments.
      3. Super amplification (short demonstration).

II. Performers had an impact by being daring, wild, and weird.
  A. Elvis Presley's gyrations banned from TV.
  B. Jim Morrison arrested for his act.
  C. Jimi Hendrix set rock afire.

Interest
  D. The Who open a new dimension of violence.
  E. Iggy Stooge used fear to become popular.
  F. Alice Cooper makes use of sadism.
  G. David Bowie captured the unreal.

III. Rock performers have changed our fashion codes.
  A. The Beatles caused the long-hair thing.
  B. Rock caused more casual dress (pictures).
  C. Rock heroes caused wilder clothes (pictures).

IV. Rock has had an impact on our moral standards.
  A. The hippie movement is related.

Vital Factors
  B. Drug use is related (demonstration of "drug music").
  C. Rock songs aid gay liberationists (demonstration).
  D. Some performers openly instigate bisexuality.

Conclusion

Reinforcement
I. Rock music has gained the attention of millions.
  A. Radio, TV.
  B. Festivals.
  C. New electronics.

II. Rock music has had a significant social impact.
  A. Brings social problems to light.
  B. Affects individual and group social behavior.

From a student speech by Robert Walker.

MOTIVATED-SEQUENCE ORGANIZATION

HERPES

General End:	To persuade.
Specific Purpose:	To persuade the audience that sexual promiscuity has a price other than pleasure.

Attention

I. An incurable virus has hit millions of Americans.
   A. A Washington lawyer, twenty-eight years old (illustration).
   B. Half a million cases are expected this year.

II. Herpes is an ancient viral infection (pictures).
   A. It is transmitted during sex.
   B. It cannot be cured.
   C. It is accompanied by sores and blisters.
   D. It was found to be a virus in the late 1960s.

Need

I. An estimated 20 million Americans have genital herpes.
   A. 51 percent are women.
   B. 95 percent are Caucasian.
   C. 80 percent are twenty to thirty-nine years old.
   D. 53 percent have completed at least four years of college.
   E. 56 percent earn $20,000 a year or more.

II. The rise in herpes.
   A. Sexual freedom.
      1. More people are involved in sex at an earlier age.
      2. Younger people are involved at an earlier age.

B. People are marrying later and divorcing more often.
C. Herpes virus can live on a towel for seventy-two hours and a toilet seat for at least four hours.
D. Ordinary cold sores can be transferred to the genitals by mouth or finger and become a venereal disease.
E. Oral sex may be a force in spreading both strains.
F. Once herpes penetrates the skin it multiplies rapidly.

III. There are two types of herpes.
    A. Type 1 (HSV-1) is more familiar.
        1. It causes cold sores on the lips.
        2. One-third of women under 24 years of age who have herpes on their genitals have type 1.
    B. Type 2 (HSV-2) is a more serious type.
        1. It typically causes genital lesions.
        2. It is very difficult to subdue.

Satisfaction

I. The herpes counterrevolution may be ushering restraint or even chastity back into fashion.
    A. Know the symptoms.
        1. A tingling or itching sensation.
        2. Blisters may appear within two to fifteen days for subsequent attacks.
        3. Blisters may be accompanied by fevers and headaches.
    B. Practice restraint.

II. Herpes won't kill you, but you won't kill it either.
    A. Herpes is not life-threatening.
    B. The virus can often be subdued.

Visualization

I. It has changed the balance between promiscuity and commitment.

II. People who contract herpes go through stages similar to mourning the death of a loved one.
    A. Shock.
    B. Emotional numbing.
    C. Isolation and loneliness.
    D. Serious depression.
    E. Impotence.

Action

I. Try restraint and chastity.
   A. The danger is real.
   B. Consider the long-term impacts.
   C. Promiscuity has a serious price.

II. If you refuse...
   A. Know your partner very well.
   B. Get a good look at your sex partner with the lights on!
      1. Look for sores.
      2. Look for discharge.
      3. Consider spermicides.

III. If you need help or information contact:
   Herpes Information
   HelPhiladelphia
   P. O. Box 13193
   Philadelphia, PA 19101

From a student speech by Jade Carter.

1. ATTENTION
2. NEED
3. PLAN
4. REINFORCEMENT
5. ACTION

BUCKLE UP AND STAY ALIVE

General End:　　　　　　　　　To persuade.

Specific Purpose:　　　　　　To persuade the audience to always use the seat belts in their cars.

Attention

I. A cure for cancer or heart disease! What excitement would be generated if medical authorities made this announcement. Mortality would be reduced to less than one fifth of the present rate.

II. For the third leading cause of death, namely auto accidents, there already exists a lifesaving device that relatively few people use.

Need

I. No medical miracle short of a cure for cancer or heart disease can save so many lives.
   A. Auto accidents are the leading cause of death between the ages of fifteen and twenty-four.
   B. The risk of death can be cut by 80 percent.

II. Most drivers don't know the facts.
   A. Ejection of an occupant is the most frequent factor in serious injury. Investigations by twenty-two states indicate that you are five times more likely to be killed if ejected.
   B. The typical victim is not a speed demon on a strange road.
      1. The National Safety Council found that three out of five fatal crashes occur on roads familiar to the driver.
      2. My accident was on a road I've been traveling all my life.
      3. The victim is more typically a young homeowner, a wife picking up her husband, or a teenager backing out of a driveway.
      4. Fifty percent of all fatalities occur at less than forty miles per hour.
      5. There is no guarantee against getting struck from behind or sideswiped.
   C. Common misconceptions set straight:
      1. You are not safer if thrown out of your car.
      2. Careful drivers are not immune to accidents.
      3. Local drivers are not immune to accidents.
      4. Driving slowly is no protection.

Plan

I. Use your seat belts at all times.
   A. An investigation of the accidents of last July fourth:
      1. There were 442 victims with no belts engaged.
      2. Belts would have prevented exactly half the deaths.
   B. These statistics are very meaningful to me because last summer I was involved in an accident in which a person without a belt was killed.

II. Seat belts are mandatory; buckling should be also.

Reinforcement

I. Some objections set straight:
    A. Don't seat belts often cause injuries?
        1. Hip bruises: my friend would have traded her fractured skull for a dozen hip bruises.
        2. Submerged in water or caught on fire.
            a. With a seat belt you are more apt to remain conscious.
            b. Seat belts can be released with one hand in two seconds.
    B. I don't drive often, far, or fast; why bother?
        1. Three of five fatal crashes are on local and familiar roads within twenty-five miles of home.
        2. Fifty percent of all fatalities are under forty miles per hour.
        3. It takes *two* to tango.

II. There are no reasonable objections.

Action

I. Safety belts have been publicized and made mandatory in cars.
    A. All car manufacturers.
    B. United States Health Service.
    C. American Medical Association.
    D. Insurance companies.

II. Always buckle up for safety to save lives and prevent serious accidents.
    A. Have everyone buckle up no matter how short the ride.
    B. It takes only six seconds to cut the risk of death by 80 percent.

From a student speech by Darlene Uten.

Appendix B
Model Campaign
Analyses

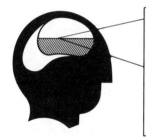

TYPICAL CAMPAIGN ANALYSIS

1. Identify the goals desired.

2. Identify the target audience.

3. Identify the persuasive strategy.

4. Implement the strategy.

5. Evaluate success.

WALTON HALL CAMPAIGN

Purpose: To become the president of Walton Hall, a residence hall at Eastern Michigan University.

Analysis: *Simons:* planning, mobilization, legitimation, promotion, activation

I. Planning
    A. Goal setting
        1. My intentions were to gain the support of as many of my schoolmates as possible.
        2. I considered my campaign efforts worthwhile whether I was elected or not because I was gaining experience in campaign techniques for later attempts to be elected to various positions.
    B. Audience analysis
        My audience analysis clearly indicated that I was running for a position that included an all-female constituency, 95 percent of whom were first-semester freshmen. The main concern of these women was to have ample extra-curricular activities in which to participate.
    C. Situational analysis
        The situational analysis was mostly self-evident. The majority of the students did not have background knowledge of EMU student government, which in any event was not critical to this situation.
    D. Research and development (handout 1)
    E. Basic strategies
        1. Media: stickers, posters, badges, etc. (visual aids).
        2. Door-to-door introductions and passing out of information (handouts 1 and 2).
        3. Speeches.

II. Mobilization
    A. Personal resources
        I offered honest representation of all the students' views and promised to keep them informed.
    B. Material resources
        All campaign funds were provided by the candidate.
    C. Communication resources
        These were provided by:
        1. The university.
        2. An organized assembly.
        3. A student-number list for the entire dormitory.

III. Legitimation
    A. Legitimacy by position
        I used my past experience as student-government president in high school.
    B. Legitimacy by endorsement
        I was a registered student, but otherwise I did not have much help. Except for a few friends no one really knew who I was. It would have been helpful to seek endorsement by resident advisors and resident advisors' assistants.
    C. Legitimacy of a cause
        I promised to try to improve EMU living conditions and educational quality.

IV. Promotion
    A. Identity
        I attempted this by introducing myself at floor meetings and by going door to

door. I used the slogan "You can't go wrong if you vote Linda Wright Walton Hall President." The play on the name made it easy to remember, and I hoped it would be remembered on election day.

B. Credibility
  1. I didn't downgrade opponents; I didn't force people to take my literature or to listen to my views; I was respectful.
  2. I maintained promises and trusts that were made during the campaign and did not promise the impossible. If I felt that I could not accomplish something, I told them so.
  3. I attempted to present a neat, attractive appearance; I was friendly and didn't act "better" than the others.
C. Case building
  1. Campaign participants
     There were only a few people who helped me with the campaign, but I made sure that they were not taken advantage of in terms of my responsibilities. I showed my appreciation and encouraged them to spread my name by word of mouth.
  2. General public
     I asked the students to actively participate in the happenings of "our" school and tried to persuade them to start by voting for the most qualified person.
  3. Key decision makers
     At the time of the election I did not know who looked at whom as an elite member of the dormitory. However, I think it could have been beneficial to consult the RAs and RAIs, as they were looked up to by most of the girls.

V. Activation
  A. Detailed action plan
     The place of the election was determined by the officers of each floor, so I encouraged voting simply by stating that locations and times would be announced by the officers on the day of the election.
  B. Preliminary commitments
     I sought commitments by asking people if they would be interested in displaying a sign on their door or if they would like to wear a badge.
  C. Follow-through
     I was concerned about irritating voters through overexposure, since other candidates hurt their campaigns that way. The voting was taking place at mandatory meetings with plenty of reminders.
  D. Penetration
     I concentrated on making my name stay in the voters' minds by the slogan "You can't go wrong if you vote Linda Wright Walton Hall President." I feel that this was good planning since most people have a tendency to associate opposites.

VI. Evaluation
   I was elected president! I should, however, have spent more time understanding the RAs and their assistants. They are opinion leaders, as described in our text. I was lucky in this respect.

From a student presentation by Linda Wright.

"GO 4 IT"

Purpose:	To increase viewer ratings at channel 4, WDIV, after Post-Newsweek bought the station.
Analysis:	"Typical" (Ross) goals: target audience, strategy, implementation, evaluation; also interviews and numerous commercials.

I. Identify the goals desired.
   A. The "Go 4 It" campaign was devised to get channel 4 back to the top in the viewer ratings. However, that was not the sole purpose behind the campaign.
   B. The people at channel 4 were also campaigning to show their interest in working with and for Detroit, the people, and the community. (public relations)
   C. They particularly featured the newscast (local quality) since that's where high-priced time is sold.

II. Identify the target audience.
   A. General description
      1. The "Go 4 It" campaign was directed toward persons ranging from twenty-five to fifty-four years old.
      2. This is because they wanted to appeal to the largest similar-age mass of people at one time, especially the baby-boom people, who were now getting older.
      3. Targeted people were those living in the greater metropolitan area.
   B. Attitudes
      1. Channel 4 was the lowest-rated of the three big stations (2, 4, 7) in the Detroit area. Attitudes were not good.
      2. Viewers were also suspicious of the new owners, since Post-Newsweek was a national, not a local company.

III. Identify the persuasive strategy.
   A. Rhetorical
      1. Please try us "just once" (go 4 it).
      2. A "two-step" opinion-leader appeal (tell someone).
      3. An image appeal (we like Detroit).
      4. Ads were directed at specific segments of viewers (visual aid).
   B. Psychological
      1. I feel they used assimilation-contrast theory. "Go 4 It" does not promise anything; they also made no wild claims (show attitude scales here). They did not promise anything with which they could not live.
      2. Both-sides persuasion was used. The campaign revealed concessions. One commercial specifically showed a man in front of three television sets watching three other *good* newscasts, but he finally "goes for it" and watches channel 4. (Play tapes if time allows.)
   C. Ethical considerations
      1. This campaign took into serious consideration the fact that a successful media campaign by "outsiders" must be *scrupulously* honest.
      2. This campaign assured choice: the audience was never high-pressured.

IV. Implement strategy.
   A. Organizational plan
      1. This campaign started out very subtly with an emphasis on the news and only later progressed into a self-fulfillment strategy (the high jump and the checkers game).
      2. They showed commercials filmed in different parts of the city to better associate themselves with Detroit and the people.

3. The commercial advertising conveyed the same message and worked creatively to avoid boring repetition.
4. They showed happy people trying new things, "going for it."
5. The campaign strategy progressed slowly to the point where they actually showed commercials of people changing the station (breaking away from the everyday routine).
6. The action in the advertising did not tell the viewers what to do. However, it showed what they could do and asked them to do it. The viewers were given a choice, but also direction.
7. (To utilize both-sides persuasion) (to gain social compliance) The attitude response was behavioral; they wanted the public to behave in an intended way by changing to channel 4.

B. Use of media
   1. I feel that this campaign has had sufficient television exposure. The commercials used were very creative, clever, and not overly repetitive.
   2. See the demonstration tape (audio-visual).

C. Ethical codes and standards
   1. The campaign strategies used were honest and ethical. The commercials followed the broadcast code.
   2. The ads were subtle, but this subtleness was not used to deceive the viewers but rather to strengthen their ideas. Both clues and choice were available.

V. Evaluate success.
   A. Behavioral
      1. The "Go 4 It" campaign has been very successful in establishing the company financially while also increasing the number of viewers.
      2. There has been drastic improvement in the ratings during the past year.
      3. People enjoyed seeing a station that was so interested in the city in which they lived, and they reported that fact.
   B. Attitudes may be inferred from the behavioral indexes above.
   C. Ethical-code compliance
      1. The "Go 4 It" campaign followed the ethical codes of professional advertising standards (see text).
      2. The campaign did not involve pressuring the public.
      3. They allowed free choice and used clue-laden, legitimate strategies.
      4. This was a very honest and fair campaign (interviews).

From a student presentation by Patty Rose.

Roadblocks (Constraints)

but use a spoon; you'll want to get every drop [for women]." They also went after the cook in the family with the notion that this soup is as good as homemade. By overcoming this roadblock they hoped to double the target audience and the sales market.

2. Another problem was that the names of the Chunky varieties would sound like the old soups, and maybe give the audience the notion that they were like the old condensed soups. For example, one brand of soup, Chunky Chicken, could be confused with the old Chicken Noodle Soup. So, the problem was to find a way to distinguish the two. They found it. They decided to make Chunky Soups NOT CONDENSED. This accomplished two purposes: One, there were no other uncondensed soups on the market, so there would be no immediate competition. Two, and more important, the consumer could distinguish between the two products. Thus, they dealt with this roadblock.

Basic Plan

H. The plan was to use mostly emotional and image appeals.
1. For the man the image was "a satisfying product that is a meal in itself."
2. For the housewife the appeal was "Your happy husband will enjoy this as if it were homemade and will feel good toward you."

II. The Promotion Stage

Resources

A. The company had many resources. One was the mass media, and they used it well. Another was an advertising agency. They hired Batten, Barton, Durstine and Osborn, a firm with a history of success. This firm was the ninth largest ad agency in America, based on total sales in 1977 (over $800 million). And, best of all, they had experience on their side. They knew what had helped and what had failed in the past. They had had experience in marketing similar products. So basically, they pooled these main resources to promote an effective campaign.

Media

B. A major effort was made through the media. Campbell decided they had a good thing going here since the sales of Campbell's other soups were media-related. To market the forty-seven condensed soups, Campbell had used television 50 percent of the time; print and radio were second and third, respectively. This was the combination that had gained them 80 percent of the old

Strategy Applied

market. Thus, the same media emphasis was planned except that more TV would be used, at the beginning.

C. Television commercials were used creatively with a split screen. To the left a chef or a mother, to the right a housewife (or any family cook). The cook would say that he or she is making homemade soup. The chef or mother at the left would act surprised and ask if certain ingredients were there. ("Do *you* use real chunks of chicken like me?" "Yep.")

D. The same format applied to the print media, and the dialogue was the same on radio. Pride was on the face of the cook, because he or she had humorously put something over on the chef or mother. Thus, the emotional need (esteem) was satisfied and the target audience was reached. Also, the soup was seen as really chunky by the consumer, and as good an impression as possible was given to the audience that the product was worth trying. Through this, Campbell hoped they would see that the soup was a meal in itself. (Play tapes.)

Credibility

E. Credibility was achieved almost immediately. All bases seemed to be touched in preparation to make the campaign seem credible. Since 1972, no real adjustments have been made in selling the product. The Campbell name helped!

III. The Follow-up Stage

Results

A. Sales figures for the company were up. Market penetration was up. After one year, Chunky Soups accounted for 16 percent of Campbell's total canned-food sales.

Ethics

B. Ethically, the campaign was fair. No evidence of deceptive advertising was found, and to me, the public was not misled by the ads. A successful, honest ad campaign for a good product.

Evaluation

C. I can honestly say that I'd do nothing to change the campaign—it was unbelievably successful. The company agrees and the campaign is now winding down.

From a student presentation by Rick Scimeca.

AN AUTO DEALER CAMPAIGN

Purpose: To increase sales of an oversupply of Chrysler
                              Cordoba and Newport automobiles.

Analysis: Typical (Ross): goals, target audience, strategy, im-
                              plementation, evaluation

I. Goals and Purposes
   A. To sell Chrysler Corporation automobiles through the Metro Chrysler/Ply-
      mouth, Inc., dealership.
   B. To increase sales of the Chrysler Cordoba and Newport models through a
      specific advertising campaign in order to relieve an oversupply of these
      models.
   C. To utilize radio spots in an effective manner.
II. Target Audience
   A. Geographic breakdown (map, visual aid).
      1. Westland/Wayne area.
         a. White-collar area (middle-upper).
         b. Blue-collar area (middle-lower).
      2. Dearborn Heights/Garden City area.
   B. Age differentiation (target groups).
      1. Twenty-one to thirty-nine.
      2. Forty and over.
   C. General demographics (chart, visual aid).
      1. Racial.
      2. Financial/economic.
      3. Single/family.
      4. Homeowner/renter.
      5. Education.

III. Persuasive Strategies
   A. Chrysler Cordoba sales strategies (radio).
      1. Styling.
         For all group breakdowns the car was pushed as sleek, aerodynamic, and
         having smart detailing, long contouring lines, and a very plush interior.
         a. "Performance and class" was the strategy for the twenty-one-to-
            thirty-nine, middle-upper groups.
         b. "Classy yet economical" was the strategy for the forty-and-over,
            family, and middle-lower groups.
      2. Price was divided into two major aspects.
         a. Middle-upper, single, white-collar: the "ultimate in options" car was
            presented.
         b. Middle-lower, family, blue-collar: affordability (V-6) and sleek economy
            were stressed.
      3. Special-features breakdown.
         a. Mileage/economy.
         b. Performance.
         c. Maintenance/upkeep.
   B. Chrysler Newport sales strategies (radio).
      1. Styling: The Newport has an image of a mature, middle-upper, "retiree"
         car. An image change was needed.
         a. First, the "family-car" image: a big, durable car for the large family who
            need space, but not a station wagon.
         b. Second, the "elegant" car: emphasizing design and impressive op-
            tions for the younger, new "executive" look of the 1980s.
      2. Price: Two images were attempted.
         a. Options and more options for the executive *class d'elegant* car.
         b. Family comfort, trunk space, durability, and long-lasting value for the
            "family" groups.

3. Special-features breakdown.
   a. Performance.
   b. Ride/comfort.
   c. Durability/maintenance.
   d. Elegance and impressive options.

IV. Implementation of Strategy
   A. Two different spots were produced, based on all the buyer-listener data compiled (radio).
      1. In spot 1 the Cordoba was presented as a multi-faceted automobile.
         a. Style.
         b. Good looks.
         c. Sporty plus economical.
      2. The Newport was presented as a car of "young elegance."
         a. Classy.
         b. Many "options."
      3. Spot 1 was recorded with a mellow pop-music background with lyrics and voice-overs.
      4. Spot 2 (commercial) dealt with the middle-lower, "family" class image.
      5. In spot 2 the Cordoba imagery was set (voice-overs) as a sporty alternative for the "blasé," small family car.
      6. The Newport was touted as the big family car.
         a. Able to take the wear, tear, and abuse.
         b. The durability of a station wagon, but with better looks, better aerodynamics, and better riding comfort.
         c. In spot 2 the music and lyrics were produced in a country, easy-listening sound matching listener-analysis patterns.
   B. Common messages in both commercials (spots 1 and 2).
      1. Location of the dealership.
      2. The quality of its service facilities.
      3. The good track record (image) of the dealership.
      4. Each was sixty seconds long.
      5. Both ran on six major stations.
      6. They were aired at different times, depending on each station's ratings guide.
      7. The campaign lasted for three months.

V. Evaluation of Success
   A. The total effect of the advertising campaign was a 17-percent increase in the dealerships' sales in the second quarter.
      1. This included service as well as car sales.
      2. This came to a three-quarters-of-a-million-dollar increase for one quarter.
      3. Specific sales statistics (visual demographics).
   B. Other variables.
      1. Related, overlapping corporation campaigns covered radio, billboards, TV, and all major newspapers and magazines (*Newsweek, U.S. News and World Report,* etc.) in the area.
      2. A major fleet sale was made at this time.
      3. Chrysler Corporation was offering a rebate deal at the time.
   C. Coordination with the corporate campaigns might have been better.
   D. More pilot tapes might have been tested.
   E. For all the "image" language, no really false claims were made.

From a student presentation by David Bork.

Index

AUTHOR

AAF, 196
ABBBI, 196
Abelson, R., 84, 88, 112
Adams, H. F., 143
Ajzen, I., 11, 55
Allport, F., 104, 116
Allport, G., 8, 37
Allyn, J., 56
Anatol, K. W. E., 28
Andersen, K. E., 28, 81
Anderson, N. H., 146
Applbaum, R. L., 28
Aristotle, ii, 73
Arnold, C. C., 183
Aronson, E., 8, 62, 87, 88, 102
ASNE, 196
Auer, J. J., 18, 22, 26, 118

Baird, A. C., 73
Baird, J. E., 113
Baker, E. E., 63
Barrios, A. A., 146
Basehart, J. R., 145, 152
Beisecker, T., 147
Bem, D., 9, 94, 162
Bem, S., 113
Benson, T. W., 76

Berger, C. R., 81
Berkowitz, L., 83
Berlo, D. K., 89, 142, 144
Bettinghaus, E. P., 28, 81, 145, 152
Beverly, G. D., 111
Binder, L., 186
Boaz, J. K., 28
Bock, D. G., 106, 113
Bock, E. H., 106, 113
Bok, S., 17
Bork, D., 228
Bostrom, R. N., 28, 81
Bowers, J. W., 183
Boynton, K. R., 60
Bradac, J. J., 62
Brady, R. M., 113
Brehm, J. W., 87, 152
Brembeck, W. L., 28, 80, 81
Brigance, W. N., 78, 79
Brock, B., iii, 182, 184, 188
Brock, T. C., 89, 145
Brockriede, W., 73, 121
Broome, B. J., 58
Brown, R., 103, 117
Bruner, J. S., 14
Bruner, K. F., 43, 65
Bryant, J., 60
Burgoon, M., 28, 113
Burke, K., 188
Burks, D. M., 120
Butler, J. L. P., 106

Cacioppo, J. T., 91, 130
Cahn, D. D., 122
Campbell, D. T., 146
Campbell, E. H., 145
Carlsmith, J. M., 95
Carlson, R. E., 120
Carter, J., 215
Cartwright, D., 83
Cathcart, R. S., 60
Chapanis, A., 88
Chapanis, N. P., 88
Chase, S., 174
Clarke, C. H., 56
Cohen, A. R., 87, 110, 142, 144, 146
Colby, M. A., 56
Cooper, J., 97
Cooper, L., 75
Corbett, E. P. J., 75
Cox Report, 9
Crockett, W. H., 145
Cromwell, H., 143
Cronkhite, G., 28, 56, 74, 162
Crutchfield, R., 3, 37
Cushman, D. P., 63

Dance, F. E. X., 63, 81
Darnell, D. K., 121
Dause, C. A., 166, 168
Davies, R. A., 62
Delia, J. G., 56
Denton, R. E., 183
Detroit Free Press, 114
Detroit News, 121
Dewey, J., iii, 133
Dietrich, D., 63
Dillard, J. P., 113
DISCUS, 191
Dollar, K., 90
Doob, L. W., 143
Doran, N. E., 113
Doyle, A. C., 169
Drefus, L. S., 117
Dublin, P., 114
Dycus, R. D., 149

Eadie, W. F., 120
Eagly, A. H., 113
Ehninger, D., 73, 137, 185
Ehrensberger, R., 130
Eisenson, J., 118
Ewbank, H. L., 18, 22, 26

Faison, E. W. J., 149
Fazio, R. H., 97
Feather, N., 83
Federico, R., 117
Feierabend, R. L., 146
Felker, D. W., 64
Festinger, L., 56, 86
Field, P. B., 110, 112
Fishbein, M., 11, 55
Flavin, J. W., 113
Flynn, L. J., 23
Foley, C., 156
Fotheringham, W. C., 186
Foy, E., 114
Freedman, J. L., 95
Freeley, A. J., 166

Gibb, J. D., 59
Gilkinson, H., 143
Goble, F., 46
Goffman, E., 57, 67
Goldman, W., 63
Greenwald, A., 89
Griffin, L. M., 184
Grimmett, R., 113
Gronbeck, B. E., 137, 184
Gruner, C., 59
Gulley, H., 142, 144

Haiman, F., 22, 54
Harary, F., 83
Harlow, A. F., 114
Hart, R. P., 120
Hartley, E. L., 147
Harvey, J. H., 96
Harvey, O. J., 111
Hass, G., 147
Heider, F., 2, 82
Helson, H., 91
Hewgill, M. A., 63
Hobbs, G., 87
Hollingworth, H. L., 104, 135
Hovland, C. I., 13, 54, 84, 109, 110, 142, 145, 147
Howell, W. S., 28, 80, 81
Hughes, H., 115
Hunsaker, D. M., 166

Ickes, W., 96
Ilardo, J. A., 28

Infante, D. A., 56, 58, 113
Insko, C., 145
Irwin, J. V., 118

Jacklin, C., 113
Jaksa, J., 20
James, W., 76, 81, 134
Janik, A., 172
Janis, I. L., 15, 36, 87, 109, 110, 112, 146, 151
Jebb, R. C., 76
Jensen, V., 172
Jersild, A. T., 142, 143
Johannesen, R., 20
Jones, R. A., 152
Judd, L. R., 113

Kagan, J., 112
Kamenetzky, J., 142
Kaplan, R. M., 59
Katz, D., 14
Kay, D., 36
Kelley, H. H., 2, 96
Kelly, G. A., 72
Kelman, H. C., 15, 17
Kennedy, A. J., 59
Kidd, R. F., 96
Kiesler, C. A., 145
Kiesler, S. B., 145
Killian, L. M., 116
Kilpela, D., 59
King, B., 87
King, B. G., 32, 35
Kirschner, P., 36
Kitchens, J. T., 113
Knapp, M. L., 62
Knower, F. H., 80, 112, 144
Kohler, J. W., 147
Konsky, C. W., 62
Krech, D., 3, 37

Larson, C. U., 28, 81, 186
LeBon, G., 115
Lee, R., 113
Lesser, G. S., 112
Levine, D., 96
Levine, J., 112
Lewis, P., 63
Linder, D., 147
Lindzey, G., 8, 102

Linthorst-Homan, B. A., 141
Liska, J., 56
Littlejohn, S. W., 81
Luchins, A. S., 145
Ludlum, T., 152
Lull, P. E., 59
Lumsdaine, A. A., 147, 151
Lund, F. H., 144

McCleaf, J. E., 56
McClelland, D. C., 41
Maccoby, E. E., 113, 147
McCroskey, J., 58, 60, 61
McDavid, J., 113
McGee, J. A., 40, 79, 137
McGuire, W. J., 8, 88, 108, 110, 146
Mainliner Magazine, 8
Mandell, W., 145
Martin, D. C., 28
Martin, E. D., 115
Maslow, A. H., 2, 43, 46
Mayo, C. W., 145
Mechling, E., 183
Miettinen, R., 207
Milgram, S., 102
Miller, G. R., i, iii, 28, 63, 81, 82, 89
Miller, N., 146
Mills, J., 62, 87
Minnick, W. C., 28
Minton, C., 112
Moe, J. D., 63
Mohrman, G. P., 184
Monroe, A. H., 40, 79, 80, 136
Montgomery, C. L., 113
Morgan, C. T., 34
Mueller, M., 90
Mulac, A., 63
Murchison, C., 8

NAAB, 197
Nathu, I. A., 56
Nebergall, R., 90, 91
Newcomb, T. M., 88, 147
Newsom, D., 195
Newsweek, 6
Nilsen, T. R., 26

Oberschall, A., 115
Ochs, D., 184
Oliver, R. T., 80

Osgood, C. E., 85
Oskamp, S., 186
Ostrom, T. M., 89

Pallak, J., 90
Pallak, M. S., 90
Parker, K. R., 56
Parson, D., 147
Pascoe, G. C., 59
Paul, I. H., 111
Paulson, S. F., 143, 152
Perloff, R. M., 89
Petty, R. E., 91, 130
Phillips, A. E., 40, 80
Pope, C., 112
Powell, F. A., 111
Powell, L., 113
Prosser, M. H., 76
PRSA, 195

Quintilian, 76

Reardon, K. K., i, 28, 81
Reed, C. R., 183
Rhodes, S., 20
Rieke, R., 172
Rife, D., 111
Roberts, W. R., 73
Rogers, C., 2
Rogers, E. M., 192
Rohrer, J. H., 111
Rokeach, M., 9, 39, 111
Roloff, M. E., 81, 89
Rose, P., 223
Rosenberg, M., 84, 88
Rosnow, R. L., 147
Ross, E. A., 115
Ross, R. S., 75, 81
Rowell, E. Z., 78

Samuels, S. C., 63
Schachter, S., 40
Scheidel, T. M., 112
Schmidt, H., 142
Schoen, L., 120
Schrier, H. N., 183
Schroeder, J. J., 55
Schwartz, J., 117
Scimeca, R., 226

Scott, A., 195
Scott, R. L., 184, 188
Seagram Distillers, 150
Sears, D. O., 95
Sears Roebuck Company, 55
Sheffield, F. D., 147
Sherif, C., 90, 91
Sherif, M., 13, 90, 91, 111
Sherwood, J. J., 64
Shoemaker, F. F., 192
Showers, M. J., 32, 35
Shulman, G. M., 122
Sikkink, D. E., 143
Sillars, M. O., 172
Simons, H. W., 28, 81, 183
Sims, B., 169
Singh, V., 112
Sitrunk, F., 113
Smith, C. B., 113
Smith, C. R., 166, 183
Smith, M. B., 14
Smith, M. J., ii, 3, 8, 72, 81
Smith, R. G., 54
Speech Communication Association, 77
Spillman, B., 110
Sponberg, H., 143
Springer, I., 116
Stewart, C. J., 182, 183, 184
Street, R. L., 113
Sullivan, J. F., 21
Sunnafrank, M., 57

Tannenbaum, P. H., 85, 88, 143
Thistlewaite, D., 142
Thompson, W. N., 28
Thonssen, L., 73
Tichener, E. B., 76
Tobacco Institute, 151
Toch, H., 102
Toulmin, S., 172
Training, 6
Turner, J., 115
Turner, R. H., 116

U. S. News and World Report, 168
Uten, D., 217

Valentinsen, B., 63

Walker, R., 212
Wallace, K. R., 77
Walster, E., 61
Watson, J. B., 77
Wayne State University, iii
Webster, B., 62
Weiss, W., 54
Wheeler, L., 104
White, R. W., 14, 43, 65
Whiting, B., 112
Widgery, R. N., 62
Williams, B. R., 60
Wilson, L., 56
Wilson, W., 145
Winans, J. A., 76
Wirth, C., 121
Woolbert, C., 77, 78
Wright, L., 221
Wulf, M. A., 60

Yoos, G. E., 162
Yost, M., 78

Ziegelmueller, G. W., 166, 168
Zillmann, D., 60

SUBJECT

Achievement motive, 41
Adaptation level theory, 91
Ad hominem, 25, 176
Adopter categories, 193
Affiliation motive, 40
Age, 111, 119
Ambiguity, 146
Analogic reasoning, 167
Analogy, 167–68
Androgyny, 113
Anonymity, 116
Antagonistic receivers, 147
Appearance, 61 (*see also* Attraction)
Argument, 169–72
  elements, 169–72
    backing, 170–71
    claims, 170–71
    grounds, 170–71
    qualifiers, 170–71
    rebuttals, 170–71
    warrants, 170–71
  fallacies, 172–77
model analysis, 170
Arrangement (*disposito*), 75, 133–56
  both-sides, 147–56
  climax-anticlimax, 142–44
  illustration, 139–41
  introduction functions, 134
  motivated sequences, 136–41
  order effects, 141–46
  primacy-recency, 144–46
  strategies, 133–56
  systems, 138
  thinking order, 133
Asignments (*see* Projects and tasks)
Assimilation tendency, 91
Attention, 134
Attitudes, 8–17
  clusters, 11–12
  defined, 8–11
  functions, 13
  latitude, 12, 90
  multiple response, 91
  range, 12
  similarity, 57
  structures, 9–10
Attraction, 57–63, 120
  appearance, 61
  attitude similarity, 57
  characteristics, 57
  clothes, 62
  common ground, 57
  communication skills, 62
  dynamism, 58
  evidence, 60
  humor, 59
  information, 60
  language, 62
  physical, 61
  recognition, 58
  self-concept, 63–67
  self-presentation, 63–67
  social adjustment, 58
  status, 58
  uncertainty reduction, 58
Attribution theory, 95
Audience:
  adaptation, 117
  age, 119
  analysis principles, 108
  antagonism, 147
  configurations, 106
  demographics, 117–20
  descriptive measures, 117
  education, 119

Audience (*cont.*)
  feedback response, 104
  gender, 120
  group memberships, 118
  hostility, 147
  interstimulation, 104
  message analysis, 118
  message relationship, 117
  nature, 102
  occupation, 119
  physical setting, 106
  polarization, 104
  proximity, 106
  receiver characteristics, 109–13
    age, 111
    authoritarianism, 111
    gender, 112
    general tendency, 109
    intelligence, 110
    self-esteem, 110
  seating arrangements, 106
  situations, 117
  social facilitation, 104
  speaker relationships, 118
  special interests, 119
  types, 104
Audience adaptation, 117
Audience analysis, 102 (*see also* Audience)
Audience psychology, 102 (*see also*
    Audience)
Authoritarianism, 111
Authorities, 163

Balance theory, 82
Begging the question fallacy, 175
Behavioral perception theories, 90–97
Beliefs, 8–17
Body systems, 33
Both-sides persuasion, 147–56
  characteristics, 152
  model outline, 153–56
  outline model, 153–56
Burke's pentad, 188

Campaign analysis models, 219–28
Campaign assignment models, 219–28
Campaign persuasion, 182–99 (*see*
    Campaigns)
Campaign report models, 219–28
Campaigns, 185–99
  adopter categories, 193

analysis models, 186–88
codes of conduct, 194–98
dramatistic analysis, 188
ethics, 194–98
importance, 6
innovation-decision process, 192
mass communication, 192–94
media, 6
model analyses, 219–28
opinion leaders, 193
psychological analysis, 189–92
regulations (*see* Ethical codes)
stages, 185
standards (*see* Ethical codes)
topics for analysis, 199
Canons of rhetoric, 73–76
Causal reasoning, 165
Choice, 3, 21
Classical rhetoric, 73 (*see* Rhetoric)
Climax-anticlimax order, 142–44
Clothes, 62
Clues, 18
Codes, 194–98 (*see* Ethical codes)
Codes of conduct, 194–98
Cognitive consistency theory, 82 (*see also*
    Consistency theory)
Cognitive dissonance, 86
Cognitive-response theory, 88
Coherence, 131
Collective behavior, 102, 115
  anonymity, 116
  contagion, 116
  psychological mechanisms, 116
  suggestibility, 116
  taxonomy, 103
Commitment, 90
Common ground, 57
Communication skills, 62
Competence, 65
Competence motive, 43
Compliance, 7, 15, 22, 87
Concessions, 149
Congruity theory, 84
Consistency theory, 82–88
Contagion, 116
Context, 96
Contrast tendency, 91
Conviction-persuasion duality, 78
Counterpersuasion, 149–51
Covariation principle, 96
Credibility, 54–57 (*see also* Attraction)
  communication skills, 62
  evidence, 60

factor analysis, 55
information, 60
language, 62
Crowds, 103, 115 (*see also* Mobs and panics)
Culpable ignorance, 22

Deception, 18
Deductive reasoning, 167
Delivery (*pronunciatio*), 75
Democracy, 5
Discounting effect, 96
Dissonance theory, 86
Dramatic realization, 67
Dramatistic description, 188
Drive-motive theory, 43–47
Drive theory, 2
Ducking the issue fallacy, 176
Dynamism, 59

Eclecticism, ii
Education, 119
Ego involvement, 90
Emotional appeals, 24
Emphasis, 129, 131
Enthymeme, 75, 89
Epistemology, ii
Esteem needs, 45
Ethical codes, 194–98
    advertising, 195
    broadcast, 197
    journalism, 196
    political campaigns, 196
    public relations, 195
Ethics, i, ii, 17–27 (*see also* Ethical codes)
    choice, 21
    culpable ignorance, 22
    emotional appeals, 24
    guidelines, 20–21
    public figures, 25
Ethos, 54
Evidence, 60
Examples, 164
    tests of, 167
Extrapolation, 174

Fair hearing, 22
Fallacies, 172–77
    begging the question, 175
    ducking the issue, 176

false cause, 174
    overgeneralization, 173
False cause fallacy, 174
False pretense, 23
Feedback response, 104
First impressions, 145
Forewarning, 145
Front, 67
Functional attitude theory, 13–17

Gender, 112, 120
Group influence, 64
Group memberships, 118
Group mind, 117

Homeostasis, 34
Hostile receivers, 147
Humanistic psychology, 2
Humor, 59

Incredulity factor, 85
Inductive reasoning, 166
Influence, 2–5
    defined, 2
    group, 64
    sources, 54–67
Information, 60
Innovation-decision process, 192
Intelligence, 110
Intent, 3
Interpersonal attraction (*see* Attraction)
Interpersonal relations, 8
Invention (*inventio*), 74

Jokes, 59 (*see also* Humor)
Jonestown, 111

Language, 62
Latitude of attitude, 90
Leadership, 7, 122
Learning postulates, 128
Lies, 17, 24–26
Loaded questions, 175
Logical supports, 162–72 (*see also* Reasoning and Argument)
    authority, 163
    examples, 164
    statistics, 164

Logos, 74
Love needs, 44

Maslow needs, 43–47
Memory (*memoria*), 75
Message arrangement, 133–56 (*see also*
    Arrangement and Message
    organization)
Message organization, 128–56 (*see*
    Organizing messages)
Mob mentality, 113, 116 (*see also*
    Collective behavior)
Model outlines (*see* Outline models)
Models:
    persuasion, 4–5
Model speech outlines, 139–41, 153–56,
    204–17
Modern rhetoric, 76 (*see also* Rhetoric)
    forerunners, 76
Motivated sequences, 80, 136–41
Motivation, 2–5
    defined, 2
Motives, 32–50 (*see also* Needs)
    inventory, 38
Movements, 182
    Griffin model, 184
    Reed model, 183
    Simons model, 183
    Stewart model, 182
Mystification, 67

Needs, 32–50
    abundancy, 37
    achievement, 41
    affiliation, 40
    avoidance, 2
    biological, 32, 36
    competence, 43
    deficiency, 37
    esteem, 45
    growth, 2
    inventory, 38
    physiological, 44
    psychological, 37–46
    safety, 44
    self-actualization, 45
    social, 37–46 (*see also* Needs,
        psychological)
    values, 38
Non sequiter, 174

Opinion leaders, 193
Opinions, 10
Order effects, 141–46
    climax-anticlimax, 142
    primacy-recency, 144
Organizing messages, 128–56
    arrangement, 133–56 (*see also*
        Arrangement)
    emphasis, 129
    learning principles, 128
    methods, 131
    motivated sequences, 136–41
    outlining, 131
    reinforcement, 129
    rhetorical principles, 130
Organizing methods, 131
Outline models, 139–41, 153–56, 204–17
Outlining, 128–56 (*see* Organizing
    messages)
Overgeneralization, 173

Panics, 114
Pathos, 74
Pentad, 188
Personal attraction (*see* Attraction)
Persuasibility, 107
    analysis principles, 108
    audience characteristics, 109–13
        age, 111
        authoritarianism, 111
        gender, 112
        general tendency, 109
        intelligence, 110
        self-esteem, 110
Persuasion:
    attribution theory, 95
    balance theory, 82
    behavioral approach, 81
    both-sides, 147–56
    choice, 3
    cognitive response theory, 88
    communication tasks, 135
    congruity theory, 84
    consistency theory, 82–88
    defined, 2–5
    democratic, 5
    epistemology, ii
    general ends, 137
    genetic approach, 79
    intent, 3
    logical, 162–72

media expenditures, 6
models, 4–5
multidisciplinary framework (*see* Preface)
philosophy (*see* Preface)
pretheoretical orientations, iii
reasoning, 162–78
rules theory (*see* Preface)
self-perception theory, 94
social judgment theory, 90
theory, 72
Polarization, 104
Positivism, 81
Post hoc ergo propter hoc, 174
Primacy-recency order, 144–46
Profanity, 106
Projectionist view (*see* Preface)
Projects and tasks:
  argument, 178
  arrangement strategy, 158
  attitudes, 27–29
  audience adaptation, 125
  audience analysis, 125
  both-sides persuasion, 159
  campaign analysis models, 200
  campaigns, 199
  cognitive consistency, 99–100
  controversial topics, 159
  credibility, 68
  definitions, 27–29
  ethical codes, 201
  evidence, 178
  fallacies, 178
  mass-media aspects, 201
  motivated sequence, 158
  needs, 50
  persuasibility, 125
  persuasion models, 27–29
  persuasion theory, 99–100
  reasoning, 178
  rhetorical sensitivity, 125
  resistance, 149
  self-concept, 68
  self-perception, 99–100
  self-presentation, 68
  social judgment theory, 99–100
  sources of influence, 68
  speech assignments, 68
  speech topics, 159
Proof, 163 (*see also* Reasoning and Argument)
Psychoanalytic theory, 2

Public figures, 25

Rapport, 135
Reactance, 156
Reasoning, 162–78
  analogy, 167
  causal, 165
  deductive, 167
  fallacies, 172–77
  generalization, 166
  inductive, 166
  logical supports, 163–72
    authority, 163
    examples, 164
    statistics, 164
  sign, 168
  Toulmin system, 169–72
Recognition, 58
Reflective thinking pattern, 133
Regulations (*see* Ethical codes)
Reinforcement, 129
Rhetoric, 73
  classical, 73
  modern, 76
Rhetorical principles, 130
Rhetorical sensitivity, 120–22
  characteristics, 122
  types, 120, 122
Role, 65, 119
Role playing, 87
Rules theory (*see* Preface)

Safety, 44
Sampling, 173
Seating arrangements, 106
Secrets, 20
Self-actualization, 45–46
Self-concept, 63–67
  influences, 64–66
    competence, 65
    role, 65
    significant others, 64
    situation, 66
Self-esteem, 110
Self-identity (*see* Self-concept)
Self-perception theory, 94
Self-presentation, 63–67
Sex, 112 (*see* Gender)
Sign reasoning, 168
Situation, 96

Slander, 25
Social adjustment, 58
Social facilitation, 104, 116
Social judgment theory, 90
Social movements, 182 (*see* Movements)
Social system structure, 194
Source credibility (*see* Credibility)
Speech assignment models, 204–17
Speech assignments (*see* Projects and tasks)
Speech outlines, 204–17 (*see* Outline models)
Speech organization, 182–56 (*see* Organizing messages)
Speech topics, 159
Standards (*see* Ethical codes)
Statistics, 164
Status, 22–24, 56, 58
Study projects (*see* Projects and tasks)

Style (*elocutio*), 75
Suggestibility, 116

Tasks (*see* Projects and tasks)
Tension reduction, 2
Timing, 177
Toulmin reasoning system, 169–72

Uncertainty reduction, 58
Unity, 130

Values, 38–39
Verbal cuing, 129, 145

Watergate, 188